# Illicit Industries and China's Shadow Economy

This book considers a wide range of illicit industries in China, exploring what drives such activities, why consumers tolerate them to differing degrees, how attempts to regulate them are implemented and how such regulation is resisted. Industries considered include human smuggling, human organs trade, illicit pharmaceuticals, smuggling of animal parts, illegal logging and trade of wood, food safety and shadow banking. Throughout, the book describes how the shadow economy works, analyses the degree to which illicit activities are regarded as criminal and highlights the importance of the shadow economy for certain regions of China and certain sections of Chinese society. In doing so, it reveals the challenges of human security posed by these industries not only for China, but also for the global community, and considers a robust governance mechanism at both national and global levels to address these challenges. Overall, the book provides a very rich picture of a key aspect of China's contemporary economy which is difficult to research.

**Victor Teo** is Assistant Professor at the School of Modern Languages and Cultures at the University of Hong Kong.

**Sungwon Yoon** is Assistant Professor at Duke-NUS Medical School, National University of Singapore.

# Routledge Contemporary China Series

**China's Regions in an Era of Globalization**
*Tim Summers*

**China's Climate-Energy Policy**
Domestic and International Impacts
*Edited by Akihisa Mori*

**Western Bankers in China**
Institutional Change and Corporate Governance
*Jane Nolan*

**Xinjiang in the Twenty-First Century**
Islam, Ethnicity and Resistance
*Michael Dillon*

**China Studies in the Philippines**
Intellectual Paths and the Formation of a Field
*Edited by Tina S. Clemente and Chih-yu Shih*

**Innovative and Creative Industries in Hong Kong**
A Global City in China and Asia
*Grace L K Leung*

**Illicit Industries and China's Shadow Economy**
Challenges and Prospects for Global Governance and Human Security
*Edited by Victor Teo and Sungwon Yoon*

**Re-engineering Affordable Care Policy in China**
Is Marketization a Solution?
*Peter Nan-shong Lee*

For more information about this series, please visit: www.routledge.com/
Routledge-Contemporary-China-Series/book-series/SE0768

# Illicit Industries and China's Shadow Economy

Challenges and Prospects for Global
Governance and Human Security

**Edited by Victor Teo and
Sungwon Yoon**

LONDON AND NEW YORK

First published 2019
by Routledge
2 Park Square, Milton Park, Abingdon, Oxon OX14 4RN

and by Routledge
52 Vanderbilt Avenue, New York, NY 10017

First issued in paperback 2020

*Routledge is an imprint of the Taylor & Francis Group, an informa business*

*British Library Cataloguing-in-Publication Data*
A catalogue record for this book is available from the British Library

*Library of Congress Cataloging-in-Publication Data*
A catalog record has been requested for this book

ISBN 13: 978-0-367-58282-1 (pbk)
ISBN 13: 978-1-138-56368-1 (hbk)

Typeset in Times New Roman
by Apex CoVantage, LLC

# Contents

# Tables

# Figures

# Contributors

**Koh Keng-We** is Assistant Professor at the Department of History of the Nanyang Technological University, Singapore. He specializes in Southeast Asian history and world history (with a focus on maritime Asia). Within these broad fields, he is interested in business and economic history, state-formation, migration history and the study of diasporic communities in Asia, religion and religious movements in Asia (especially with respect to Islam, Chinese religion and Buddhism), and aspects of popular culture. He completed his PhD at the Department of History, University of Hawaii. Prior to joining NTU, he was Assistant Professor at Seoul National University.

**Keokam Kraisoraphong** is Associate Professor at the Faculty of Political Science, Chulalongkorn University, Thailand. She is a member of the executive board and a Senior Fellow at the Institute of Security and International Studies (ISIS), Thailand; and a member of the Security Research Committee for the National Research Council of Thailand (NRCT). She is also editor-in-chief of the *World Food Policy* journal of the Policy Studies Organization (PSO), Washington DC, USA. Her latest publications include *inter alia*, "China, Japan, and the Greater Mekong Basin: A Southeast Asian Perspective" in *China-Japan Relations in the 21st Century* (Singapore: Palgrave Macmillan, 2017); "Water Regime Resilience and Community Rights to Resource Access in the Face of Climate Change" in *Human Security and Climate Change in Southeast Asia: Managing Risk and Resilience* (London: Routledge, 2012); "A Water Regime for Human Security: The Lower Mekong Basin" in *Mainstreaming Human Security in ASEAN Integration: Regional Public Goods and Human Security, volume 1* (Quezon City: Central Book Supply, 2010); "Crossing the Threshold: Thailand's Path to Rethink Security Sector Governance" in *Peacebuilding and Security Sector Governance in Asia* (Zurich: LIT VERLAG GmbH, 2014); *Conflict in Southern Thailand: Seed for Security Sector Reform* (Asia Security Initiative Policy Series no. 21, Singapore: RSIS Center for Non-Traditional Security [NTS] Studies, 2013); and "Thailand and the Responsibility to Protect" in *The Pacific Review* 20(1) (2012).

**Xiaohua Ma** is Associate Professor of Faculty of International Studies, Osaka University of Education, Japan. She teaches U.S.-East Asian relations,

International Relations and American politics. Her research focuses on World War II diplomacy, China-Japan-US relations and foreign policy, confidence-building in the Asia-Pacific region and the politics of memory. She was a visiting scholar at the Reischauer Institute of Japanese Studies, Harvard University and the School of East Asian Studies, University of Sheffield.

**Yoneyuki Sugita** is Professor of American History at the Graduate School of Language and Culture, Osaka University, Japan. He received his PhD in American history from the University of Wisconsin-Madison. He is the author of *Pitfall or Panacea: The Irony of US Power in Occupied Japan 1945–1952* (Routledge, 2003), and *Irony of Hegemony: The Asia-Pacific War and US Policy Toward East Asia* (Sekai Shisosha, 1999, in Japanese). He is also co-editor of *Trans-Pacific Relations: America, Europe, and Asia in the Twentieth Century* (Praeger, 2003).

**Victor Teo** is Assistant Professor at the University of Hong Kong. He obtained his PhD in International Relations from the London School of Economics and Political Science. His research interests are in the field of International Relations of the Asia-Pacific. At the University of Hong Kong, Victor teaches on the university's Common Core Curriculum on China and Global Issues. Victor was Japan Foundation Research Fellow at the University of Kyoto's Center for Southeast Asian Studies. He was Visiting Research Fellow at the Department of Politics and International Relations at the University of Oxford, and Doris Zimmern HKU-Cambridge Hughes Hall Visiting Fellow at the Department of Politics and International Studies (POLIS) at the University of Cambridge. He was Harvard Yenching Visiting Scholar at Harvard Faculty of Arts and Sciences and Harvard Law School, as well as Academic Research Associate at the Program on U.S.-Japan Relations at Harvard's Weatherhead Center for International Affairs. He is the author and contributing editor of six books on the international politics of the Asia-Pacific. His latest book is *Japan's Arduous Rejuvenation as a Global Power: Democratic Resilience and the US-China Challenge* published by Palgrave Macmillan.

**Sungwon Yoon** is Assistant Professor at Duke-NUS Medical School, National University of Singapore. She was previously Research Fellow with the Faculty of Medicine, University of Hong Kong. Her research interest relates to global health, especially with regards to health and development issues in China and East Asia. Prior to joining the university, she worked at various institutions in Korea including the Parliament of the Republic of Korea and the Korea Development Institute. She was awarded a Korean government fellowship to examine comparative health systems at the London School of Economics and Political Science. She was trained as a medical sociologist at Seoul National University and Ewha Womans University in Korea and subsequently completed a second doctorate in global health policy at London School of Hygiene and Tropical Medicine, UK.

# Acknowledgements

The editors thankfully acknowledge the assistance of their colleagues who have made this book possible. A great debt is owed to the School of Modern Languages and Cultures, the School of Public Health, the Common Core Curriculum Office and the Faculty of Arts at University of Hong Kong for making the logistical and academic resources available for this project. We are also grateful to the Hong Kong Research Council, the HKU Class of '82 Alumni Green Fund and the HKU Knowledge Exchange Impact Fund for helping with the research funding for some of these papers, and also for the support of a workshop that enabled the authors to come together to meet and discuss the papers. The editors would also like to thank Miss Sylvia Sun, Miss Lolo Yu, Miss Judy Shum, Miss Zhu Xuan and Miss Harmony Chan for their research assistance. The editors are also tremendously grateful to Dr Samuel Wong, Miss Zena Cheung, Miss Shirley Chan, Miss Lucilla Cheng, and Mr Eddie Lau for all their assistance in the organization of the workshop at the University of Hong Kong.

We are particularly grateful to the scholars and colleagues who have read or commented on various chapters of the book, including the referees whose comments we found invaluable. We would also like to convey our sincere gratitude to the editors and staff at Routledge, particularly Mr Peter Sowden and Miss Rebecca McPhee for their confidence in us and for making this book possible. The editors are also extremely grateful for the supportive environment and intellectual space provided by the Harvard Yenching Institute, Harvard Law School, the Duke-NUS Medical School and SingHealth so that they were able to work on the final stages and bring the project to completion. The editors would also like to express our sincere thanks to the learned scholars who have taken the time and effort to undertake the many revisions required as well as their forbearance in waiting for this book to materialize. Needless to say the errors contained therein are our own.

# 1 Illicit Industries and China's Shadow Economy: Challenges and Prospects for Global Governance and Human Security

*Victor Teo and Sungwon Yoon*

## Introduction

This volume brings together a collection of scholars from diverse disciplines in law, politics, international relations, sociology, anthropology and public health to consider the challenges stemming from the illicit economic activities in China. The Asia-based authors in this volume, from Singapore, Hong Kong, Japan, China and Thailand, have invested significant time and resources in related projects, putting them in a unique position to put forward their contributions. In particular, frequent and easy access to China meant that for most part, the authors are able overcome methodological challenges such as lack of reliable data or difficulty in accessing sources through onsite field research trips.

This idea of an "illicit" economy is a familiar phenomenon, particularly to people living in China. A literature search will reflect that even though there is an emerging body of literature[1] on the topic of the shadow economy or illicit industries, few books focus exclusively on China.[2] This is extremely regrettable since China has an illicit economy that mirrors its entire legitimate economy. There are of course reports in the media every day about various sorts of fake goods or products globally, just as there are documentaries and talk shows on the scams behind these products and services. In public narratives in China and elsewhere, Chinese products are particularly cast as low quality and inferior, depicted often to be cheap clones of genuine ones and their salvation only remains in their affordability. This is true in Nairobi, as it is in Jakarta or Cairo. This perception must be contextualized against the kind of manufacturing culture and environment in China that is remarkably different from elsewhere. There is a contemporary folk saying 'in China there are many ways to build something. It can cost 30 million, 3 million, 300,000 dollars or even 30,000 dollars. Most entrepreneurs will take your money and build according to what you pay'. Whilst admirable, this capitalistic spirit often overrides considerations of durability, standards and safety. Chinese manufacturers and service providers are amongst the quickest and sharpest in the world – very competitive and attuned to opportunities and changes in the market conditions, with many viewing what they are doing as being unregulated, as opposed to being illegal.

With the wide range of products and services that exist in the underground economy, it is often difficult to categorize whether a particular product or service is outright illegal or if its existence is illicit in nature, remaining in a legal grey zone, or if it is just something that is not regulated. For instance, would a cell phone that looks similar to an iPhone but with essentially a different operating system and physical dimensions be necessarily in breach of Apple's patent? Can a Chinese garment company be in violation of another commercial entity's right if some of their apparel designs are highly similar? Or for that matter, what about manufacturing knock-off of a foreign medicine with slightly similar active ingredients by a generic drug manufacturer? Today, in many parts of the world and particularly in Asia, most consumers are accustomed to the purchase and utilization of products which may well be genuine, but often counterfeit. They may often look legal but could be illegitimate and illicit. There is no guarantee that the consumer knows this. The operation of the underground economy is deeply intertwined with the legitimate economy, regardless of whether it is with regards to products or services, it is often difficult to decipher the integration as we see it.

The idea of an "underground economy" is an elusive one. Venkatesh[3] defines the underground economy as a 'web in which many different people, from the criminal to the pious, from the down-and-out to the bourgeois, are inextricably intertwined'. Schneider and Williams[4] suggest that shadow economy is an aggregate of:

> market based production of legal goods and services that are deliberately concealed from the authorities for the following reasons: (a) to avoid payment of income, value added or other taxes; (b) to avoid payment of social security contributions; (c) to avoid having to meet certain legal labor market standards, such as minimum wages, maximum working hours, safety standards, etc.; and to avoid complying with certain administrative obligations. This definition excludes underground economic activities associated with classic crimes, and household informal income such as babysitting.

Even though classic criminal activities such as robbery and burglary are omitted from this definition, many of the illicit activities cannot be divorced from white-collar crimes such as tax evasion, money laundering, fraud and intellectual property violations.

The volume's understanding of the shadow economy takes a more pervasive and broader definition. We suggest that the shadow economy consists of economic activities undertaken by groups of individuals, often in tandem, but ultimately in pursuit of profits that may be frowned upon by society as either illegitimate or illegal, and often both. There are, of course, categories of products and services that might be legitimate but illegal (e.g. imported cancer drugs that are not approved by local authorities) or illegitimate but not illegal (e.g. rental of boyfriends or girlfriends).

It is important to emphasize that the focus of the volume is also not concerned so much with the "grey" zone of informal work undertaken and unreported by individuals such as those engaged in home tuition, casual contractors, babysitters and ad-hoc construction workers. There is no question that this category of workers is important in the shadow economy and collectively does account for a significant portion of economic activities that go unreported and untaxed. In particular, this is significant in Third World countries such as China and much of South and Southeast Asia, where for the most part, many sectors of the economy are cash-based and informal. Not all informal economic activities are necessarily "legitimate" or seen as "casual" work. Most criminal or illicit activities are disguised in such a way that they cannot usually be documented.

## The nature of illicit industries in China

The idea of "illicit" industries in this volume at first might sound quite odd to some readers. Even though they might not be as malicious as criminal organizations that we often hear of in the mass media, still no self-respecting governments in the developed Western societies should or would tolerate the existence of these industries. It is, however, a fact that in the Third World – particularly in Asia – many aspects of the economy are informal, or at least grey. Small and medium-sized manufacturers have little notion of intellectual property rights and are often ill-versed in safety regulations. As long as it is not within the traditional notion of "crime", many of these businessmen think that it is perfectly fine to clone or duplicate products and services found in the legitimate economy for mass consumption. "Knock-offs" (i.e. imitations of genuine products), however, are different from imitations that are intentionally marketed in guise of the real product. Developing countries often exhibit this type of manufacturing just as they do in the service industry in the absence of the capacity or effort to develop new products

No one can tell for sure the magnitude of these industries – number of firms, average size, technological and cost conditions, ease of entry and exit of the industry, industrial concentration (i.e. percentage of national output by largest firms) and geospatial distribution. Unlike the firms in the real economy, the data needed to study these firms and people involved are rare, and the facts and figures only hint at the nature and magnitude of the problem as a result of successful police prosecution and detection.

This volume thus offers an introduction to the wide range of illicit industries in and related to China. Today, there is a saying in China that for every legitimate industry in the economy, may it be in the production of consumption goods or the provision of service, there will be an "illicit" mirror "counterpart". Everyone knows about the counterfeit luxury brand handbags, the melamine-laced milk powder, but what is little known is that for almost every single product that is manufactured under license in China, there will be a cheaper Chinese clone. From Pentagon-ordered made-to-specifications missile components to pharmaceuticals, from software platforms like WhatsApp to natural products such as eggs and poultry, there are clones and imitations. There are reports of clone taxi companies in Guangzhou, running a "ghost" fleet of taxis that are beyond the scope of regulation.[5]

If the cloning of Apple Stores shocks the reader, then let us look at the following incident: In 2004, there were reports of entire multinational corporations (MNCs) being cloned in Greater China.[6] NEC, the Japanese computer manufacturer, found this out when someone returned an NEC-branded computer back to the head-quarters in Tokyo which NEC had never manufactured. The illicit entrepreneurs went as far as developing an entire range of products, coordinating manufacturing across network factories and distributing the goods widely. Some of the factories and people involved genuinely believed that they were working for NEC, while some did not even know that the counterparts they were dealing with were fake. The scale and range of these illicit industries are far ranging, and those revealed in the media raise a question of the possibility that there are a lot of these industries that have not been exposed. This question – whether it is shoddy counterfeiting on a large scale or an organized crime attempting to hijack a brand – underscores the pervasive and amorphous nature of these illicit industries.

Oftentimes, the illicit industry connects legitimate economic activities with the illicit ones, linking various actors whose actions might or might not run afoul of the law, and it is these interactions that provide the sustenance and nebulousness of the industries. Throughout the manufacture of an illicit product or the provision of illicit services, it is possible that parts or services be procured from legitimate sources for the end production of illicit products or services. For instance, a sup-plier selling raw leather may not know that his material is being procured for making counterfeit bags. Similarly, an electronics shop may sell blank DVDs to a customer who, without the shop's knowledge, is a bootleg DVD pirate. Con-versely, when these illicit manufacturers want to expand their operations and therefore require more capital to rent space or buy more source materials, they borrow from legitimate bankers – or if they cannot, they will do so from shadow bankers who front them capital to rent premises. The shadow bankers in turn make the loan out of funds from depositors who are typically retirees and house-wives wishing to invest their money owing to a higher interest rate than banks. It is important to note that the capital funds derived from an illicit industry could be spent on something perfectly legitimate and legal such as rent or food, or the money could be diverted to spend on another illicit service. In short, capital itself does not have a propensity to distinguish between what is licit and illicit.

By and large, the illicit industries, especially producers of fake goods demanded by consumers (e.g. fake branded handbags), face an uphill battle because the police and the customs enforcement officers know where to go and who to look for to close down these operations. The problem is that the range of illicit indus-tries and the sheer number of actors in these industries make enforcement work look feeble. Closing down stores with physical presence in a couple of shopping centres is not hard. Rooting out and putting out entrepreneurs out of work entirely is a different story. The cloning abilities of Chinese manufacturers are legendary – from luxury bags to military hardware parts, from ubiquitous food products such as tofu and eggs to counterfeit companies, it appears that there is nothing that the Chinese are unable to copy. There are not only fake Apple Stores,[7] but also an entire corporate structure like the NEC. As one "clone taxi" driver commented, the "Chinese are only limited by their imagination, but not their abilities" (中国人只有想不到的, 没有做不到的).[8]

## *Main drivers of illicit industries*

The illicit industries are profit-driven, and the financial incentives are often so great that these varying industries offer potential for significant rewards, which is the fundamental driver for illicit industries. From being suppliers of raw materials to the manufacture and marketing of the products in various stages of the illicit services provision, the illicit industries offer exceptional entrepreneurial and economic opportunities to the willing and able, particularly in China where governance and legislation are weak. With the notable exception of some illicit industries (e.g. high-tech cloning or shadow banking), most provide low barriers for entry. This means that the illicit industries as a whole provide unprecedented economic opportunities and social mobility to people in China. This is especially attractive to people who lack skills, qualifications, opportunity or patience for honest money in the real world.

In addition to huge profits, these counterfeit industries support not only the employment of the masses, but also stand as the engines of regional development in China. In Guangdong, Fujian and Zhejiang provinces, the powerhouse of Chinese manufacturing exports, small factories counterfeit products and export them worldwide. The global demand for cheap consumer goods drives the manufacturing capabilities of many of these small industries. Although not a specified state strategy, both the Chinese people and the Chinese state understand the importance of these industries as the government cannot possibly provide employment for so many people. The enforcement of intellectual property rights through crackdowns will not only close factories employing millions of people, but has a direct impact on other industries supplying the raw materials for manufacturing to those involved in the retailing, marketing and distribution of these products. One can go further to say that it would have an impact on other legitimate economic sectors. In two of the most infamous malls in Shenzhen and Zhuhai in Guangdong province over a period of ten years with increased enforcement pressure, the editors observed that once these shops selling illicit products are closed, a remarkable downturn of foot traffic followed, with many of the shopkeepers bemoaning higher rents with less business. The shopkeepers move out or, more often than not, move their shops online platforms such as Taobao or Wechat. At times, the illicit products (Figure 1.1) move outwards in a radial pattern. Investigations indicate that pirated DVDs were being exported to Europe, the United States and East Asia. Counterfeit bags find export markets in the United States, Korea, Japan and Southeast Asia.

The consumption culture of counterfeit products in China has also driven proliferation of the illicit industries. The consumption experience in China is heavily influenced by the "Shanzhai" (山寨) industry. This simply refers to imitation or pirated goods, particularly in the electronic sectors. Euphemistically, this means "mountain stronghold" in reference to bandits or pirates who are far away from the

*Figure 1.1* Fake watches for sale in Guangdong province

control of the government authorities. Despite the intellectual property arguments put forth against counterfeit goods, Chinese people are still buying "Shanzhai" products principally because for most, the "real" products remain economically unattainable on a sustained basis (e.g. luxury handbags) and that in terms of quality, the imitation products offer almost the same functionality as the real ones (e.g. cloned mobile phones). This demand is created because of the affordability and availability issues combined with human propensity for greed. From a consumer perspective, buying pirated DVDs and cloned luxury bags at a fraction of the price of the originals might be an exercise in frugality. In many instances, one can hear Chinese friends discuss which cloned DVD stores have the best products in terms of quality and price. For that matter, no one will bat an eyelid if one were to bring home a cloned air fryer or branded watch. Most consumers are aware of the implicit intention in their act of buying a cheaper cloned product: paying less in exchange for a product of lesser quality. Chinese cloned products are sold extremely well not just in China but are exported worldwide, particularly to developing countries in Southeast Asia, the Middle East and Africa, where the newly affluent take a first step towards modern consumerism through the purveying and consumption of a range of pirated goods.

Third World societies often implicitly gain from the consumption of these products. Take software piracy for instance: In the 1990s and 2000s when software was dominantly sold on CDs and DVDs, piracy was rampant throughout the most developing world, particularly in China and Russia, to the large annoyance of multinational corporations such as Microsoft and Adobe. Even various concerned governments – including the Chinese and Russian governments – were being put under a lot of pressure, and there was little enforcement done to curb these pirates from rampantly cloning and reselling the various software suites. From Chinese shopping centres to metro stations in Moscow, Microsoft Office DVDs and Adobe System suites were going for as little as $10 a disc. As the software products are usually extremely high priced in developed countries, most ordinary citizens would not be able to afford the original software. Such pirated products do provide advantages for these developing societies, because schools are unable to purchase the software suites for education that cost thousands of dollars. It is no surprise that in general, the IT literacy rates amongst societies with the most rampant piracy problem are also the highest in the world.

It is important to note that not all illicit products or services are demand-driven. Indeed, many are supply-driven, and in many of these instances, Chinese consumers can get duped into buying the fake products because they do not know what the real products look like (e.g. Apple products for a long while before Apple China opened) or that the brand has not been introduced into China (e.g. Abercrombie and Finch). This is where we need to look at the types of illicit industries in terms of consumer perceptions.

### *Typology of illicit industries*

In understanding the nature of illicit industry activities, one should understand that many of the actors who partake in these industries are not all "evil" in the sense that they are out to deceive or harm the public. Rather, these illicit entrepreneurs often perceive the activities as a means to eke out a living. Therefore, the illicit nature of many of these industries necessarily means that it is not easy to categorize the structure and the setup of the entrepreneurs involved in these industries. They could range from a conglomerate structure (such as those involved in large-scale counterfeit DVD or electronics production) to village-level industries. One of the common features is the dominance of small household or kin-based units comprised of relatives and friends as "firms" in the industries. These kin-based units provide the secrecy, unity and adaptiveness necessary for avoiding any interference by the police. Most of these "firms" are able to establish and ingratiate themselves into the industry, precisely because of the "informal" nature to entry as well as the profitable nature. More importantly, not everyone who partakes in the illicit industries might be doing something illegal, or be conscious of the part they played in the chain of industrial activities actually contributing to the illicit industry. There is, therefore, a wide spectrum in the number of actors partaking in each industry. For instance, in the counterfeit industry, some criminals are outright passing off their products as the real thing, while others admit their products are outright copies (but not as the genuine product), and yet others who copy the concept whilst maintaining a very different product identity. Needless to say, manufacturers of genuine products will say all three categories are counterfeit.

In trying to reach a deeper understanding of the illicit industries in China, we have to be circumspect in deciphering the different categories of illicit products and services that the average consumer might have different reactions to. It is important to note that not all illicit products and services are equally welcomed by consumers, nor is their consumption necessarily voluntary. In this volume, the goods and services could be divided into three categories: those welcomed, those tolerated and those disapproved by consumers. For the first category, consumption is usually a conscious choice whereby consumers have constructive knowledge in comparing the available products and services on the market, but in fact they welcome the provision of the product or service because of the limited availability of others, often as a result of price or restriction. Businessmen reliant on shadow bankers' easy and no-questions-asked remittance service is an example in the "welcome" consumption category. In a similar light, demand for cheap seafood through illegal fishing or smuggling (e.g. cheap sea cucumbers or abalone) can be considered as a welcome category.

For the second category, the consumers tolerate the presence of this industry but see the detriments of consumption. Pirated electronic equipment, which may not be fully tested, belongs to this category (e.g. cell phone batteries, chargers), cloned household appliances (e.g. kettles, cookers) and a range of other imitation products that are priced very competitively. Other products and services that might be tolerated by the vast majority of consumers are those that are not so much in demand most of the time but might be available in the event that their services are desperately needed. Underground banking services, Chinese medicinal products with banned ingredients (e.g. endangered animal parts such as rhinoceros horns, tiger penis or pangolins) can also fall into this category. Unless there is a pressing need, these are not products that appeal to the mass consumption market. Tolerance of – or perhaps acculturation with – these services does not mean widespread approval or acceptance. The key thing here is that the consumers are conscious of the nature of the products and services, and choose to consume these services and products. To consumers, there is a significant difference between clone products (i.e. making something similar to an existing product and selling it under a different brand) and someone cloning and passing off something as the genuine product. Having constructive knowledge of a product and service of it being an illicit product and electing to consume the product or service is critical in understanding why some products and services are welcome and others not.

There are, however, some products that consumers would never intend to buy, as exemplified by counterfeit drugs and medicine as these products should not be manufactured without proper regulations. It is not too hard to imagine: medicinal products, especially those for treatment of serious illness; foodstuffs that are naturally occurring but "manufactured" such as fake walnuts, tofu made of cardboard or most incredulously, fake eggs. No consumer in the right mind would purchase or consume these.

Indeed, the revelations of the melamine milk scandals[9] in September 2008 shocked even the Chinese people who had by now become accustomed to food safety scares. Approximately 300,000 people were affected (and received compensation) (see Figure 1.2), 296,000 children had fallen ill, six babies died from kidney failure and 54,000 other babies were hospitalized. This incident was preceded by another similar episode in 2004 when "watered-down" milk had caused 13 infant deaths from malnutrition. One would think that after 2008 incident, this would have subsided, but in 2011, three children died and 35 people fell ill from

*Figure 1.2* Milk powder vendors in Shenzhen. These vendors consolidate milk powder smuggled or brought over from Hong Kong and resell it for a profit in Shenzhen, Guangdong Province. Hong Kong imposed a limit on the formula that could be legally brought out of Hong Kong after the 2008 milk powder scare in China

drinking nitrite-tainted milk in Gansu Province.[10] There are other incidents – four people died after drinking counterfeit alcoholic drinks in Guangdong in 2004; the reports of homemade oil (filtered from drains and animal carcasses) and businesses using goat/sheep urine to marinate duck meat to make them pass off as mutton.[11] It is important to point out that food safety breaches can be caused by negligence, regardless of whether the manufacturer is a licensed large-scale factory or an unregulated, home-based one. The presence of counterfeiters in the drug industry is in many ways more worrying than food safety.

Pharmaceutical drugs are essential to the well-being of the nation. When the supply of drugs is tainted by the injection of fake drugs into the supply, it has serious ramifications for the health and human security of the nation. It doesn't matter whether it is lifestyle drugs like Viagra or various vitamins or critical life-saving drugs for fighting cancer. No one of sound mind would purchase or consume these drugs. Thus, in a nutshell, most Chinese consumers generally perceive the counterfeit consumer goods or services positively if they have the knowledge of its authenticity and if they voluntarily elect to purchase the product or service with full knowledge of the pros and cons. They might even tolerate other illicit products and services as long as they offer a greater choice for consumers, regardless of their personal preference. However, when illicit products or services that are harmful and when they are consumed unwittingly, Chinese consumers will rally behind Chinese law and enforcement agencies will strike hard on these industries as shown in Table 1.1.

Table 1.1 Typology of illicit industries by consumer reaction

| Average consumer reaction | Consumer pre-knowledge | Rationale | Human security implication | Governance challenges | Example |
|---|---|---|---|---|---|
| **Welcome** | Present | Accessibility and attractive price point without significant detrimental effect on consumption. | Minor | Low | Clone of any consumer product (e.g. luxury bags, watches or consumables) that is currently being sold for high price domestically and/or not available in China; latest Hollywood movies. |
| **Tolerate** | Present | Significant Monetary savings; convenience; acceptable quality difference. Offers an option if genuine products or services are not accessible. | Moderate but can be severe in case of organ sales | Moderate | Cloned electronics with no safety or quality checks; organ sales, shadow banking services. |
| **Disapprove** | Absent | Major detrimental effect after consumption. Usually no pre-knowledge of it being fake/clone. | Severe | High | Poisonous milk powder; contaminated food products; fake pharmaceutical products. |

The aversion of Chinese consumers to "disapproved" categories of illicit industries cannot be underestimated. In the melamine milk powder case, the public outrage was real and acute across China. To the Chinese people, some of these industries are offensive simply because they are considered extremely repugnant, immoral and shocking. The widespread reporting on these incidents over the internet, often linked governmental attempts to suppress or censor the news, accentuated the difficulties as in the case of the melamine milk powder. Shunned by consumers, the domestic milk powder industry came to a standstill. Chinese citizens began to flock across the border to Hong Kong and Macau to buy milk powder, as no one trusted the milk powder supplies anymore in the mainland. The tensions had impacts in four areas: (i) direct impact on relations between Hong Kong and Chinese residents; (ii) confidence in the food supply chain in China; (iii) legitimacy of the government due to governance issue; and (iv) health and human security stemming from Chinese exports globally. This, however, is not confined to these two neighbouring jurisdictions. For example, China has been accused of exporting vegetables laced with pesticides to Korea and illegal antibiotics used in seafood sent to Singapore.

Therefore, the challenges come at different levels and in various ways, and require collective efforts involving all countries. No single government or concerned department can counter and combat the rise of a particular industry alone. Counterfeit products challenge not only international intellectual property norms, but may also come under the purview of various departments in charge of wildlife protection, environmental resource, food safety and various licensing boards. Even though the Chinese government has shown increased determination to fight against many of these industries, the government will need to select which industries should to be tackled urgently as a matter of priority. At the top of the list are those illicit industries that pose a clear and present danger to the security of China, as well as those illicit regimes that would be frowned upon and embarrass the Chinese government in a big way. The interconnectedness of the global economy means that the negative externalities alongside the redeeming features of these illicit products and services are globalized very quickly. In short, Chinese governance problems might well become issues of global governance.

## Globalization of illicit activities and human security

The idea of globalization is an amorphous one – much like other contested terms in social sciences, for instance, nationalism or democracy with a wide variety of definitions and layered meanings. For many, the idea of globalization conjures up the imagery of a compression of time and space, made most evident by the intensification and acceleration of cross-border flows of people, goods, services and ideas.[12] Needless to say, the idea of economic activities, illicit or otherwise, being contained in spatial units like sovereign entities is entirely fiction. Thus, our modern understanding of globalization could be illuminated by the emphasis of three important points as pointed out by David Held. First, there exists a dense overlap of complex networks of relations between individuals, communities, nations, states and international institutions, as well as supra-national organizations like MNCs or NGOs, and these complex and overlapping networks both empower and constrain communities, states and social forces. Second, social and political activities are stretched across the globe; and significantly, they may no longer primarily and solely be organized according to territorial principles – but at the same time, they generate pressures to be re-territorialized in the form of sub- and supra-national zones or modes of governance. Third, globalization concerns itself with the expanding scale by which power is organized – the exercise of power in one locale can have effects on another.

How do we apply this to our understanding of illicit industries and their connection to the global shadow economy? To be sure, the extent of these illicit industries that have cropped up in China is morphing into a complex weave of networks and activities that transcends national borders in Asia and is linking up criminal entrepreneurs organized and banded according to various principles (kinship or spatial-based, e.g. villages or towns, or even like-minded individuals in different localities and countries). Their illicit activities connect with the legitimate economy closely – e.g. they might be buying raw materials from entirely legitimate vendors and/or reinvesting their profits in perfectly legal enterprises within or outside their areas of operations. The illicit industry would grow to span its operations globally, just as Chinese counterfeit products are sold from Canal Street in New York to Brazzaville in the African Congo to Jakarta in Southeast Asia. The networks required to purchase, transport, distribute and retail these illicit products and services essentially suggest that they necessitate a wider community beyond Chinese illicit entrepreneurs. To that extent, as illicit entrepreneurs build and expand their business worldwide, they are always on the lookout to obtain opportunities for greater profit or further networking. Likewise, as these illicit entrepreneurs expand their networks and operations, their power grows correspondingly, making them more impervious to domestic legal infrastructure and international governance efforts. Most of these illicit industries morphed from loosely territorial-based personal network structures to deterritorialized, rational and non-kinship-based organizational structures that pride themselves on the forces of globalization for their operations. This also means that these illicit industries would face increased and concerted scrutiny because of the magnitude and range of operations, from both the domestic governments and international regimes. The spread of illicit industries and their integration into the shadow economy are fostered by unprecedented interconnectedness. As Held argues, we are now entering the age characterized by the 'widening, deepening and speeding up of worldwide interconnectedness in all aspects of contemporary social life, from the cultural to the criminal, the financial to the spiritual'.[13]

The globalization of these illicit industries in China has not only brought about an unprecedented number of problems, both in terms of scale and range, but also exacerbated existing issues by changing the nature of these industries as well as cross-linking illicit platforms to form a complex network of challenges. Globalization has five important drivers:[14] (i) changing infrastructure of global communications through the information technology revolution; (ii) the rise of a global market facilitated by new information distribution channels; (iii) changes in pressures and patterns of migration; (iv) end of the Cold War and diffusion of democratic values and consumer preferences across the world; and (v) the emergence of a new type of global civil society with the crystallization of a new global public opinion.

Illicit industries in China have taken on board these drivers and utilized them to the fullest extent. Today, both licit and illicit goods are advertised and sold on the internet through a variety of popular platforms both domestically and also internationally. Online retailers such as eBay, Taobao and even Amazon have cracked down on illicit products and services, but it might be almost impossible to verify given the massive number of retailers and partners. This, however, is nothing compared to the thousands of other sites that come online each week, with different domain names as well as the individual retailers hawking their illicit products and wares on chatting and blogging platforms. Modern advances in e-banking, modern courier delivery and shipping technologies have made the provision of these illicit products and services to far-flung remote areas as easy as it is to densely populated metropolitan areas, perhaps for a small additional fee. Illicit industries have shown that they have become remarkably adaptive to morphing into growing consumer tastes and patterns with amazing ease, even though there is growing awareness against these industries in general.

As stipulated, not each category of illicit products and services is viewed equally by consumers. Most people are normally against illicit products and services if they could afford or have access to the real products (in terms of pricing or accessibility). There are other industries that are morally unacceptable and ethically reprehensive, for instance human trafficking and organ trade. These industries have middlemen who exploit the weak and helpless; but at the same time, there are many people who go into this with eyes wide open. Many poor in Third World countries see organ sales as a legitimate way to raise cash or to meet with financial difficulties – and even if desperate buyers in the developed world pay substantial amounts to purchase a kidney, for instance, the sellers are often being ripped off by the middlemen. At the same time, numerous women from impoverished countries are tricked into the vice trade, but there are also those who voluntarily paid to be smuggled to First World cities to partake in the global vice trade, whereby they will make more money than they would make at home. Globalization not only facilitates the actual processes by which these illicit industries spread globally, but also creates the necessary public space by which actors come together to articulate their claims, defend their interests and debate about policies and justify their existence. Globalization, in short, intensified the density of social and political interactions of these actors on a global scale.[15]

Even though experts have disagreed as to whether implications[16,17] of globalization bring more opportunities[18,19] than threats,[20,21] we can agree that the globalization of these illicit industries did bring about more threats than opportunities, particularly when products and services which consumers have no interest in are exported abroad. These illicit industries exacerbate human security in all senses, ranging from economic, health, political, food, environmental and community to personal security.[22]

Take illegal immigration, for instance. Human traffickers have been providing their services to would-be migrants for decades. From the "coyotes" that bring Mexicans wanting a better life to the United States to "snakeheads" smuggling Chinese migrants from Fujian and Guangdong in China to Europe and elsewhere, illegal immigration has usually been seen as a source of problem than a benefit to host societies. Even though it has provided many migrants with an enhanced – but not necessarily easier – path to a better life, there are compelling counter-narratives of how such trafficking turned out miserably for others. Often without means and forced to survive through indentured labour, some illegal immigrants turn to organized crime or illicit activities to survive. Illegal migrants are exploited by criminal elements, discriminated against by host societies, and are often blamed by immigration and crime enforcement authorities for societal ills from crime to terrorism. The question of illegal immigration has been one of vexing concerns for various governments worldwide, and the debate on illegal immigration – particularly in the United States – has become more explicit since Donald Trump took office.

Chapter 2 on human smuggling highlights this illicit industry as a major transnational problem, with a large number of countries afflicted by it as origin, transit or destination points. To date, the scholarship has not paid much attention to the issue of Chinese human smuggling, partly because illegal Chinese immigrants have been "invisible" due to linguistic and cultural barriers erected by the Chinese communities. In light of this, Ma's chapter attempts to uncover the nature of Chinese human smuggling organizations and their operations. Focusing on illegal Chinese immigrants in the United States, Ma describes the inner structure of Chinese human smuggling networks to understand the essence of human smuggling. The connections that the industry has to other illicit industries are particularly instructive; fake passports, diversifying smuggling groups and the illegal crossing of various national borders mean that this is not a one-offence problem. Ma demonstrates that the problem surrounding human trafficking and smuggling cuts across a range of development issues, from poverty to social inclusion, to justice and rule of law issues, and human security, and thus has relevance for practitioners throughout the development community.

The exploitation of people is not just confined to trafficking of humans. Body parts from both living beings and cadavers can be commercialized. Organ transplants cannot be effected without donors. Transplant lists in developed countries, particularly those with very rigorous transplant laws and ethics considerations, are often much longer than the donors list. Compounding the situation is the fact that a successful transplant can only be done with matching tissues. The demand and supply for organs create a differential for organ transplant to become a lucrative trade, particularly when those with resources and means are able to purchase various human organs for transplant. Similarly to trafficking cases, the differential in demand, particularly between rich and poor societies, will see the rise of middlemen and those seeking to sell their body parts for profits. For families whose loved one is dying, organ brokers offer a glimmer of hope. Like the trafficking industry mentioned earlier, there are numerous stories of how it leaves the poor being exploited and vulnerable, as the brokers often make off with the majority of the money paid for the organs. This is not to mention the very often disastrous health and emotional impacts on the donors and their families.

Chapter 3 on organ trade in China provides a fuller illustration of this issue. Much of the illegal organ trade occurs in countries where law enforcement is lax or nonexistent. China, in particular, has become a major destination for transplant tourists until recently. Yoon points out that the issue of China's illicit organ harvesting, particularly from executed prisoners, has been the subject of much debate from a wide range of scholars and practitioners, but attention has been invariably paid to the ethical and moral dimension of illicit organ procurement. As a result, there is a general paucity of discussion about how such clandestine economic activities are intertwined with a series of political and socio-economic factors, both from domestic and international viewpoints. Yoon's chapter addresses this deficiency by detailing the nature of China's illicit organ trafficking practices in its broad social, economic and political context, and links this with policy and governance issues in China. She explains how the combination of various underlying factors such as punitive measures against any sign of dissent against the political system, pervasive societal divisions and gaps of deprivation accompanied by social regress in imperatives of life (i.e. healthcare) contributed to the pattern of underground organ sales in China. Yoon also illuminates how the confluence of such factors allowed the issue of the illicit organ trade to remain intact for decades despite the rigorous questioning from international community about the Chinese government's complicity in the black market. Although we witness the introduction of legal regulations of organ transplant to address the problem in China, the new measures were not without the pitfalls. Yoon highlights that the multi-faceted dimensions of illicit organ trafficking require the development of effective governance mechanism and enforcement regimes – both in China and beyond.

The negative impact of the flow of illegal immigrants or organ trade is only dwarfed by other categories of undesirable goods and products. Low-quality Chinese exports, particularly those that are manufactured under illicit conditions, have caused serious concerns during the last decade. There have been various health scares due to Chinese exports; some of these products are regular but inferiorly manufactured items (e.g. toys with lead), while others are illicit products that should never have been produced at all. Some of the scandals are attributable to negligence or incompetence of producers, while others are as a result of lax or non-existent regulatory mechanisms, or both. Yet others are due to outright illicit industries that sought to evade the oversight of authorities. Domestically, China faced severe challenges from a series of food scandals. The list of illicit food products shocked even the Chinese people, to say the very least. There have been reports of fake walnuts (made from empty shells glued together with cement and paper inside), fake eggs (gelatin, colouring and wax), fake tofu (chemicals and starch), fake rice (plastic), fake beef (pork processed with beef extract), fake mutton (rats, mink and fox meat), fake honey (sugar, chemicals and water), fake salt (industrial salt), fake rice noodles (rotten grain with additives) altered ginseng (boiled in sugar solution to increase weight), fake alcohol, and fake moon cakes, amongst others. The food safety problem certainly threatens not just Chinese people themselves, but also China's neighbours and trading partners. In Asia, virtually no country is immune to the problem as long as it imports from China to maintain a reliable and steady supply of foodstuff for their population.

Similar to Yoon's argument, Chapter 4 contends that China's rapid economic development and industrialization has come with a very high price in terms of adverse consequences to the nation, particularly in relation to the food safety issue. Drawing on the importing and exporting of vegetables as a case study, Sugita argues that as the Chinese government promotes rapid economic growth at home, it sows the seeds of its own downfall with food safety practices. Sugita goes on to describe how China's admission to the World Trade Organization (WTO) generates significant changes in government policies around food safety issues. In order to address the problem of promoting rapid domestic growth while meeting global safety standards, the Chinese government has been compelled to establish a dual economic structure – separating the food safety standard for export use from that for domestic use, and creating a highly advanced, exclusive and closed supply chain for major export-oriented companies.

The problem becomes more serious when it comes to counterfeit drugs, and in this instance, most of the consumers may not tell if they are taking the authentic medicine or if their supply has been compromised without their knowledge. This of course is on top of "traditional" drugs that are smuggled by criminal elements into the country. In recent years, the United States is seeing a surge of drugs such as fentanyl and amphetamines just as it is seeing an increase in various illicit consumer drugs and pharmaceutical products being sent or smuggled into the country.[23] In Southeast Asia, particularly in Indochinese countries such as Vietnam and Myanmar, there is an influx of fake pharmaceutical drugs into the marketplace. Most countries and jurisdictions in East Asia have strong custom regimes in place to detect and confiscate fake drugs. However, in developing countries such as Myanmar or Indonesia where regulatory mechanism is weak or non-existent, these fake drugs can find their way into the system very easily.

Chapter 5 explores the magnitude of fake pharmaceutical drug industry in China. With advances in technology and communications, the manufacturing of counterfeit drugs in China is now something that can be easily done in small warehouses and family homes. As Teo and Yoon point out, the inner workings of the industry appear to be similar to that of many other manufacturing cycles in reality in terms of the practices, value chains and production cycles. What is the most insidious aspect of this industry is that the counterfeit drugs often enter the legitimate supply chain at various stages. By providing a snapshot of successful convictions in recent times, Teo and Yoon layout the widespread nature of these criminal enterprises and discuss the serious challenges the illicit drug industry poses to both the health and human security of China and the global community as these medicines are exported worldwide. The authors suggest the need for holistic governance through legal, technical and financial mechanisms.

A lot of these "undesirable" industries are not so much "demand-driven" (since no one really wants fake medicine) as much as they are "supply-driven".

Manufacturers of fake medicine produce what is demanded in different geographical areas. In developing countries, they clone drugs that are crucial to basic survival (e.g. anti-malarial pills), whereas in developed world, drugs that are the most profitable (e.g. price inelastic drugs like cancer drugs or lifestyle drugs like Viagra) are cloned. It is one thing for sub-Saharan Africans, for instance, to obtain versions of electronics such as cheaper mobile phones or other appliances, but quite another thing for them to be supplied with fake essential drugs such as anti-malarial medicine. Due to the weak state capacity of the developing countries like those in Africa, the governments might not have the ability to deal with the influx of fake drugs into the country. Cumulatively, this is a silent crisis that is growing more serious by the day as various countries are unable to come together to deal with this problem collectively.

Africa's relationship is not only tainted by the import of fake pharmaceutical products from China, but is also weighed down by China's demand for various raw materials for its traditional cuisine and medicine. From overfishing of sharks to the poaching of rhinoceros for their horns to the indiscriminating killing of elephants for ivory, demand from East Asia, particularly from China, has been blamed for various ecological problems. The demand stimulates and encourages transnational smuggling, and there is a brisk trade for the animals and wildlife smuggled into China – dead or alive. The implication is the imbalance of the natural system and disruption of the environment: India has complained that Chinese demand for sandalwood has seen overharvesting of sandalwood trees, and Australia about its abalone stocks and deforestation; the Mongolian steppes have suffered from people's appetite for terrestrial cyan bacterium, also known as hair vegetable, popular amongst the Chinese. The ecological threats also stem from both the rearing and the consumption of animals, both within and outside of China's borders. The Cantonese appetite for wildlife, particularly for civet cats, caused the virus for the global SARS epidemic in 2003. The consumption of wildlife as part of traditional medicine, cuisine and alternative herbal remedies, and even the possession of the wildlife as exotic pets, has certainly seen the establishment of pathways for the smuggling of animals and/or their parts.

Chapter 6 on the smuggling of pangolins illustrates precisely this problem. Southeast Asia has long been an important trading partner for China, both in terms of forest, marine and mineral products from within the region, and as a transhipment centre for commodities from the Indian Ocean rim. Animal products and animal parts, in particular, have constituted an important segment of this trade, both historically and in the present. Yet, the last few decades have seen the rapid growth in the collection and trade of these animals, to the extent that many of them are threatened with extinction. The pangolin is a good example of a previously prevalent species in different parts of southern China and Southeast Asia endangered by the escalation in demand, especially in China. It has also become one of the most commonly smuggled animals in the illicit trade in animals/animal parts in Southeast Asia. Koh details the illegal trade in pangolins between Southeast Asia and China in terms of its structures, methods and flows, and its implications for the people involved in the trade. He goes on to locate the trade within its historical context and within the context of China-Southeast Asia exchanges and flows. Koh argues that it is only by adopting a more holistic approach to the socio-economic and cultural dimensions of this trade – through understanding not only the demand side in China and other East Asian and Southeast Asian countries consuming pangolin meat and scales, but also the supply side, in the collectors and hunters of these animals and parts, as well as the trade networks that facilitate these flows – that we can better tackle the challenge of curbing or even eradicating the trade.

Much of China's illicit trades are undertaken at the border, particularly with regards to the smuggling of illicit goods/services and contraband. This is particularly manifested in China's borders with Myanmar and North Korea. Both countries have come under United Nations sanctions at some point in their recent history, and both have rampant illicit trade, particularly at their borders. The China-Myanmar frontier is considered one of the world's most dangerous borders, more so on the Myanmar's side than on the Chinese side, for the simple reason that different sections of the border are under the control of different armed groups. Some of the groups co-exist with the state, whilst others are in actual conflict with the state. Areas within rebel strongholds and insurgencies often create conditions by which bilateral trade between the region and the neighbouring countries are stopped. Residents and rebels, therefore, undertake different activities to sustain their causes and livelihoods. Beyond traditional criminal activities such as drug smuggling and running gambling joints and prostitution dens, these illicit entrepreneurs often conduct illicit trade or services for the Chinese living on the other side of the border in the form of resource extraction such as illegal timber logging and smuggling of jade.[24] Rebels and separatists who fought the Myanmar government forces relied on illicit timber trade with Chinese to fund their war. The Chinese traders in turn sell the smuggled timber to the Chinese furniture makers who ferry the timber with fake papers through Chinese customs to their factories on the eastern seaboard to make cheap consumer furniture for export to United States or Europe.

Chapter 7 on logging provides an interesting case to consider. The Greater Mekong Basin (GMB) has been one of the most important sources of high-value hardwoods for China's market over the past decade. Kraisoraphong reviews the situation of the alarming surge in demand for the rosewood species, and the associated illegal trade, which has occurred under poor governance within the Mekong countries. She discusses the case of Siamese rosewood (*Dalbergia cochinchinensis*) listed in Appendix II of United Nations Environment Programme's Convention on International Trade in Endangered Species of Wild Fauna and Flora (CITES), and the challenges to effective implementation of CITES. Drawing from a theoretical framework on international institutions and national policies, the chapter argues that CITES can influence national compliance through alternative mechanisms, which refers to non-state actors and domestic mechanisms.

Depending on legal jurisdictions, the legality of a product or service could change. Marijuana is illegal in many countries, while in the Netherlands, it could be consumed like a cigarette in most coffee shops for less than 20 Euros. The ability to criminalize an activity or outlaw a product is one of the most potent arsenals in a state's ability to fight illicit activities and criminal enterprises. Yet, it is also this ability to create differentials across different legal jurisdictions that accentuates demand and supply of illicit activities and services. When news of the melamine-laced milk powder scandal broke, demand for foreign-manufactured milk powder soared because no one had the confidence to buy domestic milk powder. In order to prevent mainland Chinese from buying up all the milk powder in its stores, the Hong Kong government legislated that all persons could not carry up more than 1.8 kg of powder formula a day across the border. Offenders might be jailed for two years or fined HKD$500,000. From a legal framework that might work, but smugglers resorted to using the elderly, the unemployed and workers who cross the border on a daily basis to bring back the milk powder. Legislation provides teeth to law enforcement, but often it drives illicit activities underground – making them harder to control, much less eradicate.

The problem with legal jurisdictions may also create adequate opportunities. Other than physical products, entrepreneurs might capitalize on the differential to generate even more profits. Chapter 8 on shadow banking illustrates exactly how this industry can manage. Regardless of the illicit industries one is involved in, these grey economy entrepreneurs would need to have access to banking services and products, just like ordinary entrepreneurs. Illicit entrepreneurs are often unable to get a loan from high street banks or perform certain transactions such as remittances, foreign exchanges and transfers of money abroad. The development of the shadow banking industry is therefore one of the most important dimensions that supports most of the illicit industries in China. In particular, the ability to funnel profit out of China to be laundered is one of the most important functions in the People's Republic. Through this chapter, Teo surveys the overall state and the development of shadow banking in China. By consolidating various views and perspectives, the chapter presents the diverse activities and practices in the industry, and in turn, looks at how the government has attempted to rein in these activities. Teo goes on to detail how unlicensed money changers acting as remittances help to funnel money in and out of the country. All these cases illustrate the difficulties of the individual states and their agency to handle and rein in these illicit industries, and allude to the importance of having the states come together to handle these challenges.

## Illicit industries, shadow economy and global governance

There is no question that these industries need to be managed and curbed – domestically in China, regionally in Asia and globally. However, the connection between illicit industries and the global clandestine economy cannot be separated that easily. As much as the governments agree on the need to co-operate, the notion of sovereignty necessitated by the Westphalian system[25] means that current attempts to combat these transnational ills remain fraught with difficulties. The absence of an overarching authority in the international system also means that anarchy is a central element in the international system, suggesting that any meaningful dialogue, whether it is conflict and collaboration, can only take place between states. There are four difficulties[26] with the traditional interpretation of International Relations in regards to interstate relations. First, there is no clear demarcation between intergovernmental agencies, as their mandates and functions often overlap or conflict, and consequently, objectives get blurred. Second, very often because of bureaucratic inertia or reasons, these agencies fail to address their collective objectives. Third, many issues are characterized as intermestic; that is, issues are both international and domestic at the same time. Fourth, there is an accountability deficit in the shaping of global politics and practices. It is not immediately clear how decisions surrounding global policy reflect the balance of power among states as well as between state and non-state actors. Existing international institutions and regimes do not seem to be able to tackle these dangers posed by these illicit industries adequately.

### *Why current international cooperation cannot work*

The ineffectiveness of current international cooperation means that today, the dangers of illicit industries are spilling into areas which modern states have not prepared for.[27] Although some of these international groupings, organizations or regimes have had some success in creating global consensus, legitimacy and coordination around certain issues, there still exist many areas which these groupings cannot collectively address.[28]

The first of these areas is the transnational and human security issues poised by the illicit industries. This is not surprising, since many of these regimes are not created specifically to deal with illicit industries.

Second, due to the sheer number of international groupings, states, regimes and other actors, they often have conflicting aims and strategies which might cancel out each other's efforts. Even when they are not, their goals might not be harmonized enough to provide a coherent solution. For instance, even if the WTO and other NGOs lobby for better environmental governance, they often also lobby for an increase in global trade.[29] Illicit industries would thrive under such a liberal trading environment, too.

Third, given that many transnational businesses – licit or otherwise – are never under the regulatory frameworks (often by the state), it would be extremely difficult for states to enforce laws and regulations against these illicit industries. Different legal regimes, the inability of law enforcement agencies to undertake cross-border and transnational operations, and the lack of successful cross-jurisdiction prosecutions (due to cost, time and technical difficulties) all make things very difficult.

Fourth, there are endogenous reasons related to each illicit industry. Profits, employment and knock-off effects for local economies, and the inability of the entrepreneurs to switch to other forms of work, would contribute to the persistence of the industry.

Fifth, the illicit industries react to the state's attempt to govern, and in turn the state is often circumscribed by the need for the existence of these industries whereby consumption of products are not harmful but often aid in the economy for the reason of the supply of jobs and income. The counterfeit industry in Southern China is an extremely good example.

Sixth, the competition within these industries is driving innovation within each of these industries to both compete amongst themselves and also to survive from the attempts to shut them down. There are innovations in materials design, cloning techniques and even marketing. For instance, today's fakes are increasingly hard to discern. Many watch retailers and pawnbrokers in Macau are being scammed by people selling fake watches to them, as the quality of the fakes are so good that often only manufacturers themselves can distinguish the fake from the genuine. These products are either smuggled or exported to countries as far away as Africa and the United States.

Seventh, illicit industries use different methodologies and strategies to thrwart the state's attempt to grapple with them. The criminal innovation in the enhancement of products and services is only surpassed by the innovation in self-preservation strategies to overcome the attempts to control and eradicate them. They operate nimbly across jurisdictions and present real challenges for law enforcement, particularly as these illicit entrepreneurs interact, collaborate and innovate. The approaches to handling these illicit industries and transnational security remain relatively weak, incoherent and reactive.

### *Global governance and the way forward*

There have been intense discussions of how global governance is required to help combat precisely the kind of challenges illicit industries pose for us today. It is, however, not instantly clear what the term "global governance" means, as most scholars cannot grapple with the entirety of what is going on at the global level.[30] In theoretical terms, *governance* differs from *government*, the latter implying sovereign prerogatives and hierarchical authority. Thus, global governance does not equate to world government.[31] Global governance is characterized by a multiplicity of actors, with no overarching authority and inability to construct a coherent agenda. Globalization has established transnational spaces that prevent the aggregation of interests at this level, and this in turn encourages the interaction between state and non-state actors that limits the political options of states.[32] It is therefore a process of cooperative leadership that brings together national governments, multilateral public agencies and civil society to achieve commonly accepted goals.[33] This cooperation should be characterized by inter-sectoral, inter-ministerial and inter-institutional exchange and collaboration, though the rationalizing of actions among sovereign states[34] to incorporate actors and communities from underrepresented states. The constituent membership of existing multilateral institutions should be updated to better represent people and regions not represented. These steps improve the "democratic deficit" of existing international regimes.

Today, economic globalization is the most common form of globalization, as represented by multitude of MNCs and financial institutions, which coexist side by side with international regimes. Public and private interests are usually more represented in the agendas of these international organizations as opposed to global interests. Illicit industries occur clandestinely, allowing them to expand with impunity. As demonstrated, transnational security problems – particularly those posed by these illicit industries – are problems that exceed the capacity of one state, organization or individual community to tackle. The provision of global public goods such as the combating of environmental ills, tackling global and transnational crimes or grappling with public health scares transcend that of traditional security concerns. Human security, therefore, provides an excellent paradigm compatible with global governance regimes because it responds to transnational, multi-dimensional threats that a single country cannot manage. The problems and challenges posed by the illicit industries in the global underground economy are often insidious, amorphous and have a complexity that defies easy categorization, often involving actors at various levels.

At the holistic level, the authors in this volume agree that an enhanced global governance mechanism is necessary to tackle all these issues. There are three important principles that the new governance system must adopt to tackle these issues. First, there cannot be a one-size-fits-all approach in trying to address these challenges, and that relevant sets of actors from IGOs, NGOs and concerned governments to local institutions must come together to coordinate their actions and strategy for the purpose of combating these challenges in a more sustainable and coordinated manner. All chapters speak of the importance of novel global concerted efforts to address common challenges. Second, in order to develop effective countermeasures for dealing with the ills from these industries, the governance mechanism must be able to stay in line with the innovation of these illicit industries. This innovation means that there must be accurate intelligence on the ground of evolving methodologies, trends and strategies of the criminal entrepreneurs working in various industries. Naturally, it would also be accompanied by rapid change and response in both policing and enforcement methods at the level of transnational, national and subnational institutions. Most importantly, the legislation must change and adapt to ensure that appropriate enforcement is followed through. Third, the new global governance mechanism should work in tandem within the existing framework of the international system. Unlike many other scholarly pieces, authors in this volume suggest that even though a new innovative governance system must supersede the kind of international cooperation predominant in the international system today, this superseding should and must reinforce the existing mechanisms of the Westphalia system. Whether it is the compliance with international legislations, strengthening enforcement efforts or running educational campaigns against intellectual property thefts and cultural proclivities to consume wildlife, all these efforts require the acquiescence and compliance of national authorities, not without.

Using the "consumer reaction" model proposed (Table 1.1), the volume suggests that one of the most urgent tasks for global governance efforts to focus on should be those illicit industries that are disapproved by both the state and the public (consumers). This category of products and services constitutes an immediate menace to humanity. Therefore, human security should precede national sovereignty considerations and be the fundamental basis for the objectives of policy and cooperation at regional and global levels. In tackling these industries, the focus of the global governance efforts should be targeted at the supply side of the equation, i.e. the manufacturers and those who distribute the products. Taking the example of the fake pharmaceutical industry, this could be done through a few measures. First, all stakeholders should understand that the quality of global governance will improve greatly with the acquiescence of the relevant countries to play a greater role. In this instance, the Chinese government should be invited to increase governance capacity and champion the cause in combating the production and distribution of fake pharmaceuticals not just in China but also elsewhere. Second, relevant IGOs should try to persuade China to harmonize the penalties and enforcement efforts to tackle these industries at the source through the establishment of ongoing dialogue and discussion, and strengthening of domestic law. For instance, large-scale export of counterfeit medicine could be covered by parts of terrorism legislation across states, and this would render the state authorities greater leeway for investigation, prosecution and enforcement. Further regulation could also be considered for institutions liable for the facilitation of the export of illicit items. National authorities should strengthen the regulations regarding the negligence of courier companies for the transportation of illicit products, increasing the liability of couriers, airliners and shipping companies. Legislation could be strengthened for inter-agency cooperation for cross-border taskforces and right of hot pursuit to track these illicit entrepreneurs across borders. Third, global governance efforts should rethink the prospects of enhancing the penalties for people, particularly those with fiduciary duties in breaching the medical supply. In this instance, healthcare workers such as doctors and nurses could be dealt with under legislative provisions. This is of course in addition to the various measures discussed in the chapter, but the point here is that the Chinese government should not be viewed as an adversary in the fight against fake pharmaceutical products, but an important ally. Even though China might be reluctant to admit that it is the source of these drugs, it would be in China's interest to work with relevant international institutions such as Interpol and other states for two reasons: First, this directly impinges on China's international image as a peaceful rising power capable of shouldering more international responsibilities. Second, it is in China's self-interest to ensure that producers of fake drugs are being brought to justice – particularly to secure their own drug supplies in an effort to prevent this epidemic from growing at an exponential rate. Given that the illicit pharmaceutical business is known to be one that has the profitability of the drug business without the corresponding risk, the rational thing perhaps is to consider increasing the "risk" of people who partake into the industry. Cooperating with international regimes and allowing foreign investigations can lead to successful prosecutions and would send a message of the enhancement of governance efforts to the global community.

Needless to say, some of these recommendations also extend to the fake "food" industry. As Sugita notes, government leadership, corporate conscience and consumer supervision are extremely important to build a secure food supply system.

In China, the circumstances are quite different. It appears that the government is determined to address this issue, and law enforcement has no problems taking down manufacturers who endanger food safety. For instance, the manufacturers of the melamine-laced milk powder were quickly located and brought to justice. The real problem is that in China, most of these offending industries are not exactly "corporate" in nature. From fake eggs to fake beef, many of these setups are usually cottage industries that have cropped up over the years in backyards and makeshift factories in disused buildings and village spaces.

The important ingredient missing in the governance of these industries is the lack of strong national bodies that govern the various standards of food safety, and the number of home-based informal food producers who remain outside the remit of these governing bodies. Granted, the founding of the State Food and Drug Administration of China in 2003 (国家食品药品监督管理总局) to look after food and drug safety is an important and positive step forward, but much remains to be done. China still suffers from criticisms about bloated bureaucracy, the lack of coordination between the national and provincial agencies, the lack of effective "food" legislation and most importantly, the deficiency of effective monitoring systems that focuses on "prevention" above everything else. In other words, food safety in China today still appears to be more about damage control and after-the-fact enforcement rather than a coherent system with a well-thought-out strategy to insure the safety of the people. This impression might not be a fair critique, but the press reports of food safety problems certainly seem to give that impression.

This is not surprising, since the unethical producers are often small scale and undertake activities that even deny the imagination of most common people. It is hard to see how the Food and Safety Agency can foresee that illicit vendors would "manufacture" walnuts with walnut shells glued back with stones in them or look for rice manufactured out of plastic. Enforcement is particularly difficult as many of these backyard industries are not licensed in the first place (i.e. they are off the radar) and they would quietly hawk or distribute their products directly to end users, often bypassing retail outlets. Until they are reported by consumers, the authorities would not be able to act. Thus, one of the most important mechanisms to tweak is the provision of a more centralized monitoring and reporting system that puts consumers, including the mass media and online platforms, at the forefront of reporting errant food and drug vendors. Better global governance with regards to the food exports from China can only be achieved with better cooperation with the Chinese state, not against it. Thus, regional countries should engage and interact with the Chinese government, encouraging Chinese authorities to emulate the systems that other developed countries have in place. They could look to the United States, Germany, Britain, Japan, Singapore or even Hong Kong to pick and choose features that they would like to adopt. It would be in the interests of regional states to help China, not to criticize it, and this can be done through low-profile frequent exchanges and discussions.

Beyond this, a broader question that needs to be addressed here is the element of greed. Traditional suggestions of building more effective monitoring standards, instituting stricter food safety regulations with regards to the manufacturing of food products and additives cannot substitute for ethics, self-restraint and social responsibility. All these are social and cultural attitudes that can only be changed if there is a corresponding change to the idea of relentless pursuit of material wealth and profits at a societal level.

The picture is different for the category of goods and services that are "welcomed" by consumers. This would be the category of consumer goods that provides an "additional" choice for consumers such as cloned electrical appliances described earlier, even though manufacturers and law enforcement have a problem with that. In targeting industries that infringe intellectual property laws, China should also think about seizing the profits made from these industries in addition to imposing stiffer custodial sentences for major offenders. At the same time, enhancement of economic growth for more employment opportunities, upskilling of the workforce in tandem with technological advancement, and promoting an increase in public awareness of intellectual property rights are important steps forward.

For those industries that are "tolerated" by consumers, it would be important to consider the industries on a case-by-case basis. The existence of these industries does not necessarily offend all consumers in China, as they usually cater to a specialized category of clientele (e.g. those looking to migrate without paperwork or those looking to purchase a kidney or move money illicitly overseas). These industries do not offend the large number of other consumers, and very often receive some sympathy from the general public. In order to tackle each of these illicit industries, it is important to understand what drives the suppliers and consumers in each industry. The organ trade system is easy enough to understand. Desperately sick people in developed countries (or even in developing countries) with sufficient means attempt to skirt the law to purchase an organ needed for the transplant. It is hard to see how global governance can eradicate the demand when demand always outstrips supply. The organ trade in China is a "tolerated" industry, because most people have no use for it usually, but would consider this industry an "optional" one because there might be a chance that they seek to join the queue for one. The Chinese nation is an unlikely place for supply to meet the demand because of Chinese perchance for "complete bodies" when one dies. A more troubling issue is related to the middlemen who scam the poor for their body parts to sell in neighbouring countries such as India or the Philippines.

A controversial but possibly safer way out for the poor might be for states to harmonize the prospects of a transnational body overseeing international donor and recipient lists, with the possibility for the donor to provide some sort of consideration donation to the recipient's family or community. This might effectively eliminate the middlemen, ensure that the financial incentives to go the right people, increase the list of donors and – most importantly – allow the authorities to control the "trade". This proposal of course needs to be studied carefully and all safeguards put in place, but the essence of this solution is to crack down on the unethical middlemen who exploit the poor. Legislating this trade might provide more control and protect both the interest of donors and recipients. In other instances, such as the shadow banking, it would be incumbent for states and relevant actors to come together and consider licensing some of these trades in order to control them.

Like the organ trade, moving overseas to work to strive for a better life is not something that is out of place for many Chinese. Today, this practice of moving without legitimate paperwork is usually confined to the poor or the unskilled who view that their prospects of life are much better in the target countries. They form the bulk of work of the snakeheads who traffic humans for a living. This form of migration is now usually voluntary and brings more problems for host country than the donor country. The negative externalities of the human trafficking industry, like that of the organ trade countries, is felt more outside of China than inside China. The most interesting aspect for global governance with regards to human trafficking is that this is an industry that is very contingent on social networks and word-of-mouth contacts. This is not surprising since the bulk of transpacific or transatlantic migration from China to United States or Europe has been of people from certain areas in China, notably Fujian and Guangzhou provinces. Tackling these issues would require not only a harmonization of legislation and enforcement mechanisms, but also a deep-rooted approach that understands the dynamics of social networks and the mobilization of these workers. Like the bulk of the illicit industries in this category, a significant percentage of those who procures the services of snakeheads does so out of desperation or misinformation. Thus, in addition to the harmonization of laws and enforcement efforts, tougher penalties and seizing of profits from these middlemen are critical to the tackling of these industries.

Lastly, global governance could be enhanced if the cultural dimensions of these illicit industries are taken into account. In Hong Kong, campaigners have mounted a ferocious movement against the consumption of shark fin as an environmental issue. Beyond educating the general public regarding the ills of the industry for African countries and the general shark population, the campaign also works against a more deep-seeded cultural proclivity of ostentatious consumption. This is the flip side of quest for ever-increasing amount of profits. Cultural proclivities reinforce ostentatious consumption, which in turn necessitates huge profits. To break this cycle, education and reasoned thinking need to be injected in public and state policy.

Taken together, there is an urgent need to change our worldview and goals pertaining to the control of illicit industry activities in China by incorporating the notion of global public good. This requires a drastic re-orientation in the way states, societies and people conceive of these industries – they should be viewed as an issue of human security and global governance, as opposed to disparate domestic issues with international implications or public ethical problems with no recourse. Indeed, the illicit industries in China are a manifestation of complex issues spanning from legal, ethical, economic and political dimensions to transnational and domestic phenomenon. A number of obstacles stand in the way of China making an effort to address these massive and multifarious issues. However, in the absence of agreed-upon rules, enforcement mechanisms and objectives on a global scale, these illicit industries will continue to flourish and globalization will drive this trend further. It is tremendously important that countries including China focus more attention on making their involvement in cooperation more effective. They could make sure their policies and laws are harmonized so that their commitments made have positive impacts on strengthening punitive regimes. How China responds and curbs the activities of these illicit industries remains to be seen, but only through global governance efforts can we defeat the threats posed by the illicit industries. Responding effectively to the threats has now become the burden and opportunity for China and the global community.

## Notes

1 For instance, see R. Neuwirth, *Stealth of Nations: The Global Rise of the Informal Economy* (New York, NY: Pantheon Books, 2011); M. Niam, *Illicit: How Smugglers, Traffickers, and Copycats Are Hijacking the Global Economy* (New York, NY: Anchor Books, 2005); J. Henry, *The Blood Bankers: Tales from the Global Underground Economy* (New York, NY: Four Walls Eight Windows, 2003).

2 D. McMahon, *China's Great Wall of Debt: Shadow Banks, Ghost Cities and Massive Loans and the End of the Chinese Miracle* (Boston, MA: Houghton Mifflin Harcourt, 2018); A. Collier, *Shadow Banking and the Rise of Capitalism in China* (Singapore: Palgrave Macmillan, 2017).

3 S. Venkatesh, *Off the Books: The Underground Economy of the Urban Poor* (Cambridge: Harvard University Press, 2009), p. 371.

4 F. Scheider, and C. Williams, *The Shadow Economy* (London, UK: Institute of Economic Affairs, 2013), www.iea.org.uk/sites/default/files/publications/files/IEA%20 Shadow%20Economy%20web%20rev%207.6.13.pdf

5 "Guangzhou gears up clone taxi crackdown", *China Daily*, 23 October 2014, www. chinadaily.com.cn/china/2014-10/23/content_18791114.htm

6 D. Lague, "Next step for counterfeiters: Faking the whole company", *The New York Times*, 1 May 2006, www.nytimes.com/2006/05/01/technology/01pirate.html

7 "Chinese authorities find 22 fake Apple stores", BBC, 12 August 2011, www.bbc. co.uk/news/technology-14503724

8 This comment was made to one of the editors (Victor Teo) during a research fieldwork trip in Shenzhen.

9 See "Timeline: China milk scandal", BBC, http://news.bbc.co.uk/2/hi/7720404.stm

10 "Milk poisoning kills children in China", *The Guardian*, 8 April 2011, www.guardian. co.uk/world/2011/apr/08/tainted-milk-china-kills-three

11 ＜大厨自曝"厨房黑幕" 鸭肉泡羊尿冒充羊肉＞ [Chief reveals kitchen scandal of marinating duck meat in goat urine to pass off as mutton], *Xinhua News Net*, 15 March 2003, http://news.xinhuanet.com/life/2009-03/15/content_11014862.htm

12 D. Held, A. McGrew, D. Goldblatt, and J. Perraton (eds.), *Global Transformations: Politics, Economics and Culture* (Cambridge: Polity Press, 1999), pp. 15–16.

13 Ibid, chapter 1, in particular p. 27.

14 D. Held, "Reframing global governance: Apocalypse soon or reform!", *New Political Economy*, 11(2) (2006): 157–176.

15 J.G. Ruggie, "Reconstituting the global public domain – Issues, actors and practices", *European Journal of International Relations*, 10(4) (2004): 499–531.

16 For example, see C. Dahlman, "Technology, globalization, and international competitiveness: Challenges for developing countries", 2007, www.un.org/esa/sustdev/publi cations/industrial_development/1_2.pdf

17 L.E. Davis, "Globalization's security implications, Rand issue papers", 2003, www. rand.org/content/dam/rand/pubs/issue_papers/2005/IP245.pdf; also see Werlhof,

C., "The consequences of globalization and neoliberal policies: What are the alternatives?", *Centre for Globalization Paper*, 2008, www.globalresearch.ca/the-conse quences-of-globalization-and-neoliberal-policies-what-are-the-alternatives/7973

18 Depending on the individual state's attributes, including its size, relative power and economy structure, globalization is thought to have very different implications for different countries. See T.L. Friedman, *The Lexus and the Olive Tree: Understanding Globalization* (New York, NY: Picador, 2000).

19 J. Bhagwati, *In Defense of Globalization* (Oxford: Oxford University Press, 2007); also see W. Chamberlain, J. Bhagwati, and P. Armington, *Globalization, Free Trade and World Health: Set the People Free* (North Charleston: Create Space Independent Publishing Platform, 2012).

20 F. Mishkin, *The Next Great Globalization: Disadvantaged Nations Can Harness Their Financial Systems to Get Rich* (Princeton, NJ: Princeton University Press, 2008), chapters 4 to 7 in particular discuss the challenges financial globalization brings to emerging markets.

21 N. Serra, and J. Stiglitz, *The Washington Consensus Reconsidered: Towards a New Global Governance* (Oxford: Oxford University Press, 2008).

22 United Nations Development Programme Human Development Report Office, *Human Security*, http://hdr.undp.org/sites/default/files/human_security_guidance_ note_r-nhdrs.pdf

23 S. Jiang, "China says US not doing enough to cut demand for opioids", *BBC News*, 28 December 2017, www.cnn.com/2017/12/28/asia/china-drugs-us-intl/index.html

24 Fieldwork interviews, along the China-Myanmar border, summers of 2015 and 2016.

25 The modern nation-state system is underpinned by the legal principle of sovereignty that each nation-state has exclusive sovereign rights over its territory. To that end, all states are regarded as equal in international system, and have a few common characteristics: a well-defined territory occupied by a population with a common history and shared cultural characteristics; a central government supported by a functioning bureaucracy that must have a monopoly to the legitimate use of force and be able to exert this force to the further extent of the nation-state's territorial limits; and that this state must be recognized by other sovereign states; it must therefore be able conclude international treaty and wage wars.

26 D. Held, "Reframing global governance: Apocalypse soon or reform!", *New Political Economy*, 11(2) (2006): 166–167.

27 J. Stiglitz, *Globalization and Its Discontents* (New York, NY: W.W. Norton and Company, 2002).

28 D. Cameron, "Governance for growth: Building consensus for the future", *Report Submitted to the 2011 G20 Cannes Summit*, November 2011, www.g20.utoronto. ca/2011/2011-cameron-report.pdf

29 P. Newell, "The political economy of global environmental governance", *Review of International Studies*, 34(3) (2008): 507–529, http://sro.sussex.ac.uk/12575/1/S0260 210508008140a.pdf

30 T. Weiss, "Governance, good governance and global governance: Conceptual and actual challenges", *Third World Quarterly*, 21(5) (2000): 795–814.

31 *Global Governance 2025: At a Critical Juncture*, p. 17, www.iss.europa.eu/uploads/ media/Global__Governance_2025.pdf

32 W. Hein, and S. Moon, *Informal Norms in Global Governance* (Aldershot, UK: Ashgate, 2013), pp. 18–19.

33 J. Boughton, and C.I. Bradford, "Global governance: New players, new rules: Why the 20th-century model needs a makeover", *Finance and Development*, quarterly magazine at IMF, www.imf.org/external/pubs/ft/fandd/2007/12/boughton.htm

34 Ibid.

# 2 Human smuggling

## The case of illegal Chinese immigrants in the United States

*Xiaohua Ma*

China's rapid economic development helps improve economic and political ties between China, Central and Southeast Asia, Europe, and the Americas. However, whilst the improved trade and transportation networks facilitate legal trade and migration, they also facilitate the trade of grey market goods, illegal products and immigration, which collectively make up the shadow economy. China's massive population has resulted in an increase in its disposable income, and its consumer market is increasing accordingly, with business both legitimate and illicit attempting to obtain global market share. Driven by huge profits, once human and transportation networks are established, the shadow economy grows accordingly because more people are forced outside the legitimate economy to find new products and business out of the country. Smugglers and criminal organizations establish networks and control the flow of illicit products in and out of the country. Shadow economy works on the same basic economic principle of illicit goods work to meet consumers' demands outside of government control.

Human smuggling is a global concern, with a large number of countries affected by it as origin, transit or destination points. Even though there is a large and growing literature on human smuggling, the literature still lacks systematic research of theoretical and conceptual approaches.[1] The process of human smuggling is still not well understood, stemming from the difficulties in observing, measuring and precisely obtaining reliable data.

China, the most populous country in the world, has been criticized for its acts on human rights due to its different social and political systems. The latest U.S. State Department report released in 2017 condemned China as "among the world's worst offenders for allowing human trafficking".[2] The issue of Chinese human smuggling has been frequently mentioned, but scholarship has long ignored, partially because illegal Chinese immigrants have largely been "invisible" due to linguistic and cultural barriers erected by Chinese communities. Some study identifies basic features of Chinese human smuggling and provides valuable empirical knowledge about smuggling operations, but does not go far enough.[3]

This chapter attempts to uncover the nature of Chinese human smuggling organizations and their operations. First, it explores the inner structure of Chinese human smuggling networks to understand the essence of human smuggling. Second, it examines how illegal Chinese immigrants have been smuggled globally and how the Chinese smuggling business is operated. Since the United States is widely regarded as a main destination country for human smuggling, the focus is on the illegal Chinese immigrants in the United States.

## The difference between human trafficking and smuggling

Human trafficking and smuggling is a highly attractive market for criminal organizations. It has become one of the fastest-growing illicit industries in the world. According to a survey conducted by the United Nations in 2012, human smuggling and trafficking has become a thriving business that generates a total of US$32 billion in profits each year.[4] The worldwide trade in human smuggling and trafficking is now the third largest source of profits for organized crime, behind drugs and weapons.

The problem of human trafficking and smuggling cuts across a range of development issues, from poverty to social inclusion, to justice and rule of law issues, to human security, and thus has relevance for practitioners throughout the development community. The accepted international definition of human smuggling and trafficking was not devised until the end of the 1990s. Human smuggling and trafficking are covered under the two Protocols to the Convention Against Transnational Organized Crime, which was negotiated in Vienna under the United Nations Commission on Crime Prevention and Criminal Justice.

Human smuggling and trafficking are often used synonymously in public discussions and the media. However, the two terms are different. Human trafficking has many faces: forced labour, domestic servitude and forced marriage; organ removal, the sex trade, warfare, etc. Due to statistical bias and national legislation, sexual exploitation (79%) is by far the most commonly identified form of trafficking in persons, followed by forced labour (18%).[5] Millions of men, women and children become victims of human trafficking for sexual, forced labour and other forms of exploitation worldwide every year. The costs of human capital are probably impossible to quantify.

The Trafficking in Persons Protocol defines trafficking as:

> the recruitment, transportation, transfer, harboring or receipt of persons, by means of the threat or use of force or other forms of coercion, of abduction, of fraud, of deception, of the abuse of power or of a position of vulnerability or of the giving or receiving of payments or benefits to achieve the consent of a person having control over another person, for the purpose of exploitation.[6]

The Protocol to Prevent, Suppress and Punish Trafficking in Persons, Especially Women and Children, supplementing the United Nations Convention against Transnational Organized Crime, contains the first internationally agreed upon definition of trafficking in persons. The Trafficking in Persons Protocol entered into force on 25 December 2003, and 143 countries ratified or acceded to it by February 2011.

The Protocol against the Smuggling of Migrants by Land, Sea and Air, supplementing the United Nations Convention against Transnational Organized Crime, entered into force on 28 January 2004, and 127 countries ratified or acceded to it by February 2011. The Smuggling of Migrants Protocol deals with the increasing problem of migrant smuggling, often committed by transnational organized crime groups at high risk to the migrants and at great profit for the offenders. The definition of smuggling of migrants in the Protocol is as follows:

> Smuggling of migrants shall mean the procurement, in order to obtain, directly or indirectly, a financial or other material benefit, of the illegal entry of a person into a State Party of which the person is not a national or a permanent resident.[7]

Thus, trafficking in persons and smuggling of migrants are two completely different concepts. However, they are easily confused because of some similarities and partial overlap often existing between the two phenomena. Human trafficking and smuggling have common elements, but still some differences between the two criminal activities exist. The major differences between the two concepts:

1) *Agreement:* The smuggling of migrants, whilst often undertaken in dangerous or degrading conditions, involves migrants who have consented to the smuggling. Trafficking victims, on the other hand, have either never consented or, if they initially consented, that consent has been rendered meaningless by the coercive, deceptive or abusive actions of the traffickers.
2) *Ways of exploitation:* Smuggling ends with the arrival of the migrants at their destination, whereas trafficking involves the ongoing exploitation of the victims in some manner to generate illicit profits for the traffickers.
3) *Trans-nationality:* Smuggling is always transnational, whereas trafficking can be national or transnational. Trafficking can occur regardless of whether victims are taken to another country or only moved from one place to another within the same country.

From the definitions of the two offences, the conclusion can be drawn that the main difference is in the exploitation aspect of trafficking which is absent from the smuggling operation. However, making a profit is the main goal of both traffickers and smugglers. Similarities can also be found in their organizations, ranging from small-scale to large-scale businesses.

The United States is widely regarded as a destination country for both human trafficking and smuggling of migrants, but the exact number of human trafficking and smuggling victims within the United States has remained largely undetermined. Due to the covert nature of the crimes, accurate statistics on the nature, prevalence and geography of human trafficking and smuggling are difficult to calculate.

## A hidden path to "American Dream": smuggling of migrants into the United States

For centuries, people from all over the world have arrived on American shores with little more than a suitcase and a dream of a better life. The promise of freedom and opportunity lures a great number of foreigners to the United States, even though hardship and barriers exist. Political instability, increasing population, environmental degradation, widening economic disparities between countries and a worsening unemployment crisis have exacerbated global population mobilization. Furthermore, rapid technological developments have accelerated globalization and international migration.

During the 1990s, an average of 700,000 illegal immigrants entered the United States each year. The rate went up to 817,000 by 1998 and increased to one million in 1999. The foreign-born population of the United States amounts to a total of 33 million up to now, which equals 11% of the overall population. However, the U.S. Census Bureau estimates that 8–9 million of the foreign-born are illegal immigrants.[8] A 2010 statistic indicates that more than 11 million illegal immigrants resided in the United States.[9] They made up over 3% of the total population. In 2011, the U.S. Immigration and Naturalization Service released a survey and the number of illegal immigrants had increased to a total of 11.5 million (Figure 2.1).[10]

Illegal immigrants in the United States come from all over the world (see Table 2.1). It is estimated that 8.9 million (77%) of the total 11.5 million illegal immigrants living in the United States in 2011 were from North America, including Canada, Mexico, the Caribbean and Central America. The next leading regions were from Asia (1.3 million) and South America (0.8 million). Mexico is the leading country of origin with estimate of 6.8 million in 2011, which comprises 59% of the total illegal immigrant population in the United States. From 2000 to 2011, the Mexican-born population increased by 2.1 million, or an annual average of 190,000. The next leading source countries were El Salvador (660,000), Guatemala (520,000), Honduras (380,000) and China (280,000).[11] It is estimated that approximately one million foreigners illegally enter the American border each year. As Figure 2.2 indicates, the number of illegal Chinese immigrants in the United States is relatively small compared to the millions of Mexicans and Central Americans who enter the country illegally every year.

*Table 2.1* Country of birth of the illegal immigrant population in the United States

| Country of birth | 2000 | 2000 (% of total) | 2011 | 2011 (% of total) |
|---|---|---|---|---|
| **Mexico** | 4,680,000 | 55 | 6,800,000 | 59 |
| **El Salvador** | 430,000 | 5 | 660,000 | 6 |
| **Guatemala** | 290,000 | 3 | 520,000 | 5 |
| **Honduras** | 160,000 | 2 | 380,000 | 3 |
| **China** | 190,000 | 2 | 280,000 | 2 |
| **Philippines** | 200,000 | 2 | 270,000 | 2 |
| **India** | 120,000 | 1 | 240,000 | 2 |
| **Korea** | 180,000 | 2 | 230,000 | 2 |
| **Ecuador** | 110,000 | 1 | 210,000 | 2 |
| **Vietnam** | 160,000 | 2 | 170,000 | 2 |
| **Other countries** | 1,940,000 | 23 | 1,750,000 | 15 |
| **All countries** | 8,460,000 | 100 | 11,510,000 | 100 |

(Source: U.S. Department of Homeland Security)

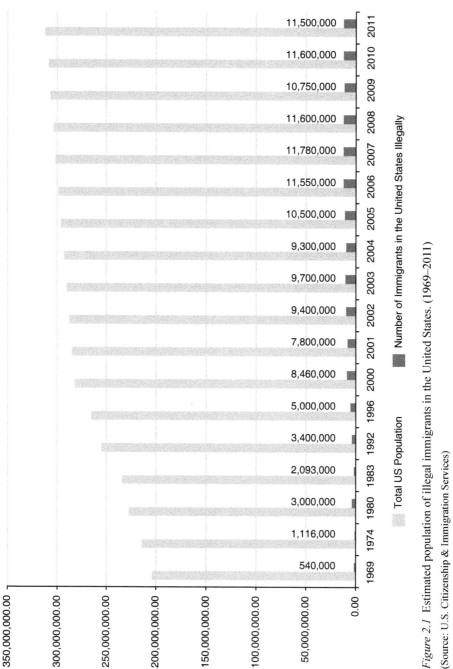

*Figure 2.1* Estimated population of illegal immigrants in the United States. (1969–2011)

(Source: U.S. Citizenship & Immigration Services)

## Human smuggling and illegal Chinese immigrants in the United States

Although narratives describing the first wave of immigration to the United States often focus on the people from Europe, Chinese drawn by the economic opportunity associated with California Gold Rush in 1849 were also among the country's early immigrants. The Chinese Exclusion Act of 1882, however, prohibited Chinese immigration to the United States, and legal opportunities for Chinese to emigrate to the United States did not occur until the fundamental reform of American immigration laws in 1965.[12] The number of Chinese immigrants in the United States has increased after the immigration legislation reform in 1965, particularly after Sino-U.S. diplomatic normalization was established in 1979, when the population of the Chinese Americans stood at just under 100,000 in the 1960s, to reach 1.8 million in 2010. According to the 2010 U.S. Census, the population of the Chinese Americans numbered approximately 3.8 million.[13] The Chinese represented the second-largest immigration group in the United States after the foreign-born from Mexico in 2010, and accounted for 4.5% of the total foreign-born population of the country. As Figure 2.2 demonstrates, a majority of Chinese Americans came to the United States after 1980 and the population has been rapidly increasing. Chinese immigrants, however, are highly concentrated in two states, California and New York.

Because of the limited immigration quota for Chinese nationals, few have a legitimate opportunity to emigrate to the United States. The restrictive immigration policies have resulted in a lucrative business whereby enterprising agents and

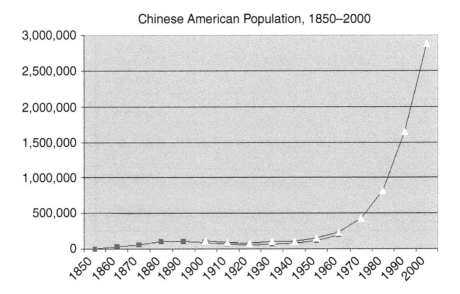

*Figure 2.2* Population of Chinese Americans (1850–2000)

(Source: U.S. Citizenship & Immigration Services)

contractors charge fees to transport Chinese nationals illegally. People in China, a country with a population of 1.3 billion, who believe that they can enjoy a better opportunity in the United States than their own country, seek to move to the United States to secure better lives and realize their "American Dream". Smugglers take advantage of the large number of people willing to take risks in search of a better life when they cannot access legal channels of migration. A significant number of Chinese who fail to enter the United States via legal channels consequently become clients of human smuggling. In fact, Chinese entering the United States illegally is not a new phenomenon. Nevertheless, organized Chinese human smuggling is relatively a new issue.

The Chinese smuggling issue did not make the news until 1993. Organized Chinese human smuggling aroused American attention in 1993 after the Honduran ship *Golden Venture* ran aground in New York Harbour with 286 undocumented Chinese aboard. The American public became aware of the fact that illegal Chinese immigrants were flowing in by sea.[14] In 1994, the United States Congress enacted the Violent Crime Control and Law Enforcement Act to punish the smuggling of migrants.[15] Federal authorities have also successfully prosecuted several smuggling organizations as racketeering business. However, the wave of illegal entry of Chinese nationals into the United States does not terminate. Instead, global smuggling networks have emerged.

### The strategy of Chinese human smuggling

Organized Chinese human smuggling onto American shores has been conducted over two decades. Since the 1990s, Chinatown in New York City has witnessed a large flow of Chinese immigrants from Fujian Province. Walking down East Broadway in New York's Chinatown, one can easily see many shops, restaurants and employment agencies (Figure 2.3) run by Fujianese. Some scholars argued that it is impossible to study modern Chinatown without a careful analysis of the Fujianese community.[16] Some even pointed out that the "new blood" of Fujianese immigrants has challenged the old Chinese community, whose people originally came from Guangdong and Taiwan.[17] A survey found that the number of Fujianese in New York's Chinatown reached over 200,000 in 2000.[18] A great majority of them were facilitated by human smugglers, whom the Chinese called "snakeheads", or *Shetou* in Chinese. Though it is difficult to obtain an accurate number of Fujianese population in the United States, conservative estimates suggest that more than 30,000 illegal Chinese immigrants have been brought to the United States annually.[19] How can these illegal immigrants be transported to the United States from China?

The vast majority of illegal Chinese immigrants are smuggled by someone they know through personal or community connections. Smugglers do more than just help people to get across borders. They are essentially brokers, making money from everyone involved in the irregular labour markets. Smugglers or snakeheads who act as recruiters understand the situation in China, and they have established

*Figure 2.3* A typical scene of the Fujianese Employment Agency in New York's Chinatown
(Source: Photograph by Xiaohua Ma)

a close relationship with brokers and employers in Chinatown. Thus, social networks are key to linking the immigrants and the smugglers.

Tens of thousands of Chinese have entered the United States illegally through a sophisticated worldwide network of direct or indirect routes each year. Unlike illegal immigrants from Latin America who enter the United States at little cost, each illegal Chinese immigrant must pay snakeheads a huge fee from $20,000–140,000, depending on their transportation methods.[20]

Several strategies have been utilized to transport Chinese nationals into the United States. A traditional strategy is to travel to Canada or Mexico and then illegally cross the borders into the United States.[21] Those who crossed into the United States on land faced risks and hardships. The majority of them had travelled to Mexico or Canada by sea. They suffered not only during the long sea journey, but also whilst crossing the border. A second strategy is to fly into the United States either directly or via several transit ports outside China. Many Chinese illegal immigrants hold some fraudulent documents to board the aeroplanes and enter the country. A third strategy is to transport Chinese nationals on freighters into the United States.[22] Most of Chinese illegal immigrants start in Fuzhou, capital city of Fujian province, or other coastal towns in Fujian province. From there, they are sent by freighter, by air with false visas or hidden in cargo containers. Cargo containers are often used to transport Chinese directly into the U.S. ports. The role of Chinese smugglers – snakeheads – is to

*Figure 2.4* A corner of Little Fuzhou in New York's Chinatown
(Source: Photograph by Xiaohua Ma)

provide fraudulent documents, advice on bribing officials in transit countries and passage across the Canadian or Mexican border to enter the United States successfully.[23]

A majority of Chinese illegal immigrants leave China legally from Fujian province and have legitimate passports and visas to countries other than the United States. Many of them go to Thailand first on legitimate visas. In Bangkok, they make contact with local snakeheads who provide them fraudulent documents then fly to a third country, where they wait for a couple of weeks or months and subsequently go to the United States. The whole journey may take several months, or even a year or two. One major route passes though Bangkok, Karachi, Madrid and London before finally arriving in New York City (Figure 2.4). Some Chinese even travel from Latin American countries such as Dominican Republic into Puerto Rico, where they can fly to the U.S. mainland without passing through immigration control.[24]

Many employment agencies in this area attempt to help the newly arrived immigrants to find jobs in the Chinese communities. After the *Golden Venture* incident in 1993, it became rather difficult to drop immigrants off in U.S. ports by boat. There have been several changes in the methods and routes that are used by snakeheads to transport Chinese nationals into the United States. The preferred method became smuggling Chinese to Central America or Mexico, where they could make their way overland to the United States. In recent years, Chinese human smugglers have been increasingly going to peripheral locations to unload the human cargoes, such as the U.S. Virgin Islands and Guam, Ensenada (Mexico) and British Columbia

(Canada).[25] Chinese snakeheads have also developed other sophisticated methods for breaking the defence lines erected by the U.S. Coast Guard. The routes change frequently depending on what the snakeheads think will work efficiently.

On the other hand, the strategy has been changed, as well. Many would-be immigrants now demand either a direct flight from China to the United States, namely as members of a business delegation, or using "legal" immigration procedures, for example as spouses of American citizens through false marriage to enter the United States. This route is the most expensive, some even paying more than $140,000 for a transportation fee.[26]

The smuggling business is extremely lucrative since the fee is expensive. It has been increasing rapidly in recent years. According to a court testimony of Chinese smuggler Cheng Chui-ping, who was well-known as "Big Sister Ping" in New York's Chinatown and regarded as one of "the most powerful and successful alien smugglers" in the United States, the fee she charged for would-be immigrants for the journey from Fujian to New York was $18,000 in the 1980s, and it increased to $35,000 in the 1990s.[27] The fee charged for the journey to the United States increased to $60,000 in 2000.[28]

In short, there are many different means of transportation. The level of safety and ease of reaching the destination are dependent on the amount of money paid. A fake business visa or a false marriage visa (or as spouses of F-1 visa holders) may cost even more, over $100,000.[29] Those would-be immigrants do not need to pay until they have reached their destination successfully, although a small amount of down payment – approximately $3,000 – is necessary before the trip starts.[30]

Furthermore, there is also a big change in the geographical origins of the smuggled Chinese immigrants. In the past, the U.S. Immigration and Naturalization Service estimated that more than 95% of illegal Chinese immigrants came from Fujian Province. Recent research shows that the population of illegal Chinese immigrants from Wenzhou of Zhejian province has been increasing. In addition, a new group of illegal immigrants from northeastern provinces is rapidly growing in New York's Chinatown.[31] A survey found that the total number of illegal Chinese immigrants reached to 350,000 in the United States in 2006.[32]

In sum, the smuggling of Chinese immigrants is more diversified and dynamic in regional and cultural backgrounds. Moreover, the smugglers have become more capable of using multiple sophisticated routes, methods and strategies to transport Chinese nationals into the United States illegally.

### The nature of Chinese human smuggling: a sophisticated social network

Organized human smuggling is no longer a simple activity to help immigrants across national borders for $100, due to the greater distance of many sending regions. The smuggling of immigrants is a complicated and difficult operation that cannot succeed without an extremely cautious scheme and cooperation around the globe. Chinese snakeheads are much more sophisticated than the coyotes who help people cross the American borders. Their organizations are transnational and have access to the most advanced technology for communication. Their passport and visa factories have the capacity to make fraudulent passports of any country, fake visas to the United States and other necessary documents. They are also able to obtain the latest information and arrange the best possible routes for smuggling people.

Therefore, the organization of Chinese human smuggling requires multiple players in different regions and countries. In the case of Fujanese immigrants, the smuggling process starts operation in the communities in Fuzhou, Fujian province, where smugglers can recruit potential immigrants nearby the area. Recent survey demonstrates that smugglers have a dense network that reaches every corner of the world: Fujjian, Taiwan, Hong Kong, the Golden Triangle – a northern mountain region of Myanmar, Thailand and Laos – Latin America, Africa, Europe, and New York's Chinatown.[33]

The smuggling business is a complex process. However, it is not difficult to start because there are no qualifications or special skills required for snakeheads to operate the enterprise. People of diverse backgrounds participate in the smuggling business. Most of the snakeheads are regular people working in the restaurants, shops or factories in Chinese communities. The most important premise for the Chinese smuggling organizations is to use the social networks efficiently.

Chinese snakeheads in the smuggling business are normally from a close social network, namely a regional association, or *Tongxianghui* in Chinese (Figure 2.5).

*Figure 2.5*  The largest Fujianese Association in New York's Chinatown, Fujianese *Tongxianghui* Association, located on East Broadway in Manhattan's Chinatown, has become a central hub for Fujianese immigrants in the United States

(Source: Photograph by Xiaohua Ma)

The majority of the smuggling organizations belong to a family or a close regional association. The smuggling process consists of various social networks and regional associations based on geographical, cultural and linguistic similarities. Smugglers become involved in the business through relatives, friends or business partners, in addition to direct recruitment. Since Chinese snakeheads and would-be immigrants originally come from the same village or the same town and speak the same dialect, a special partnership can be easily established on the foundation of the same cultural background. These special social ties are dispensable for immigrants and snakeheads.[34]

Therefore, Chinese human smuggling operations depend on unique social networks rather than individual agency. The social relations and network ties of family, friends and villagers have been central to understanding of migration and Chinese transnational human smuggling. The proximity and solidarity of the special social ties are crucial for regular migration and human smuggling, as well.

Chinese human smuggling is often described as "well organized with sophisticated global networks".[35] The smuggling process is composed of several networks, each is responsible for the eventual goal of landing clients in the United States. There are many players in the organizations, but no one has been manipulated by the other. Moreover, no one has absolute control over entire smuggling business. Comparing to the traditional criminal organizations, Chinese smuggling organizations are not hierarchical, the division of labour is well developed among the smugglers and their roles are different during the whole transportation process. The major divisions of the smuggling activities can be summarized:[36]

1) **Recruiters** are often relatives or close friends of the would-be immigrants who know the smugglers.
2) **Coordinators** are central figures in the smuggling business since they need to communicate and provide necessary services for the whole transportation process.
3) **Transporters** help those would-be immigrants to leave China and enter other countries, and finally land in the United States.
4) **Document vendors** are able to produce documents (both legal and illegal) to facilitate the transportation of the would-be immigrants.
5) **Corrupt officials** are the authorities in China and other transit countries who are paid to assist the Chinese.
6) **Crew members** are employed by snakeheads to work to run the smuggling ships.
7) **Guides** are responsible for moving the Chinese from one transit point to another, or assisting the would-be immigrants to enter the United States.
8) **Local staffs** in *Tongxianghui* of Chinese communities help the would-be immigrants to find jobs in the shops, restaurants or factories in Chinatown.
9) **Debt collectors** are responsible for the would-be immigrants to be safe in the United States, and supervise and inspect them for paying the smuggling fees.

Each role is by no means exhaustive. The specific role required for a smuggling operation may differ, depending on its transportation method and complexity. It might be more complicated if the transportation method becomes more diversified, since the whole process needs smugglers' inseparable contacts and cooperation in different regions and countries.

Motivated by profit, Chinese smugglers are more concerned about the process of the work and even the responsibilities to their clients than about the morality of their activities. Chinese snakeheads consider themselves as free agents and describe others in their networks as friends, fellows or business partners. None of the smugglers consider themselves criminals, although they realize the illegal nature of the smuggling activities. The relationship between snakeheads and would-be immigrants is perceived as strictly contractual and not exploitative. Naturally, they view themselves as making an honest living since they are trying to help their friends, relatives and villagers to move into the United States. Thus, snakeheads generally regard themselves as "regular" and "honest" business people.

On the surface, the relationship between Chinese smugglers and their clients is somewhat based on a kind of reciprocal assistance. The would-be immigrants trust the smugglers, and some even show great admiration for them. For example, "Big Sister Ping" – one of the most prolific and notorious Chinese human smugglers, or "Mother of All Snakeheads" who was arrested in the United States in 2000, was widely respected in the Fujianese community in New York's Chinatown. Ironically, she was even regarded as a "Living Buddha" in her hometown of Shengmei, a village near Fuzhou City, Fujian province, since over 90% of the villagers was successfully transported to the United States and finally realized their "American Dream" owning to her assistance.[37] Undoubtedly, this view helps to explain why so many otherwise law-abiding people become involved in the human smuggling business.

It is worth mentioning that one phenomenon is obvious in the Chinese human smuggling business. Unlike those involved in traditional organized gang crime, a great number of the snakeheads are female like Big Sister Ping.[38] Those female snakeheads are found at different levels of the smuggling business. Some are very successful, whilst others are merely part-time recruiters. Some scholars have pointed out that Chinese human smuggling had relations with the traditional gang crimes in the Chinese community.[39] However, recent research found that the majority of Chinese smugglers had nothing to do with traditional crime organizations.[40] More research into this matter is still required.

## Conclusion

Human smuggling is a global phenomenon which has remarkable geographic and organizational diversity. Profit-seeking criminals smuggle people across borders and between continents. Assessing the real size of this crime is a complex matter because of its underground nature and the difficulty of identifying when illegal migration is being facilitated by smugglers. Evidence suggests that the crime is significant and increasingly growing as the development of the global markets. After 11 September 2001, the U.S. government strengthened the border control system and enacted The Homeland Security Act in November 2002 to protect its borders. Ending human trafficking and smuggling is among the top priorities of President Donald Trump's administration as those practices are perceived to seriously violate human rights and threaten national security. Even with top-notch technology and large numbers of customs agents, however, it is extremely difficult to stop human smuggling and illegal immigration.

There are many reasons. Smuggling operations around the world are extremely profitable, which naturally attracts the attention of organized crime. Once these organizations see profits, they begin to solidify their control, expand their reach and build their networks. As different regions are connected to one another, it becomes easy for the criminal organizations to control entire networks, from supply to market. These criminal organizations can become so powerful that they rival local and state governments for power. In some regions or countries, for example in Southeast Asia and Central America, human smuggling is handled by organized criminal organizations both local and international, local governments and possibly military networks. Thus, it is not difficult for organized criminal organizations to establish routes to transport illicit goods and human smuggling globally. Corruption is a major and serious problem at border crossings and ports, which not only increases the difficulty of interdiction, but also negatively affects border security. It is no surprise that, looking at the global context of illegal smuggling, organized crime groups are increasing their control of the transportation routes and networks connecting Asia to Europe and the Americas.

Undoubtedly, strict laws and regulations will decrease the crime. Combating human smuggling is extremely challenging, although there are many strict laws preventing human smuggling and its victims from being abused. Even countries that are resolute in the fight against illicit trade and human smuggling encounter daunting obstacles. The real nature of the problem lies in the enforcement of the laws. Apart from it, moral education is pivotal. For cross-border illicit trade and crimes, the need for transnational cooperation, including evidence sharing across different legal systems, impedes legal enforcement. Therefore, it is indispensable to increase international cooperation, reinforce transnational efforts, strengthen moral education and ensure that the laws in the countries involved are harmonized to close loopholes.

There is no doubt that human smuggling distorts global markets, undermines the rule of law and spurs transnational criminal acts. It is a serious transnational crime and a gross violation of human rights. It threatens national security and public safety and represents serious dangers to both single states and the global community. This transnational organized crime involves the planning and execution of illicit business ventures by many social networks or groups of individuals working in. More and more people are becoming aware of the horrors of human smuggling.

Although human smuggling persists in the world, we can reduce the crime with strong laws, sufficient punishment and good moral education. We should use all possible measures to minimize the increasing crime.

# Notes

1 The best treatment of human smuggling can be seen in D. Kyle, and R. Koslowski (eds.), *Global Human Smuggling: Comparative Perspective* (Baltimore, MD: Johns Hopkins University Press, 2001 and 2011) and S.X. Zhang, *Smuggling and Trafficking in Human Beings: All Roads to America* (Westport, CT: Praeger Publishers, 2007).
2 G. Harris, "China is among worst human trafficking offenders, State Department says", *The New York Times*, 27 June 2017 (online). https://www.nytimes.com/2017/06/27/world/asia/china-human-trafficking.html
3 For example, S. Zhang, *Chinese Human Smuggling Organizations: Families, Social Networks and Cultural Imperatives* (Polo Alto, CA: Stanford University Press, 2008), and K.L. Chin, *Smuggled Chinese: Clandestine Immigration to the United States* (Philadelphia, PA: Temple University Press, 1999).
4 "U.N.: 24 million human trafficking victims", *USA Today*, 4 March 2012, http://usatoday30.usatoday.com/news/world/story/2012-04-03/
5 United Nations Office on Drugs and Crime, *Global Report on Trafficking Persons* (New York, NY: United Nations Press, 2012), p. 13.
6 United Nations Office on Drugs and Crime, *United Nations Convention Against Transnational Organized Crime and the Protocols Thereto* (New York, NY: United Nations Press, 2004), p. 5.
7 Ibid, p. 41.
8 M. Hoefer, N. Rytina, and B. Baker, "Estimates of the unauthorized immigrant population residing in the United States", *Population Estimates*, March 2012, pp. 3–4, www.dhs.gov/xlibrary/assets/statistics/publications/ois_ill_pe_2011.pdf
9 J. Preston, "11.2 million illegal immigrants in U.S. in 2010, report says; no changes from '09", *New York Times*, 2 February 2011. https://www.nytimes.com/2011/02/02/us/02immig.html
10 M. Hoefer, N. Rytina, and B. Baker, "Estimates of the unauthorized immigrant population residing in the United States: January 2011", *Population Estimates*, March 2012, pp. 6–7. http://www.congressandimmigration.com/2011_report.pdf
11 Ibid, p. 4., http://www.congressandimmigration.com/2011_report.pdf
12 For the historical formation of American discriminative policy towards Chinese immigrants, see X. Ma, "The Sino-American Alliance during World War II and the lifting of the Chinese Exclusion Acts", *American Studies International*, 2 (June 2000): 39–61.
13 U.S. Census Bureau, *The Asian Population: 2010*, March 2012, www.census.gov/prod/cen2010/briefs/c2010br-11.pdf
14 Among the 286 undocumented immigrants aboard the *Golden Venture*, ten died attempting to swim to shore; 246 were from Fujian Province and 40 were from Wenzhou of Zhejian Province.
   There was a wide coverage of the Chinese smuggling issue in 1993, for example, "The Golden Venture, plus 100,000", *The New York Times*, 9 June 1993, www.nytimes.com/1993/06/09/opinion/the-golden-venture-plus-100000.html; and P. O'Shaughnessy, "The Golden Venture tragedy: From hell at sea to the American dream", *New York Daily News*, 8 June 2008, www.nydailynews.com/news/golden-venture-tragedy-hell-sea-american-dream-article-1.294299
15 U.S. Congress, *Violent Crime Control and Law Enforcement Act of 1994*, H.R. 3355, 103rd Congress (Washington DC, 1994). https://www.congress.gov/bill/103rd-congress/house-bill/3355
16 P. Kwong, *The New Chinatown* (New York, NY: Hill and Wang, 1996).
17 J. Li, "The new blood in Chinatown, on the eve of Hong Kong takeover, a revolution takes hold in lower Manhattan", *The New York Times*, 22 June 1997.
18 K. Murphy, "Smuggling of Chinese ends in a box of death, squalor", *Los Angeles Times*, 12 January 2000, http://articles.latimes.com/2000/jan/12/news/mn-53272

19  W. Criffith, "Chinese immigrants find faith in America", *CBS News*, 26 December 2011, http://www.cbn.com/cbnnews/us/2011/June/

20  These numbers are based on author's interviews with Chinese newcomers working in New York Chinatown in 1996 and 2003.

21  "Smugglers use Mexico as gateway for Chinese immigration", *Los Angeles Times*, 21 June 1993, http://articles.latimes.com/1993-06-21/news/mn-5468_1_illegal-immigrants

22  S. Zhang, and K.L. Chin, "Chinese human smuggling in the United States of America", *Forum on Crime and Society*, 2(1) (2000): 33, http://www2.tku.edu.tw/~ti/Journal/8-1/812.pdf

23  B. Mo, *Shadou: Chugokujin mikkosha o owu* [Snakehead: Chasing Chinese Illegal Immigrants] (Tokyo: Shinchosha, 1999).

24  P.R. Keefe, *The Snakehead: An Epic Tale of the Chinatown Underworld and the American Dream* (New York, NY: Anchor, 2010).

25  "Pingjie Guoji Touduwang Baoguang: Maitong Haijun, Renshe Xuesa Bu Gui Lu" [Exposure of Sister Ping's smuggling network: Bribing naval officials and clients go to a road of no return], http://news.xinhuanet.com/overseas/2005-06/03/content_3040657.htm

26  S. Zhang, and Khin, "Chinese human smuggling in the United States of America", p. 38.

27  J. Preston, "Trial starts with details of immigration smuggling", *The New York Times*, 17 May 2005, www.nytimes.com/2005/05/17/

28  Z. Liang, and W. Ye, "From Fujian to New York: Understanding the new Chinese immigration", in D. Kyle and Koslowski, eds., *Global Human Smuggling: Comparative Perspective* (Baltimore, MA: John Hopkins University Press, 2011), p. 223.

29  "Cong Fujian Cunguo dao Toudu Huanghou: Shetou Dajie Ping Fumoji" [From a regular female villager to queen of human smuggling: Full collapse of Snakehead big sister Ping], *Fazhi Ribao*, 1 April 2006, http://news.sina.com.cn/o/2006-04-01/11258586462s.shtml

30  S. Zhang, and K.L. Chin, "Chinese human smuggling in the United States of America", pp. 31–52.

31  K.L. Chin, *Smuggled Chinese: Clandestine Immigration to the United States*, p. 13.

32  "Meiguo Feifa Huayi Yimin, Piaobai haishi Qiansong" [Illegal Chinese immigrants in the United States: Americanized or repatriated, *Guoji Xianqu Daobao* [Newspaper of International Pioneer], 30 May 2006, http://news.xinhuanet.com/overseas/2006-05/30/content_4619893.htm

33  D. Kyle, and R. Koslowski (eds.), *Global Human Smuggling: Comparative Perspective*, p. 220.

34  For Fujianese *Tongxianghui* and its roles in transporting Chinese nationals to the United States and the relationships between the old Fujianese community and the new immigrants, see Yoshihara Kazuo, "San Francisco no kajin shinyimin dantai ni okeru sougo fujo to koukyosei: Fukkenkaikan o jirei ni" [The organizations of Chinese new immigrants in San Francisco and their commonality of reciprocal support: A case study of Fujianese Associations], in Fujita Hiroo, ed., *Higashi ajia ni okeru koukyosei no henyo* [Transformation of Commonality in East Asia] (Tokyo: Keio University Press, 2010), pp. 347–361.

35  S. Zhang, and K.L. Chin, "Characteristics of Chinese human smugglers", *Research in Brief*, 7 August 2004, www.ncjrs.gov/pdffiles1/nij/204989

36  The data is mainly based on author's interviews carried out in March 2012 with Fujianese who resided in New York's Chinatown and participated in the smuggling business.

37  M. Sha, "Toudu Yougong? Cunminmen wei Pingjie Kuahai Shengyuan", [Contribution to smuggling of migration? Villagers cross the sea to support big sister Ping], http://news.xinhuanet.com/overseas/2005-06/23/content_3124330.htm

38 S. Zhang, and K.L. Chin, "Women's participating in Chinese transnational human smuggling: A gender market perspective", *Criminology*, 45 (2007): 699–733.

39 M. R.J. Soudijin, and E. R. Kleemans, "Chinese organized crime and situational context: Comparing human smuggling and synthetic drugs trafficking", *Crime, Law and Social Changes*, 52 (2009): 457–474.

40 Y.R. Wang, "Human smuggling, illegal Chinese immigrants and crime – An examination of the American experience", *Tamkang Journal of International Affairs* (2004): 45–66.

# 3 Black market trade of human organs in China and its implications for global governance

*Sungwon Yoon*

## Introduction

Human organ transplantation has become a successful medical procedure during the past few decades. Thousands of patients at risk of death are given new life through the transplantation of healthy organs. According to the World Health Organization (WHO), 98 countries have organ transplantation services.[1] Regrettably, very few countries have sufficient organs to meet patients' needs. The demand for organs far outstrips the supply. The shortage of human organs is a global issue leading the death of thousands of patients on the list awaiting organ transplant.[2] In desperation, many patients resort to unethical supply of organs – namely, organ transplant tourism – thereby encouraging organ trafficking and exploiting the vulnerable as a source of organs. At present, it is estimated that almost 10,000 organs are purchased on the black market annually.[3] Whilst the growing rates of illicit organ trafficking raise concerns for the victims of the organ procurement, mounting media reports on the black market in organs indicate that the illegal organ trade seems only likely to grow. Much of the illegal organ trade occurs in countries where law enforcement is lax or nonexistent. China, in particular, has become one of the popular destinations for transplant tourists until recently. The issue of China's illicit organ harvesting – particularly from executed prisoners – has been the subject of much debate from a wide range of scholars and practitioners, but attention has been invariably paid to the ethical and moral dimension of illicit organ procurement. As a result, there is a general paucity of existing discussion about how such clandestine activities are intertwined with a series of political and socio-economic factors both from domestic and international perspectives.

This chapter investigates the nature of China's illicit organ trafficking practices in their broad social, economic and political contexts, and links this with policy and governance issues in China. Specifically, it examines the combination of various underlying factors reflected in the pattern of underground organ sales in China, and explains why the issue of illicit organ trade had remained intact for decades despite rigorous questioning from international community about the Chinese government's complicity in the black market. Recent introduction of legal regulations of organ transplants to address the problem is then discussed, along with the pitfalls of the new measures in cracking down the enduring illegal organ trade practice in China. The chapter concludes with some policy implications of the multi-faceted dimensions of illicit organ trafficking for the development of an effective governance mechanism both in China and beyond.

## Globalization of the black market organ trade

The nature of the clandestine black market of human organ trade is closely linked with globalization. Globalization has facilitated both the humanitarian dimension of organ transplantation and the illicit aspect of this undertaking. In an era of globalization, knowledge knows no boundaries and procedures once thought to have been "miracles" can now be performed in many countries. This important life-prolonging method is now available to most of the world (Figure 3.1). Regrettably, the technological innovations in science have been subjected to an adverse feature of globalization, a propensity to commodify and find marketable values in human body parts. What was previously a scientific and medical activity is increasingly transformed into the commercial language of supply and demand, contract, trade and reimbursement.

And from this commercialization, implicit in the removal of organs and the handling of the donor as a natural resource, come the profiteering and illicit exploitation that has tainted this great scientific process. The 21st century provides ease of transport across national boundaries, assistive technology such as computers and mobile phones, all of which expedite and provide opportunities for traffickers to practice their trade without much risk, making the business of organ trafficking highly lucrative and as infamous as international slavery, drug trafficking and exploitative child labour. Preying on the anxieties and desperation of both the sick and the poor, organ traffickers can take advantage of both elements and profit hugely in the process. As the United Nations admitted in its Millennium Declaration: "While globalization offers great opportunities, at present its benefits are very unevenly shared, while its costs are unevenly distributed".[4]

Underlying these profit-making clandestine activities is the unmatched supply and demand in human organs. As medical science has provided the means to prolong life, the demand for transplants has grown by approximately 33% each year. However, the availability of donors has only risen by about 2%.[5] This gap opens the door for illicit activity to meet the demand and make lucrative profits.

The WHO estimated that approximately 66,000 kidney transplants, 21,000 liver transplants and 6,000 heart transplants were performed in 2005 across the globe.[6] Kidney transplants appear to be the most prevalent, and are carried out in over 90 countries. Similarly, the Global Observatory on Donation and Transplantation estimated that about 100,000 solid organ transplantations (not including corneas, heart valves and tissues) are performed yearly worldwide.[7] As of 2015, there were 84,347 kidney transplantations, 27,759 liver transplantations, 7,023 heart transplantations, 5,046 lung transplantations and 2,295 pancreas transplantations.[8] According to the Netherlands Health Council, about 25,000 transplants are performed yearly in the United States and approximately 16,000 in Europe.[9]

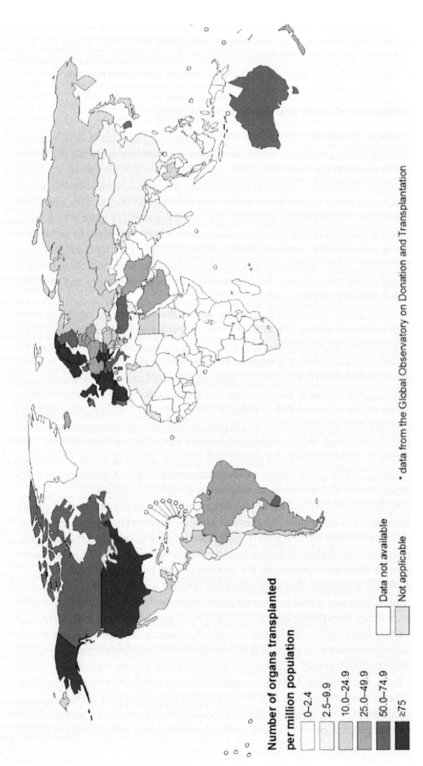

**Number of organs transplanted per million population**

- 0–2.4
- 2.5–9.9
- 10.0–24.9
- 25.0–49.9
- 50.0–74.9
- ≥75

Data not available

Not applicable

\* data from the Global Observatory on Donation and Transplantation

*Figure 3.1* Global transplant activities of solid organs in 2014

Observatory on Donation and Transplantation (2016). Available at www.transplant-observatory.org/)

Unfortunately, the number of transplants has not kept pace with the markedly increased demand. There are more patients waiting to receive transplants than there are deceased donors or even living donors to provide the required organs. In Europe, there were 40,000 people waiting for a kidney for transplant[10] and only 10% of the demand for kidneys was fulfilled.[11] As of 2014, 63,000 Europeans were waiting for transplants and 4,100 died due to the shortage of organs. The waiting time for Europeans hoping for an organ transplant is expected to increase to ten years.[12] In 2018, 115,039 patients were on waiting lists for transplantation in the United States[13] and the daily death rate from this cause was estimated to be 20.[14] In the United Kingdom, more than 5,000 patients were waiting for a kidney transplant in 2017,[15] whilst the number of deceased donors has barely increased. As a result, the demand for kidney transplant is projected to increase at 8% annually.

Asia is not exceptional in the race to search for organs, which is also allegedly regarded as one of the world's most abundant sources of human body parts for transplants. In China alone, it is estimated that 1.5 million patients need organ transplants, whereas only 19,000 operations are performed annually.[16] This shortage has been explained as due, 'in part, to religious beliefs that the body should be buried intact and in part to a fear of hospitals intentionally allowing patients to die to harvest their organs for paying patients'.[17] In Japan, there are approximately 12,000 patients on the waiting list for transplant but only 10% of those receive transplants.[18] The huge gap between supply and demand has prompted a great number of illicit actors who see the commercial trade and trafficking of human organs as an easy and quick profit-making business with very little effort.

The organ brokers, not bound by either legal or ethical imperatives, look for the cheapest sources of organs, often exercise force and violence, and sell in the affluent markets, making vast profits without much fear of being caught. At present, nearly half of all transplanted kidneys were estimated to come from living donors, and that the figure increased to over 80% in countries of social insecurity and economic abandonment. With the increasing burden of chronic diseases as a result of ageing population worldwide, growing wealth, and the ease of international travel, demand for transplantation is expected to increase. In the absence of an adequate global regulatory framework, the shortage of available human organs will therefore undoubtedly facilitate organ transplant tourism and illicit organ trafficking and sales. Tourism for overseas commercial transplants raises particular concerns about the victims of organ procurement in underground sale of organs. Studies that documented organ trafficking showed that living vendors were either coerced or paid little, and often left with no follow-up care, leading to physical disabilities and depression.[19,20,21] Studies also demonstrated that purchasing transplants overseas is reportedly associated with a higher risk of serious complications, especially infections such as human immunodeficiency virus (HIV) and Hepatitis B.[22]

Due to the nature of such illegal activities, characterized by inherent concealment and deceit, an estimation of the scale of the organ trafficking or an assessment of the global picture is hard to achieve. The United Nations stated that the scope of organ trafficking is difficult to estimate as the subject had not been closely scrutinized by member states.[23] The WHO estimates that 10% of the over 63,000 kidneys transplanted annually from living donors have been trafficked. It is also reported that brokers charge US$70,000–160,000 to organize a transplant procedure. The donor could receive US$1,000–5,000 for a kidney[24] (see Table 3.1 on page 55). The WHO admits that the 'lack of documentation makes it difficult to estimate the extent of ethically unacceptable practices or the relative efficacy and safety of transplantation for the treatment of various conditions and in various settings'.[25] Hence, much of the evidence is anecdotal, and whilst the figures provide a hazy picture which is nonetheless alarming, substantial information on the actual nature of this illicit underground business is difficult to come by.

There can be little doubt, however, that organ trafficking, like any other criminal enterprises such as human trafficking and the drug trade, flourishes in a globalized economic system where notions of national sovereignty appear outdated and are belied by the fast pace and transport of goods, services and money from one country to the next. The black market of human organ trade in China comes in this context of global picture.

## Organ trafficking in China: the contextual background

China had for decades allegedly been one of the most popular destinations for human organ tourism.[26] The scarcity of organs worldwide and the readily available body parts allegedly procured from executed prisoners in China have created a widespread international suspicion that China is part of the illicit global economy of organ trade. Little information is publicly available about China's involvement in this clandestine enterprise due to, similar to other "sensitive" issues, the country's policy on restricting freedom of speech and public debates on subjects of controversy and uncertainty. Before we examine the details of China's organ trafficking practices, this section outlines the backdrop of wider political, economic and public health issues behind China's involvement in illicit human organ trade.

First, from a political perspective, China has displayed an aggressive pursuit of national interests, militarization and elimination of dissent. Consequent to the Communist takeover of China in 1949, the government has emphasized an assertive form of nationalism that manifests itself in various ways ranging from a defensive reaction when any allegations surface in the Western media about significant corruption in the Chinese government, punitive measures against any sign of dissent against the political system, and judicial conviction and capital punishment to a great extent. Chinese authorities have zero tolerance for crime. As one media report puts it, the Communist Party leaders wanted "police to strike hard to smash blackness and wipe out evil".[27] The government believes that the death penalty is necessary to enforce its laws and for citizens of China to retain a peaceful existence.

Under such political circumstances, the system of organ procurement was, according to Chinese dissidents and human rights activists, state-sanctioned and state-supported. The harvesting of the body parts from executed prisoners from a country that routinely executes more people than the rest of the world was not inconceivable. As this chapter will examine in the next section, the Chinese information was largely made up of allegations that were strenuously denied and denounced by the Chinese government. Criminal activity, particularly when civil servants appear to be profiteering, was concealed and covered up with a degree of thoroughness. Only occasionally did the Chinese government admit the existence of the problem, and when it did, it acted in a rapid fashion to deal with it.

Second, economically, however, the situation is entirely different. China has in recent decades converted a socialist economy into a global economic market-place that manufactures a significant portion of the world's consumables and has become one of the leading economies in the new century.[28] China's economic policy was very successful. Whilst prior to the economic reforms, China's economic growth was 6% a year (though not every year), in the aftermath of the economic changes, China has achieved a spectacular average annual growth rate of 10% in 1990–2010. As of 2017 estimates, China has emerged as the world's largest economy, with US$12 trillion of gross domestic product (GDP), over-taking United States. China has become the largest exporter and second-largest importer of goods in the world.[29]

However, there is a more depressing aspect of the positive growth of the Chinese economy. The U.S. National Intelligence Council emphasized China's growing gap between the rich and poor, the social safety net, corruption and environmental damage.[30] The benefits of this rapid progress have not penetrated to the 61 mil-lion Chinese believed to be below the national poverty line. The World Bank estimated that 219 million Chinese lived on less than US$1 per day, China has paid a significant price for its economic development and although the economic reforms have lifted millions of its people out of poverty, the costs are manifesting themselves daily across the country.[31] Therefore, whilst China may be the world's largest economy, it is also ironically the country with the second highest level of economic inequality in Asia.

Organ trafficking in China can be considered one manifestation of the perva-sive societal divisions, gaps of deprivation and destitution that motivate people to take desperate measures to survive. Within a country where the governing idea involves the importance of making money, the commodification of every item would appear to be inevitable. The activities of traffickers demonstrate a continu-ing problem of corruption as well as ignorance of the rights of people and of the law.[32] Despite the strict controls over freedom of expression, occasionally a story surfaces that highlights the type of desperation that prompts people to engage in organ trafficking.

Third, economic progress in China has been accompanied by social regress in imperatives of life such as healthcare. The conversion to a capitalist economic structure has led to serious inequities in the distribution of wealth generated by the new system. The WHO survey measuring the equality of medical treatment placed China 187th out of 191 countries. Driven by private enterprise and a profit-oriented economy, the government spending on basic healthcare expenditure dropped from 36% in 1980 to 17% by 2006.[33] The consequence has been that transplant tourism became an important business venture and a vital avenue for the survival of healthcare providers in a rapidly privatizing economy.

The decline of public spending on healthcare forced hospitals and physicians to raise revenues through profitable enterprises such as transplant tourism, accepting bribes, ordering unnecessary tests for a patient and prescribing medications, as more medicine doctors prescribed, the more they earned. Hu Weimin, a cardiovascular doctor, disclosed that hospitals in China had no choice but to chase profit in order to survive. The World Bank study found that 20% of China's poor blamed healthcare costs for their financial straits. The Chinese Community Party (CCP) government admitted that as of 2006, 80% of Chinese citizens had no medical insurance.[34] In January 2009, the government embarked on serious healthcare reform of universal healthcare system, allocating US$125 billion with an aim to extend medical insurance coverage to 95% of its population and improving access to hospitals and clinics.[35] A recent report indicates that under-funding of healthcare facilities and growing disparity in quality of healthcare persisted.[36]

It should therefore come as no great surprise that China would enter with enthusiasm into the business of providing medical facilities and human organs for foreign transplant tourists who saw the price acceptable and did not enquire about the source of their new organs.

### The extent of the illicit organ trade and China's limited openness

The illicit organ trade thrived in China since late 1990s that particularly catered to transplant tourism from overseas. Transplant operations in China was first performed during the 1960s, and since then China experienced rapid growth in organ transplantation. In particular, the period from 2000 to 2005 represents a time of rapid increase in the number of organ transplant operations. National statistics show that surgeons performed approximately 11,000 organ transplants in 2004.[37] The figure includes 7,300 kidney transplants, more than 2,500 liver transplants and over 100 heart transplants. The number of registered liver transplant facilities increased from 19 in 1998 to 52 in 2000 and 500 in 2005.[38,39] In the United States, there were 100 hospitals qualified to perform liver transplants.[40] Accordingly, China boasted the largest deceased donor renal and liver transplant programme in the world as of the mid-2000s.[41]

Oddly, however, Chinese cultural values do not seem to be compatible with the donation of human organs. Chinese people in general believe that humans should die intact, and as such, there is a general unwillingness to donate the organs of their deceased family members. Even kidney donation from living relatives represented only 0.6% of 40,393 transplants between 1971 and 2001.[42] This universal unwillingness towards organ donation amongst the Chinese, when matched against the massive number of transplant surgeries performed annually, was perplexing for many. It is inconceivable to see the high transplant volumes if the supply of organs is unpredictable and depends on the timing of death or living donation. This unusual feature of organ transplants in China suggested that it was fundamentally a supply-driven market. Human rights activists, Chinese dissidents and other sources claimed to have strong evidence that pointed to the likely commission of illicit practices against Chinese prisoners by members of the medical, legal, police and judicial professions.

Dr Harry Wu, one of China's most prominent dissidents, revealed in testimony before the U.S. Senate Committee on Foreign Relations that 'China's problems with organ transplants have resulted in the harvesting of organs from bodies of executed prisoners, and a flourishing illicit trade in donations among the general population'.[43] Wu stated that in China 'the harvesting of organs from executed prisoners proceeds as an entirely government owned and controlled operation'.[44]

Whilst the precise number of executions was shielded as a state secret, Amnesty International estimated in 2001 that China's average execution rate was 40 citizens per week. According to the organization, between 1990 and 1999, China imposed 27,599 death sentences and executed more than 18,194 persons.[45] The five-year average between 1995 and 1999 was 1,680. In 2005, the number of executions was 1,770. Correspondingly, the number of liver transplants increased from 118 in 1999 to 4,000 in 2005.[46] The organization commented that China was 'performing executions to expand the organ trade from executed prisoners'.[47] The country defended what it considers to be its very limited use of the death penalty.[48] The Chinese government insists that even if organs were taken from executed prisoners, the practice only proceeded after the prisoner or their family consented.

International human rights groups and activists began questioning China's commercial organ collections and sales extensively in the early 1990s, highlighting the country's practices to the international community for the first time.[49] Yet it was not until 1997 that the U.S. Federal Bureau of Investigation (FBI), in response to information submitted by the Justice Department regarding China's death row organ trade, began to investigate these allegations.[50] In 2001, a congressional subcommittee in Washington, DC rigorously questioned Chinese government representatives regarding China's commerce in organs from death row inmates.[51]

The Chinese representatives unequivocally denied the existence of the clandestine enterprise.[52] An official from the Justice Ministry maintained that harvesting from death row prisoners was not a usual practice, and that it was carried out with the "presumed consent" of the prisoners when it did happen.[53] Although the Chinese government claimed this practice rarely occurred, it refused to disclose any information on the number of organs extracted from the death row prisoners.[54] The Chinese embassy in Washington, DC asserted, 'the so-called sale of criminals' organs in China is a deliberate fabrication with ill intentions'.[55] Zhang Qiyue, the Foreign Ministry spokeswoman, declared that the major source of human organs comes from voluntary donations from Chinese citizens and any claim on China's illegal organ trafficking was 'a vicious slander' against China.[56]

The nature of underground organ trade was also explained to a Congressional Committee on Human Rights in the United States in 2001 by a Chinese doctor, Wang Guoqi, who applied for political asylum. He testified that prisoners were 'executed so that their organs can be transplanted into wealthy recipients from the West and Far East'. According to Wang, a former military physician who had participated in the removal of nearly 100 organs from death row convicts, prisoners selected to be donors were tested before execution for suitability. He noted that rich foreigners paid over US$15,000 for transplants and the 'sale of organs netted huge profits for the People's Liberation Army'.[57] The Chinese Government accused Wang of 'fabricating appalling lies' with an aim at acquiring political asylum in the United States.[58]

The growing evidence about China's practice of organ harvesting from executed prisoners, including Wang's testimony, prompted international criticism. Critics argued that such practice compromised the legitimate administration of China's penal process and resulted in brutal forms of prisoner abuse. Human rights activities pressed China to change both the organ procurement and death penalty practices. In 2006, harvesting of the organs of executed Falun Gong adherents – reported by David Kilgour, a former Member of Parliament of Canada, and David Matas, an international human rights lawyer – attracted major international attention. They released two investigative reports in 2006 and 2007 that found systematic organ harvesting on a massive scale from thousands of involuntary Falun Gong practitioners detained in China's prison system. Again, this allegation continued to be strenuously denied by Chinese authorities.[59]

In 2006, by one estimate, approximately 4,000 prisoners were executed and "donated" about 8,000 kidneys and 3,000 livers, mainly to foreign purchasing patients.[60] In 2008, Asma Jahangir, United Nations special rapporteur on freedom of religion, and Manfred Nowak, United Nations special rapporteur on torture, demanded that 'China explain the dramatic increase in organs used for transplantation from 2000 to 2005, and the mismatch between the high number of transplants and the relatively few known donor sources'. It was implied that the persecution of Falun Gong prisoners coincided with a 'surge in organ transplantation in China' during that time period.[61] The Chinese Government allegedly claimed that it had no transplant statistics for the period in question.[62]

Similarly, the World Medical Association that listed China as one of five organ trafficking hot spots adopted a resolution[63] condemning 'any practice in violation of ethical principles and basic human rights, and ensure that Chinese doctors were not involved in the removal or transplantation of organs from executed prisoners'. The media reported in 2006 that China's 'organ transplant industry has become big business',[64] and the same year, British transplant surgeons condemned the removal of prisoner organs as a breach of human rights. International human rights organizations also accused 'China of harvesting organs from executed prisoners for transplant without the consent of the prisoner or his or her family'.[65] The Japanese Society for Transplantation has disallowed transplant tourism to China in light of this use of prisoner organs, and the Japanese Ministry of Health has warned hospitals not to assist organ trafficking.

It is apparent that organ procurement practices in China generated grave concerns and condemnations by the international community.[66] In the absence of reliable information released by the Chinese government, numerous reports produced from various sources led to the conclusion that state-sanctioned organ harvesting of death row convicts was prevalent in China for more a decade. The figure for the procurement of organs from prisoners was estimated to be as high as 95% with

*Table 3.1* Black market organ trade: all-inclusive transplant packages in China

| Name of organization, website | Transplant package |
| --- | --- |
| BEK-transplant (http://ww.bek-transplant.com/joomla/ index.php) | Kidney (US$70,000) Liver (US$120,000) Pancreas (US$110,000) Kidney and pancreas (US$160,000) |
| China International Transplantation Network Assistance Center (http://en.zoukiishoku.com/) | Kidney (US$65,000) Liver (US$130,000) Lung (US$150,000) Heart (US$130,000) |
| Yeson Healthcare Service Network (http://yeson.com/index.htm) | Kidney, liver, heart and lung |

(Source: World Health Organization (Shimazono Y [2007]. *The State of the International Organ Trade: A Provisional Picture Based on Integration of Available Information*, 85 Bulletin of the World Health Organization))

over 60,000 Falun Gong prisoners allegedly accounting for the source of transplants. Given China's tendency to conceal any contentious nature of issues from international scrutiny, it is not surprising that the Chinese leadership was overly defensive denying that the practice even did not occur or acknowledging that only willingly donated prisoner organs were transplanted in 'a very few cases'.[67,68]

## The 2006 reversal and challenges ahead

Expressions of outrage, concern and repugnance around the world about China's apparent involvement in organ trafficking eventually had an impact on the Chinese central government. Amid persistent pressure and condemnation from the international community, the Chinese government officials began to admit the existence of the black market organ trade and to change its policy and practice.[69]

At a conference of surgeons in Guangzho in 2006, Deputy Health Minister Huang Jiefu – a former surgeon specializing in kidney transplantion – acknowledged the flourishing sales of human organs to foreigners in China. He publicly stated that most of the organs from cadavers in China are obtained from executed Chinese prisoners and that the prisoners are not an appropriate source of organs for transplantation.[70] Whilst Huang raised this information in the context of a call to stop the illegal organ trade, his statement is one of the first admissions by high-ranking officials that this practice exists.[71] The public remarks by Huang appear to mark a new approach by the Chinese government, an acknowledgement that indicated future eradication of the illicit activities of organ trafficking. Subsequently, Huang acknowledged in an article in the medical journal *The Lancet* that over 90% of transplanted organs in China were obtained from executed prisoners.[72] The article went on to state, 'China is planning regulations for the new phase of transplantation, which will largely conform to international standards'. This has signified, from a perspective of commentators and international medical community, a new openness in China's official position regarding underground economy of organ sales.

Huang's public acknowledgement of the extent of black market organ sales particularly the unlawful extraction of organs from executed convicts was followed by several legislative and policy changes. For example, all organ transplant operations should be granted by the Ministry of Health's committee on the clinical application of technologies of human organ transplantation, the human organ transplant branch of Chinese medical association.[73] The committee is tasked to ensure that the organs used were voluntarily donated and not sold or removed randomly.[74] Medical procedures were standardized for organ transplants and hospitals had to establish competence with appropriate equipment, adequate management, qualified physicians and a medical ethics committee. Henceforward, organ trafficking was banned in China and organs would have to be allocated according to need.[75] Most importantly, The Supreme People's Court in China began reviewing some death penalty cases.

The Regulation on Human Organ Transplantation issued by the State Council of the Chinese government prohibited, effective 1 May 2007, all forms of trafficking and limited donations to defined familial and blood relatives.[76] The ban did not apply to tissue transplants, corneas or bone marrow. Additionally, selection criteria for a potential donor are scrutinized. People under the age of 18 are not allowed to donate organs, and only those who are capable of making their own decisions and are willing can be selected. The new regulation also banned the sale of organs to foreign patients.[77] New penalties were introduced for doctors involved in organ trafficking: Physicians who try to profit from the sale of organs would have their medical licenses revoked, and officials convicted of this trade would be fired.[78] Transplants could only occur at specified locations, and a limited number of hospitals were licensed for the procedure.

Immediately after the introduction of the new rules, organ traffickers were arrested for violations of the transplant tourism provisions and hospitals had their licenses withdrawn for involvement in foreign transplants. The number of institutions performing transplants (Figure 3.2) appeared to be markedly decrease.[79] In particular, kidney and liver transplant operations have drastically reduced since the passage of the legislation. The WHO commended the new measures, as 'altruism and not financial compensation became the driving principle for organ donors'.[80] In 2009, the Chinese government created a registry for organ donors and recipients, a vital step in gaining some level of regulatory control over the illicit practices that have so denigrated the international reputation of that country. In 2010, the government also piloted a voluntary donation system in 16 of 31 provincial-level regions in the hope of easing the burden of organ transplants.[81]

It seems apparent that China has heeded the criticisms about the extraction of and trafficking in prisoners' organs after execution, and sought to rehabilitate its international reputation in this regard by displaying a more open acknowledgement of the problem. Huang noted at the Madrid conference on organ donations and transplants organized by the WHO and the European Union that: 'The trading of human organs emerged in China in an under-regulated environment, forming a tremendous profit chain that is against the principles of equality and the goal of building harmonious society in China'.[82] Similarly, Wu Mingjiang, vice-president

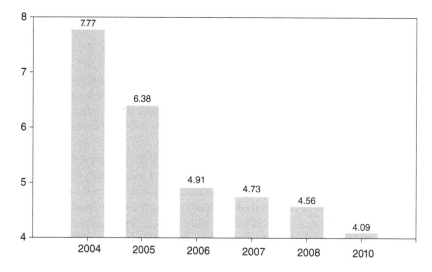

*Figure 3.2* Kidney transplant activity in China before and after the introduction of a new regulation

(Source: Organ Procurement and Transplantation Network. Available at http://optn.transplant.hrsa.gov/)

and secretary general of the Chinese Medical Association, endorses its official policy position that 'the Chinese medical Association will through its influence further promote the strengthening of management of human organ transplantation and prevent possible violations of the regulations made by the Chinese Government'.[83]

The challenge was that whereas law enforcement led to a decrease in deceased organ transplants, an indication of the gradual separation between transplantation and the prison system, new markets emerged to replace old practices. Chen Zhonghua, deputy director for transplantation of the Chinese Medical Association, explained that with the crackdown against transplant tourism by foreigners and organ harvesting from death row prisoners, organized criminals 'have procured organs from the poor and jobless by making them relatives of organ recipients by forging documents with the help of lawyers and medical workers'.[84] This illegal exercise had increased the rate of transplants from living donors, a figure that was 15% before the legislation, had reached 50% after the passage of the law. At the same time, media reports indicate that cases of prisoner organ harvesting were persisting. Huang told the media that two-thirds of organs used for transplantation were taken from executed prisoners. Disapproving the practice, he added, 'some people just ignore legal procedures regarding organ donations from executed prisoners and make a fat profit'.[85]

Whilst the introduction of new measures may curb the practice of organ retrieval from executed prisoners, the country does not yet have an open and transparent system when it comes to organ transplantation. Commentators maintained that the new regulations did not take into account the secretive executive system, particularly the 'issue of the provenance of the organs'.[86] Likewise, rights groups and activists criticized that the new procedure did not fully answer the international community's concerns since the regulations are not substitutes for an open and transparent system [of organ procurement].[87] It becomes clear that the implementation of national laws in China lies at the local level and is in the hands of numerous civil servants, police authorities, judicial officials, physicians and hospital administrators, and the sheer numbers of such persons renders monitoring against corruption extremely difficult.

In response, the central government revised the *PRC Criminal Law* in 2012 which for the first time categorized organ trafficking as a crime. The following year, the government announced that the central authority planned to abolish the practice of harvesting organs from death row prisoners and move to a voluntary donation-based system, a step that would address what for decades has been one of the country's most criticized human rights issues. In a press conference, Huang commented, 'the pledge to abolish organ donations from condemned prisoners represents the resolve of the government'.[88] The central government also prosecuted organ traffickers and conducted a multi-province crackdown on organ trafficking rings. Nonetheless, there continue to be reports of some hospitals trading with illegal organ agencies.[89,90] Dr Luc Noel of the WHO stated that there had been a sign of resurgence of illicit organ trafficking in the past two or three years. Military hospitals were believed to have carried out the transplants.[91]

It remains to be seen if the new regulations and other policy changes will make a difference in the practice of organ procurement in China. Evidently, the illegal trade appears to have fallen back into place immediately after the introduction of the new regulations. Notwithstanding that, until an open and accountable system emerges, the dearth of publicly available information will render all Chinese sources dubious or at best unconvincing. It may well be that the Chinese leadership is aware now that illegal harvesting of organs is universally condemned, that the condemnation of China's reputation internationally is not worth the continuation of this practice. Huang's recent publication clearly represents the importance of China's reputation in international political economy: 'With the rise of China's international status, an organ transplantation system replying on death row inmates' organs harms our national image as a civilized nation and political power'.[92] If the central government can be persuaded that a more open approach and less defensiveness might yield even greater respect from other countries, then that might help facilitate the progress of China's efforts to end the illicit conduct of organ procurement.

## Towards global governance of organ transplantation

This chapter has demonstrated a shift in the position of the Chinese government on organ trafficking from total denial to limited but public acknowledgement. It appears that China became more receptive to admitting that the country had a problem that requires a solution. Whilst there is a need for more transparency, the statements and actions of the Chinese government appear to be forward looking. At least, in the minds of Chinese leadership, there is a realization that no country eager to be a player in a globalized world can keep itself isolated and secretive without paying a price both in terms of its economic progress and its international relations and reputation. At the same time, the case of China illustrates an absence of governance and legal framework at national, regional and global levels.

There has been a growing international consensus that would seek the eradication of the organ trafficking and advancement of protective measures for both donors and recipients, so that organ donation can revert to the scientific breakthrough and life-enhancing measure it was intended to be, not the tainted practice it has become. The United Nations organizations have made concerted efforts to combat the practices of organ trafficking. In 1991, the World Health Assembly approved the WHO set of guiding principles on organ transplantation.[93] These guidelines prohibited commercial sales of human organs, but left enforcement methods up to individual countries. In view of the global increases in organ trafficking, the World Health Assembly adopted an amended version of the principles in 2004. It urged member states to act against transplant tourism and international organ trafficking.[94] The following year, the WHO Western Pacific Regional Office, where countries of allegedly facilitating organ trade, were located convened a consultation meeting. The meeting condemned commercial sales of organs and urged transparency about transplantation practices. In May 2008, the executive board of the World Health Organization presented its Updated Guiding Principles on Human Cell, Tissue, and Organ Transplantation. These updated principles were based on extensive stakeholder consultations and attempted to 'provide an ethical framework for transplantation in response to transplant commercialism'.[95] The World Health Assembly placed on its agenda of a detailed resolution on organ transplantation in 2009, which expressed opposition to financial gain in transactions involving human body parts and urged healthcare professionals to report on such activities.[96]

Separately, the Transplantation Society and the International Society of Nephrology convened an international summit in Istanbul, Turkey in 2008 to address the unethical practices associated with transplantation. The universal expressions of concern from over 150 members of the scientific and medical community representing 78 countries resulted in the creation of the Declaration of Istanbul,[97] a significant attempt to help countries to eliminate organ trafficking. Although the Istanbul Summit drew an international membership, the Declaration of Istanbul bowed to the inevitable importance of state sovereignty in calling for each country to implement programs to deal with the problems associated with organ trafficking in their territories. Compared with the international guidelines, the Declaration of Istanbul can be viewed as an important way forward toward a clear stand by the international community of medical professions against transplant tourism and illicit organ trafficking.

To date, however, these efforts have been met with limited implementation success at both national and global levels. The key challenge is that current framework lacks direct and effective enforcement mechanisms. Whilst the traffickers and black market facilitators have gained an international canvas for their business, individual jurisdictions remain powerless in the enforcement of such illegal enterprises. By nature, trafficking is a transnational activity involving multiple countries. Therefore, it is difficult – and almost impossible – for national and sovereignty-focused jurisdictions to enact bans against the transnational criminal conduct. Therefore, if any form of organ trafficking is considered a crime against humanity, it is time to strengthen the global governance framework to address illicit organ trafficking and transplant tourism within and across borders.[98,99] The establishment of an effective governance framework and enforcement regime may spur and complement the strengthening of national legislation in individual countries.[100]

This chapter on China's illicit organ trade underlines the urgent need for the implementation of binding international convention on organ trafficking. An exploration of existing international law will reveal the flaws that exist, particularly as national legislation cannot handle all that effectively against transnational activities. At a national level, a more open channel of discussion is required – particularly in China, which has a long-held policy of maintaining secrecy and defending views on national sovereignty, and has not been entirely forthright with its past involvement in illegal organ enterprises – to encourage the country to strengthen the existing organ procurement laws and promote the adoption of international standards and resolutions.

## Notes

1  B. Mahilo, M. Carmona, M. Alvarez, S. White, L. Noel, and R. Matesanz, "2009 global data in organ donation and transplantation: Activities, laws and organization", *Transplantation* 92(10) (2011): 1069–1074.
2  O.S. Surman, R.F. Saidi, R. S. Purtilo, M. Simmerling, D. Ko, and T.F. Burke, "The market of human organs: A window into a poorly understood global business", *Transplantation proceedings*, 40 (2008): 491–493.
3  D. Campbell and N. Davison, "Illegal kidney trade booms as new organ is sold every hour", *The Guardian*, 27 May 2012.
4  United Nations, "United Nations millennium development goal", www.un.org/millenniumgoals/
5  E. Burke, "Alarming rise in illegal organ trade", www.abc.net.au/news/2012-06-22/an-illegal-organ-trading/4086096
6  Y. Shimazono, "The state of the international organ trade: A provisional picture based on integration of available information", *Bulletin of the WHO 955*, 85 (2007): 955.
7  T. Deen, "Health: Study faults unregulated trade in human organs", *Allbusiness*, www.allbusiness.com/medicinehealth/medical-treatments-procedures-surgery/13252107-1.html
8  World Health Organization, "Organ donation and transplantation activities", 2014, www.transplant-observatory.org/organ-donation-transplantation-activities-2015-report/
9  A. Lita, "Organ trafficking poses global challenges", *American Humanist Association*, http://americanhumanist.org/hnn/archives/index.php?id=314&article=5
10 C. Nullis-Kapp, "Organ trafficking and transplantation pose new challenges", *Bulletin of the WHO 715*, 82 (2004): 715.

11  A. Cholia, "Illegal organ trafficking poses a global problem", *Huffington Post*, 24 August 2009, www.huffingtonpost.com/2009/07/24/illegal-organ-trafficking_n_ 244686.html

12  European Commission, "Organ donation and transplantation: Recent facts & figures", 2014, https://ec.europa.eu/health/sites/health/files/blood_tissues_organs/docs/ ev_20141126_factsfigures_en.pdf

13  *United Network for Organ Sharing*, 2018, https://unos.org/data/

14  Ibid.

15  NHS UK, "Kidney transplant", 2018, www.nhs.uk/conditions/kidney-transplant/

16  C. Paddock, "China launches pilot scheme in bid to fight transplant organ trading", *Medical World News*, 27 August 2009.

17  A. Aronowitz, *Human Trafficking, Human Misery: The Global Trade in Human Beings* (Westport, CT: Praeger Publishers, 2009), p. 121.

18  A. Kokubo, "The interaction of the international society concerning kidney transplants – A consideration of diseased kidney transplants in Japan and transplant tourism over the world", *Legal Medicine*, 11 (2009): s393–395.

19  T. Bakdash, and N. Scheper-Highes, "Is it ethical for patients with renal disease to purchase kidneys from the world's poor?", *Plos Medicine*, 3(10) (2006): 1699–1702.

20  D.A. Budiana-Saberi, and F.L. Delmonico, "Organ trafficking and transplant tourism: A commentary on the global realities", *American Journal of Transplantation*, 8(5) (2008): 925–929.

21  F.L. Delmonico, "The Pakistani revelation", *Transplant International*, 20(11) (2007): 924–925.

22  Y. Shimazono, "The state of the international organ trade: A provisional picture based on integration of available information".

23  A. Aronowitz, *Human Trafficking, Human Misery: The Global Trade in Human Beings*.

24  C. Nullis-Kapp, "Organ trafficking and transplantation pose new challenges".

25  WHO Secretariat, "Human organ and tissue transplantation: Report by the Secretariat", *WHO DOC. EB113/14*, 27 November 2003, pp. 1–2.

26  K. Juan, "Organ trafficking stirs concern", *Global Times*, 24 August 2009, www. globaltimes.cn/china/society/2009-08/460386.html

27  "Executions top 1,200 in one year", *South China Morning Post*, 24 March 2001.

28  C. Zissis, and J. Bajoria, "China's environmental crisis", *Council on Foreign Relations*. https://www.cfr.org/backgrounder/chinas-environmental-crisis

29  W.M. Morrison, "China's economic rise: History, trends, challenges, and implications for the United States", *Congressional Research Service, RL 33534* (2018), https://fas. org/sgp/crs/row/RL33534.pdf

30  "Gap between China's rich and poor can't be hidden in Chongqing," *The Globe and Mail*, www.theglobeandmail.com/news/world/the-china-diaries/gap-between-chinas-rich-and-poor-cant-be-hidden-in-chongqing/article7571019/

31  World Bank, Results profile: China poverty reduction, www.worldbank.org/en/news/ feature/2010/03/19/results-profile-china-poverty-reduction

32  "Corruption in China: checked and balanced?" *The Economist*, www.economist.com/ blogs/analects/2013/05/corruption-china

33  L. Lim, "The high price of illness in China", *BBC News*, 2006, http://news.bbc.co.uk/2/ hi/asia-pacific/4763312.stm

34  Ibid.

35  "China plans universal healthcare", *New York Times*, www.nytimes.com/2009/01/22/ world/asia/22iht-beijing.1.19590543.html

36  World Health Organization, *World Health Statistics 2013* (Geneva: World Health Organization, 2013).

37  J. Huang, et al., "Government policy and organ transplantation in China", *The Lancet*, 372 (2008): 1937.

38  C. Shi, "China medicine news: Current organ transplant status in our nation", *Biotech Information Net*, 2 December 2002.
39  X. Shaowen, "Profit drives White-Hot organ transplantation market: Competition without regulation raises concern", *The First Financial Daily*, 5 April 2006.
40  Z. Feng, "New rule to regulate organ transplants", *China Daily*, 5 May 2005.
41  Ibid.
42  "Current organ transplant status in our nation", *China Pharmacy Net*, 2 December 2002.
43  "China should heed WHO warnings on transplant organs", *Epoch Times*, 21 January 2004, www.rfa.org/english/news/126287-20040121.html
44  Ibid.
45  "China tops execution tables", *BBC News*, 21 March 2001, http://news.bbc.co.uk/2/hi/asia-pacific/1234000.stm
46  Amnesty International annual reports- China cited by D. Kilgour, and D. Matas, "Bloody harvest: Revised report into allegations of organ harvesting of Falun Gong practitioners in China", 2007.
47  W. Michael, "China announces a system for voluntary organ donors", *N.Y. Times*, 27 August 2009, www.nytimes.com/2009/08/27/world/asia/27china.html
48  "Mass Execution in China", *BBC News*, 27 August 1998, http://news.bbc.co.uk/2/hi/asia-pacific/159667.stm
49  C. Smith, "Quandary in U.S. over use of organs of Chinese inmates", *New York Times*, 11 November 2001.
50  L. Blumenthal, "FBI hears report that China executes prisoners to sell their organs", *Freno Bee*, 23 October 1997.
51  "Organs for sale: China's growing trade and ultimate violation of prisoners' rights: Hearing before the Subcommitee on Int'l Operations and Human Rights", *Commission on Int'l Relations, 107th Congress*, 24 (2001).
52  N. Scheper-Hughes, "Postmodern cannibalism? Organ transplants in the globalocal market", *Whole Earth Review* (Summer 2000).
53  D. Rowan, "A pound of flesh for sale", *Times (U.K.)*, 21 February 2004.
54  J. Huang, et al., "Government policy and organ transplantation in China".
55  C. Smith, "Quandary in U.S. over use of organs of Chinese inmates".
56  Ibid.
57  "China fury at organ snatching lies", *BBC News*, 28 June 2001, http://news.bbc.co.uk/2/hi/americas/1411389.stm
58  Ibid.
59  Press Release, "Organ harvest investigation", *Matas/Kilgur Release New Evidence on Organ Harvesting in China*, 22 August 2008.
60  F.L. Delmonico, "The implications of Istanbul Declaration on organ trafficking and transplant tourism", *Current Opinion in Organ Transplantation*, 14(2) (2009): 116–119.
61  S. Yu, "China denies having organ transplantation statistics between 2000 and 2005", *International Federation for Justice in China*, 7 September 2008, www.theepochtimes.com/news/8-7-8/73169.html
62  Ibid.
63  P. O'Neil, China's doctors signal retreat on organ harvest, *Canadian Medical Association Journal*, 177(11), 2007: 1341.
64  "Organ sales 'thriving' in China", *BBC News*, 27 September 2006, http://news.bbc.co.uk/2/hi/5386720.stm
65  "China to ban human organ trafficking from May 1", 7 April 2007, *Channel News Asia*. http://www.channelnewsasia.com/stories/ afp_asiapacific/view/269026/1/.html.
66  T. Diflo, "Use of organs from executed Chinese prisoners", *The Lancet*, 364 (2004): 30–31.
67  "China bans transplant organ sales", *BBC News*, http://news.bbc.co.uk/2/hi/asia-pacific/4853188.stm

68 "Duncan Hewitt, Shanghai balks at organ donation", *BBC News*, http://news.bbc.co.uk/2/hi/asia-pacific/1032537.stm

69 M. Magnier, and A. Zarembo, "China admits taking executed prisoners' organs", *L.A. Times*, 18 November 2006.

70 J. Huang, "Ethical and legislative perspectives on liver transplantation in the People's Republic of China", *Liver Transplantation*, 13 (2007): 193–196.

71 L. Beck, "China says to ban sale of human organs", *Reuters*, 28 March 2006.

72 J. Huang, et al., "Government policy and organ transplantation in China", p. 1937.

73 World Health Organization, *WHO Guiding Principles on Human Organ Transplantation Report of the Regional Meeting* (Manila: World Health Organization Western Pacific Region, 2009).

74 Z. Feng, "New rule to regulate organ transplants", *China Daily*, 5 May 2005, www.chinadaily.com.cn/china/2006-05/05/content_582847.htm

75 J. Zhu, *Country Progress, Legislative Framework: China, in Second Global Consultation on Critical Issues in Human Transplantation: Towards a Common Attitude to Transplantation* (Geneva: World Health Organization, 2007), p. 12.

76 K. Juan, "Organ trafficking stirs concern", http://english.peopledaily.com.cn/90001/90776/90882/6737416.html

77 M. McDonald, "Report of organ tourism stirs new Japan-China controversy", *New York Times*, 17 February 2009, www.nytimes.com/2009/02/17/world/asia/17iht-organs.1.20242560.html

78 J. Watts, "China introduces new rules to deter human organ trade", *The Lancet*, 369 (2007): 1917–1918.

79 F.L. Delmonico, "The implications of Istanbul Declaration on organ trafficking and transplant tourism".

80 "China hopes organ donor system stops trafficking", *CNN*, 26 August 2009, http://edition.cnn.com/2009/WORLD/asiapcf/08/26/china.organ.donation/

81 J. Huang, "A pilot programme of organ donation after cardiac death in China", *The Lancet*, 379 (2012): 862–865.

82 O. Thibault, "Transplant tourism causing international concern: Experts", *AFP*, 25 March 2010.

83 P. O'Neil, "China's doctors signal retreat on organ harvest", *Canadian Medical Association Journal*, 177(11) (20 November 2007).

84 J. Kang, "Organ trafficking stirs concern", *Global Times*, 24 August 2009, http://english.peopledaily.com.cn/90001/90776/90882/6737416.html

85 T. Hubert, "China acknowledges death row organ trafficking", *World Coalition Against the Death Penalty*, 28 August 2009, p. 361.

86 J. Watts, "China introduces new rules to deter human organ trade", p. 1918.

87 G. Wong, "China issues human organ transplant rules in attempt to clean up industry", *AP Features*, 7 April 2007.

88 K. Bradsher, "China moves to stop transplants of organs after executions", *The New York Times*, 23 March 2012.

89 N. Davison, "In China, criminals fill the kidney donor deficit", *The Guardian*, 27 May 2012.

90 M. Palin, "The living dead: Prisoners executed for their organs then sold to foreigners for transplants", *News Australia*, 3 June 2017.

91 D. Campbell, and N. Davison, "Illegal kidney trade booms as new organ is sold every hour", *The Guardian*, 27 May 2012.

92 J. Huang, "Pragmatic solution for organ donation in response to challenges faced by the Chinese society: Summary for the National Donation after Circulatory Death Pilot Program", *Chinese Medical Journal*, 126(3) (2013): 569–573, 569.

93 World Health Organization, "Guiding principles on human organ transplantation", *The Lancet*, 337 (8755) (1991): 1470–1471.

94 World Health Organization, "Human organ and tissue transplantation", *WHO 57.18*, 2004, www.who.int/ethics/en/A57_R18-en.pdf?ua=1

95   World Health Organization, "Human organ and tissue transplantation: Report by the Secretariat", *WHO DOC. EB123/5*, 18 April 2008.
96   World Health Organization, "Human organ and tissue transplantation: Report by the Secretariat", *WHO DOC. EB124.R13*, 26 January 2009.
97   *The Declaration of Istanbul on Organ Trafficking and Transplant Tourism*, www.declarationofistanbul.org/
98   T.H. Jafar, "Organ trafficking: Global solutions for a global problem", *American Journal of Kidney Diseases*, 54(6) (2009): 1145–1157.
99   F. Ambagtsheer, and W. Weimar, "A criminological perspective: Why prohibition of organ trade is not effective and how the Declaration of Istanbul can move forward", *American Journal of Transplantation*, 12 (2012): 571–575.
100  F. Delmonico, B. Dominguez-Gil, R. Matesanz, and L. Noel, "A call for government accountability to achieve national self-sufficiency in organ donation and transplantation", *The Lancet*, 378 (2011): 1414–1418.

# 4 China's food safety problems and the establishment of a dual economy

## A case of vegetables

*Yoneyuki Sugita*

## Introduction

The main research question addressed in this chapter is: Why does China suffer from a serious lack of food safety? A secondary question is also investigated: What are the implications of this situation? This chapter uses vegetables as a case study because they have become one of the most important food exports with a competitive edge. My working hypothesis is that the Chinese government policies that tried to promote rapid economic growth at home set the groundwork for food safety problems as the country faced the simultaneous need to adjust its exports to meet international food safety standards. The implication is that the Chinese government, in order to address the problem of promoting rapid domestic growth whilst meeting global safety standards, has been compelled to establish a dual economic structure: separating food safety for export use from food safety for domestic use, which created a highly advanced, exclusive and closed supply chain for major export-oriented companies.

Whilst laws and institutions for dealing with food safety problems are well established in China, the editorial board of *Shoku no Kagaku* argues that what Chinese people must acquire is ethics and morals.[1] The General Administration of Quality Supervision, Inspection, and Quarantine (AQSIQ) – a ministerial-level department established under China's State Council in April 2001 to hold responsibility for food safety – held an international commodity safety meeting in Beijing in May 2007. More than 300 people from in excess of 30 countries participated. These participants apparently believed that concerns about commodity safety in China resulted primarily from the existence of producers with low levels of morality who pursued only profit maximization and from a national consciousness with little concern for product safety.[2] Syoichiro Kawahara correctly argues that ensuring food safety requires three major elements to function in an integrated way: government leadership, corporate conscience and consumer supervision. China, he says, possesses the first element, but lacks the second and third elements. Kawahara writes, 'It is no exaggeration to say that the most important challenge to achieve food safety in China is to reform Chinese people's consciousness of food safety'.[3] Ying Hong also argues that declining moral standards in China are the cause of many problems: 'a major overhaul is needed in the ethical perspectives of many people in business'.[4] According to these arguments, the food safety problem in China derives not from any socio-economic or political structure, but from people's mentality. Consequently, according to those arguments, if the nation changed its mindset, the food safety problems would be resolved.

Indeed, the Chinese mentality toward food safety may be an important cause of the nation's food safety problems, but it is not an exclusive cause. People outside China, especially those in capitalist nations, share the Chinese mentality of putting emphasis on profit maximization; however, their activities are constrained by state policies. Because some Chinese government policies have had significant effects on the country's food safety problems, this chapter focuses on those policies that showed little regard towards the Chinese people's destiny in terms of food safety.

Introducing a market economy in the era of globalization in the 1980s, the Chinese government employed a "get-rich-quick" policy that has encouraged giving top priority to immediate economic performance over mid- and long-term non-economic elements, including food safety.[5] In December 2001, China joined the World Trade Organization (WTO). As a full member, China became obliged to observe international standards of food safety – at least as far as its exports were concerned. Joining the WTO made the Chinese government ensure the safety of exported foodstuffs, compelling China to establish a dual economy: separating food safety for export use from food safety for export use, which created a highly advanced, exclusive and closed supply chain for major export-oriented companies.[6]

## Chinese government's domestic policies for rapid economic growth

In the 1980s, China introduced a market economy as an important measure to promote reform and door-opening policies. China changed its food policy emphasis from grain production to the production of other cash crops such as vegetables and fruits in the mid-1980s. As a result, land used for vegetable production rapidly increased from 4.1 million hectares in 1983 to 8.08 million in 1993 and 13.35 million in 1999.[7]

According to China's official statistics, the average land area per farming household as of the late 1980s and the 1990s was tiny, just over 50 acres, about one-third of that of Japan.[8] Chinese farmers used a small amount of pesticides and chemical fertilizers until the 1970s, but the Chinese government has encouraged their use since the 1980s in order to cultivate farmland as productively as possible and to maximize crop output.[9] The amount of pesticides and chemical fertilizers has rapidly increased year by year. The Food and Agriculture Organization of the United Nations indicates that China increased its use of inorganic fertilizers by about 100 times in about 45 years (1949–1995).[10]

Since the 1980s, Chinese agriculture has been increasing its product output through its bold commercialization and liberalization processes. In particular, from 1994 to 1996, the Chinese government rapidly pushed forward food production measures such as increasing province-level subsidies, intensifying administrative decrees and raising the prices paid by the state for grain. Because of these government stimulus policies, the volume of food production reached over 500 million tons for the first time in history and China was able to keep this level of production for the next four years.[11] As a result of this rapid and consecutive increase of food production, China faced a new problem: the combination of overproduction and the decline of market prices on their agricultural products. After 1995, vegetable prices gradually declined.[12] Chinese vegetable farmers tried to overcome the decrease in market prices not by adjusting their production output downward, but by increasing production – partly because of a lack of useful market information and partly because of the failure of coordinating organizations representing the farmers. Unfortunately, because many farmers thought the same way, overproduction continued and further decreased market prices. Because of the worsening financial conditions, the Chinese government in the year 2000 abandoned its protective policy of buying wholesale products at a price higher than the market rate.[13]

In order to increase food production, the government encouraged farmers to use chemical pesticides. In just over 20 years (1985–2006), China's production of chemical pesticides increased by nearly 700% from 0.20 million tons to 1.38 million tons.[14] With the government's encouragement, China has become the world's No. 1 user, producer and exporter of chemical pesticides since the 1980s. Trying to overcome the overproduction problems by producing more vegetables also meant that the nation used more pesticides and chemical fertilizers. According to the National Bureau of Statistics of China, as Table 4.1 indicates, the amount of pesticides and chemical fertilizers being used roughly doubled from 1990 to 2007.[15]

However, the increasing usage of pesticides and fertilizers also had a negative effect on China as a whole. Approximately 100,000 consumers were affected annually by pesticide residue and chemical additives, and 300–500 farmers were actually killed by improper use of dangerous pesticides.[16] There was widespread use of strong chemicals that left toxic residues on food. The government eventually banned all dangerous toxic agricultural chemicals, but they were still available via underground vendors in less expensive but ineffective forms. In addition, because of rapid industrialization, water, air and soil had become contaminated, which significantly affected all vegetables and other crops, as well as the food processing factories.[17]

According to China's Ministry of Health, over 600 food poisoning cases involving over 20,000 people were reported in 2001. As Table 4.2 shows, three years later in 2004, the food poisoning cases jumped to more than 2,300 with about 43,000 people involved.[18]

*Table 4.1* The change in consumption of chemical fertilizer and agricultural chemicals in China (10 thousands)

|  | *Consumption of chemical fertilizer (10,000 tons)* | *Consumption of agricultural chemicals (10,000 tons)* |
|---|---|---|
| **1990** | 2,590.3 | 73.3 |
| **1995** | 3,593.7 | 108.7 |
| **2000** | 4,146.4 | 128.0 |
| **2006** | 4,927.7 | 153.7 |
| **2007** | 5,107.8 | 162.3 |

(Source: Kazutsugu Oshima, "Chugoku ni okeru seitai kankyo no akka to junkangata nogyo shisutemu kochiku no hitsuyosei", [Deterioration of ecology in China and the necessity of establishing recycling agricultural systems] *Momoyama Gakuin Daigaku Keizai Keiei Ronshu* 53, no. 2 (October 2011): 26)

*Table 4.2* Serious food poisoning cases issued by MOH from 2001 to 2004

| Year | Food poisoning cases | Involved persons | Deaths number |
|---|---|---|---|
| 2001[a] | 624 | 20,124 | 143 |
| 2002[a] | 464 | 11,572 | 68 |
| 2003[a] | 1,481 | 29,600 | 262 |
| 2004[b] | 2,305 | 42,876 | 255 |

a Source: Statistical Bulletin of China's Health Service (2001–2003), MOH, www.moh.gov.cn/
tjxxzx/tjsj/tjgb/index.htm
b Source: Document [2005] no. 58 issued by Ministry of Health

Food poisoning was a serious problem in China. In December 2008, China's Ministry of Health reported that infant milk formula adulterated by melamine killed six infants and caused 300,000 children to suffer from kidney ailments.[19] These are some of the most common illicit practices that have been taking place in China.

China's rural areas lack an effective socio-economic infrastructure. Chinese farmers are not well organized.[20] China has no well-established agricultural-related organizations to provide farmers with competent training for the safe and effective use of pesticides and chemical fertilizers, to diffuse environmentally friendly techniques and to offer other useful agriculture-related information. This is in stark contrast to Japan, which offers these services through agricultural technique extension centres – which are affiliated with prefectural governments and the Japanese agricultural cooperatives – and other private organizations.[21] Without these kinds of agricultural organizations, it would be next to impossible to disseminate necessary technical and market information, proper usage of pesticides and fertilizers, and other agriculture-related information.

In addition, according to the statistics from 2009 compiled by China's Ministry of Agriculture, of 490 million workers in rural areas, only 13% had high school diplomas, 36.7% received elementary-level education or less, and fewer than 5% have received agricultural technical education. Consequently, these workers have little knowledge about food safety, the effective management of pesticides and chemical fertilizers (let alone good agricultural practices), and the methods of land use that can best achieve the objectives of agronomic and environmental sustainability.[22]

Agricultural markets are not well organized or regulated. In agricultural marketing, traders and farmers are likely to engage in business transactions on a cash basis without documentation. They are seldom interested in establishing long-term business relationships based on business ethics and mutual trust. Once farmers sell their products at the market, they are free from all accountability, and even if contaminated products are found, it is impossible to trace them to the original producers.[23] This ineffective market system does not provide these producers with incentives to grow safe products. Under this system, those who are willing to cheat will profit and those who are honest and who pride themselves on their safe products may face low profitability or lose money. It is this system, not the producers' conscientiousness, that is the fundamental issue to be addressed in China.

China's food processing industry achieved rapid development on an annual growth rate of 13.5% from 1980 to 2004.[24] However, the nation has 353,000 small-sized food processing companies with ten or fewer employees, constituting 78.8% of the entire food processing industry. These companies are the most likely to engage in processing food with less sophisticated technology, inadequate sanitation standards and no or fraudulent licenses.[25] People in charge of these companies tend to be less educated and have little concern for the proper use of preservatives.[26]

Due to the combination of large pesticide consumption, low technology and inadequate knowledge of safety management, agricultural pollution such as pesticide residues and the misuse of dangerous chemicals has become a major problem. There were reports of contaminated vegetables in the 1990s in Hong Kong and in 2000–2001 in China.[27]

The Chinese government prohibited the use of the five most dangerous pesticides in January 2007, but companies are still manufacturing and distributing them in the domestic market because they are more effective and less expensive than those pesticides that are legally available.[28] Although the Chinese government is serious and has made robust policies, regulations, and institutions consistent with international standards, this does not mean that the local authorities will follow the regulations. In fact, local authorities still have incentives to not obey these regulations strictly. Small food processing companies and family workshops that cannot meet the standards set by these regulations are not permitted to carry out their businesses or are denied market access. Strict observance of these regulations would therefore decrease local gross domestic product (GDP) growth as well as raise serious unemployment problems.[29] Local officials are placed in a dilemma: On the one hand, they have to observe food safety regulations; yet, on the other hand, they have to promote local economic development to prevent unemployment problems and to increase GDP because good governance is equated with an increasing GDP.[30] Because the GDP growth of their regions normally occupies about 70% of local officials' annual performance assessments, their most rational choice is to apply the regulations in an ineffective way or to ignore the regulations outright in favour of increasing regional GDP growth.[31]

China has achieved rapid economic development; however, industrialization has brought environmental pollution to the nation. There has been massive excretion of three major industrial effluents: exhaust fumes, wastewater and solid waste. These, as well as waste generated in urban areas, have introduced large quantities of toxic material to the rural soil, as well as bacteria and heavy metals into the drinking water.[32] Over 70% of China's river systems are contaminated by industrial liquid waste, and 40% of the water cannot be used for drinking or food production and processing.[33] In April 2007, the Ministry of Land Resources claimed that 30.4 million acres, over 10% of China's arable land, as well as 13 million tons of grain, had been contaminated by heavy metals.[34]

Poor handling, storage and distribution systems with inadequate temperature-controlled infrastructure and the use of cheap, but unsafe, additives and toxic dyes to preserve food and improve its appearance also contributed to the issue of food pollution.[35] The inadequate distribution systems gave incentives to illicit producers and processors to take improper measures to maximize their profits. Food processing companies sometimes offer local supervising officials a bribe in exchange for certificates or leeway to run their business operations without proper safety conditions. The central government enacts food safety laws, but local authorities are primarily responsible for enforcing them.[36]

The Chinese government's "get-rich-quick" policy has encouraged giving top priority to immediate economic performance over mid- and long-term non-economic elements such as health, environment and food safety.[37] This policy has provided illicit food producers and processors with a golden opportunity to use unsafe pesticides, chemicals and additives to maximize profits. Their incentives include the reduction of production costs, improvements to the appearance of products and an extension of the shelf life of products.[38]

## Admission to the WTO and its implications

China has not paid much attention to food safety, although it began to take some measures in the 1990s. The China Green Food Development Centre, affiliated with China's Ministry of Agriculture, was established in November 1992 and offered a "Green Food" certification to ensure food safety. The Organic Food Development Centre, affiliated with China's State Environmental Protection Administration, was established in 1994 and offered more robust standards. The Ministry of Agriculture introduced a "Pollution-Free" program in 2001, designating Beijing, Tianjin, Shanghai and Shenzhen as model cities where the government conducted sample examinations for pesticide residues and antibiotic substances in various places such as production facilities, wholesale markets, retail markets and slaughterhouses. This program aimed to monitor the production and distribution of agricultural products with a reduced amount of pesticides and chemical fertilizers.[39] It was only in the 21st century that external pressure forced China to take serious measures to improve its food safety.[40] In December 2001, China joined the WTO (cf. p. 2). As a full member, China became obliged to observe the functions, values and norms of a free market.[41]

According to statistics from China's Ministry of Health, food poisoning cases dropped sharply from 2001 to 2002. Joining the WTO had a short-term influence of reducing cases of food poisoning, but this effect did not last. The figures surged in 2003 by more than three times and continued to increase in 2004.[42] According to the Chinese government's statistics in 2003, between 53,300 and 123,000 people were poisoned by pesticides each year.[43] A study conducted by China's Ministry of Environmental Protection in 2003 showed that 400,000 people died from air pollution every year,[44] and a Chinese journalist critical of the Chinese government reported that between 200,000 and 400,000 people suffer from contaminated food every year in the country.[45] In April 2004, fake and substandard infant milk formula killed at least 12 babies, and hundreds of infants suffered from serious malnutrition in Fuyang in Anhui province. The Chinese government later found a large amount of fake and substandard infant milk formula in at least ten other provinces.[46]

One of the first difficulties that China faced when joining the global market-place was the requirement of meeting the international sanitary and phytosanitary (SPS) standards. China's Ministry of Commerce has indicated that about 90% of China's exporters of foodstuffs were adversely affected by international SPS standards, and the losses amounted to $9 billion in 2002. China's foodstuffs have had SPS problems for a long time, but once the country became a full WTO member, the international community paid more serious attention to the issue.[47] It was time that China's bare-knuckle economic growth strategy gave way to complying with more law-abiding global standards.[48]

With admission to the WTO, China placed more emphasis on labor-intensive farm products such as vegetables and fruits, which had comparative advantages in the international market for export.[49] In February 2002, a test conducted by the Nouminren Food Research Laboratory in Japan found residual pesticides in spinach, a discovery that garnered wide media coverage. In April, Japan's Ministry of Health, Labor and Welfare implemented monitoring on 100% of spinach imported from China. On 17 July, the Ministry of Agriculture, Forestry and Fisheries publicly announced that it found pesticides that were 180 times over the acceptable levels stipulated by the Food Sanitation Act, and that the pesticides were detected in frozen spinach imported from China. This incident swayed Japanese public perception toward believing that food produced in China was of a substandard quality and presented risks to those who consumed it.[50] Japan stopped importing frozen spinach from China from July 2002 through February 2003. Further detection of pesticide residue at levels higher than permitted again stopped Japan from importing from the period of May 2003 through June 2004.[51] Japan was the largest customer for Chinese vegetable exports, and these Japanese safety measures placed pressure on China to rectify the situation.

Exports from China to Japan decreased sharply. This spinach incident was a shock to the Chinese authorities. Since 2002, China has been serious about tackling its food safety problems, especially safety standards for exports within all points of the supply chain.[52] The AQSIQ is primarily responsible for exported food safety. With this centralized department, the Chinese government tried to ensure the safety of exporting foodstuffs by establishing a dual economy, separating food safety for export use from food safety for domestic use, which created a highly advanced, exclusive and closed supply chain for major export-oriented companies.[53] Food export companies are required to meet the following standards in order to acquire export permission:

1) Strict control over all records of purchase, management and status of use regarding pesticides in registered databases.
2) Installation of pesticide residue testing equipment and regular implementation of pesticide residue testing.
3) Documentation of testing results.
4) Securing a minimum of 20 hectares of farmland for exclusive use.
5) Stationing at least one professional agricultural engineer on the exclusive plot of farmland.[54]

These companies maintain world-class sanitation standards, hire highly qualified employees and are required to establish a system that ensures that exported
products are of a certain standard – which they accomplish by cultivating agricultural products on their exclusive plot of farmland – and that the processors monitor residual pesticides themselves.[55]

In other words, these export-oriented companies tend to implement vertical
integration: securing raw materials, transporting them to food processing factories, producing safe processed foods, and exporting these food products abroad
themselves. The Chinese government has established strict rules and regulations
for the purpose of regulating the export-oriented food processing companies. In
order to deal with the pesticide-residue problem, the AQSIQ promulgated a new
law in 2002 to test and quarantine exported and imported vegetables. This law
required the affected companies to have production bases of a designated size, to
manage pesticides, and to record usage conditions. To ensure food safety, the law
also prohibited these companies from procuring agricultural products in wholesale markets.[56] It is no exaggeration to say that export vegetables bound for the
Japanese market are protected by the highest quality-control measures among
vegetables produced in China.[57]

Since 2002, exporters of fruits and vegetables have been required to obtain certification for Hazard Analysis and Critical Control Point (HACCP), a system designed
to help food processors examine how they handle food to make sure it is produced
safely and in good quality.[58] Since January 2003, companies exporting vegetables
have been required to register the production bases of their agricultural products.[59]
AQSIQ and China's entry-exit inspection and quarantine administrations, the administrations that actually inspect companies exporting vegetables from local areas,
have been requesting export companies to establish a thorough food safety system.[60]

In January 2003, each food processing company engaging in exports was
required to write the registration number of the production base in its export documentation in accordance with standard international regulations, which are based
on traceability.[61] With a series of laws and regulations, as well as various food
safety standards, China possesses a solid food safety legal system and institutions
capable of improving food quality and maintaining the trade order for exporting
and importing foodstuffs. China's food processing technologies and equipment
are close to reaching or have already reached the requirements set by international standards. Quality control of food processing companies is more scien-
tifically classified, and an increasing number of companies are acquiring official
certificates to prove the safety of their products; however, the country still faces
a serious problem in effectively implementing these regulations.[62] China lacks
competent, non-corrupt, and independent inspectors and administrators at local
levels. China also suffers from a lack of well-trained chemical, pesticide, and
agricultural/food science experts. It is doubtful that every lot has been sampled
prior to export. In addition, falsified export certificates seem widely available.[63]

In April 2007, President Hu Jintao held a collective study meeting of the Polit-
buro of the Communist Party at which he emphasized the importance of food
safety in China.[64] The Chinese government has been trying to solve these serious

problems by legal, institutional and administrative measures.[65] China's agricultural production bases for exports allegedly have the world's safest management system.[66] In theory, China developed competent laws and institutions to ensure food safety; however, a substantial reduction of food pollution did not follow.[67] China has already established enough legislation in terms of quantity, but carrying out strict implementation of the legislation has been difficult, punishment of illegal conduct is inadequate and the power of local supervising authorities is weak and sometimes compromised.[68] Chinese farmers and food processing companies were largely capable of adjusting themselves to the changing needs and requirements of the market after joining the WTO, but the Chinese market system is still inadequate and the government's administrative and supervising capabilities are still of a poor standard. Under conditions that lacked both corporate social responsibility and market information, people selfishly pursued their own interests and gains, which eventually led to failures within the market and government.[69]

After its admission to the WTO, the Chinese government was compelled to address its many food safety issues. Considering the importance of food exports, the Chinese government established a dual economic structure, separating food safety for export use from food safety for domestic use, which created a highly advanced, exclusive and closed supply chain for major export-oriented companies. The government believed that this would provide a safer and more quality-controlled environment for produce to be exported around the world.

## Concluding observations

Getting back to the original research question: Why does China suffer from a serious lack of food safety? The short answer is that the Chinese government's domestic policies aimed at trying to promote rapid economic growth set the grounds for numerous food safety issues. In other words, the Chinese government's domestic policies provided Chinese food producers, processors and vendors with many opportunities and incentives for illicit practices, transactions, and operations. Globalization pushed China to join the WTO, which made the Chinese government work to ensure the safety of exported foodstuffs. The combination of the "get-rich-quick" policy and membership in the WTO compelled China to form a dual economy, separating food safety for export use from food safety for domestic use, creating a highly advanced, exclusive, safe and closed supply chain for major export-oriented companies.

## Notes

1 Shoku no Kagaku Henshubu, "Chugoku 'san no mondai' to Nihon eno eikyo", [China's 'triple agriculture-related problems' and their impacts on Japan], *Shoku no Kagaku*, 339 (May 2006): 28.
2 "Chugoku, Shoku no anzen kakuho to hinshitsu kojo kyoka e", [China, securing food safety and intensification of quality improvement], *Chikusan no Joho*, 213 (July 2007): 23.
3 S. Kawahara, "Chugoku no shokuhin anzen seido", [China's food safety system], *Norin Suisan Seisaku Kenkyujo Review*, 12 (June 2004): 44. See also: Syoichiro

Kawahara, "Chugoku no shokuhin anzen mondai", [China's food safety problems] *Gekkan Shokuryo to Anzen*, 9 (December 2011): 40–41.

4  Y. Hong, "The practice of business ethics in China: we need a parent", *Business Ethics: A European Review*, 10(2) (April 2001): 90.

5  Y. Akiyoshi, and T. Mashiko, "Shoku no anzen ni okeru seisakuteki torikumi ni kansuru ichi kousatsu Nihon, Amerika, EU, Chugoku no jirei ni tsuite", [A study on food safety approach with reference to Japan, USA, EU, and China], *Macro Review*, 22(1) (2009): 8–9.

6  M. Sato, "Chugoku no Noyaku Jijou to Shoku no Anzen", [Conditions in pesticides in China and food safety], *Nihon Noyaku Gakkaishi*, 31(1) (2006): 60.

7  Y. Miyazawa, and T. Ohtahara, "Chugoku ni okeru yushutsu muke 'yuki yasai' seisan no haikei to kigyo senryaku: Santonsho no kako kigyo wo jirei toshite", [The background and corporate strategies of 'organic vegetable' production for export in China: A case study of processing companies in Shandong Province], *Hokkaido Daigaku Nokei Ronso*, 58 (March 2002): 124.

8  From Chinese statistical yearbooks cited in T. Yutaka, and X. Sun, "Chugoku ni okeru tainichi yushutsu yasai no seisan/ryutsu no genjo to tenkai hook", [Current status and development direction of production and distribution of exporting vegetables to Japan in China], in Susumu Fukuda, ed., *Higashi ajia ni okeru fuudo shisutemu no kosa* [Intersection of Food System in East Asia] (Fukuoka: Kyushu Gakujutsu Shuppan Shinko Centre, 2004), pp. 70–71; K. Oshima, "Chugoku no Nogyo/Shokuhin Sangyo to Anzen Kanri Seisaku no Doko", [China's agriculture/food industry and development of safety management policies], *Seikyo Sogo Kenkyujo Seikatsu Kyodo Kumiai Kenkyu*, 395 (December 2008): 17.

9  Oshima, "Chugoku no Nogyo・ Shokuhin Sangyo", p. 20.

10  S.C. Wong, X.D. Li, G. Zhang, S.H. Qi, and Y.S. Min, "Heavy metals in agricultural soils of the Pearl River Delta, South China", *Environmental Pollution*, 119 (2002): 34.

11  K.Oshima, "Chugoku no Nogyo・ Noson no Chokumen suru Kadai to Tenkai Hoko", [Issues that Chinese agriculture and agricultural villages face and their development direction], *Kokusai Josei*, 75 (February 2005): 32–33.

12  Y. Miyazawa, and T. Ohtahara, "Yushutsu muke yuki yasai seisan no kigyo senryaku", [Corporate strategy of export-oriented organic vegetable production], in H. Sakazume, Hong Park, and Akihiko Sakashita, eds., *Chugoku yasai kiigyo no yushutsu senryaku – zanryu noyaku jiken no shogeki to kokufuku katei* [Export Strategy by Chinese Vegetable Enterprises: Impacts of the Residual Pesticide Problem and the Overcoming Process] (Tokyo: Tsukuba Shobo, 2006), pp. 67–68.

13  K. Oshima, "Chugokusan Nosanbutsu no Zanryu Noyaku Mondai to Tainichi Yushutsu Senryaku", [Pesticide-residue problems of agricultural products made in China and the exporting strategy to Japan], *Gekkan Nosei*, 57(2) (February 2005): 21.

14  J. Zhou, and S. Jin, "Safety of vegetables and the use of pesticides by farmers in China", *Food Control*, 20 (2009): 1043.

15  K. Oshima, "Chugoku ni okeru seitai kankyo no akka to junkangata nogyo shisutemu kochiku no hitsuyosei", [Deterioration of ecology in China and the necessity of establishing recycling agricultural systems], *Momoyama Gakuin Daigaku Keizai Keiei Ronshu*, 53(2) (October 2011): 25–26.

16  L. J. Ellis, and J. L. Turner, *Sowing the Seeds: Opportunities for U.S.-China Cooperation on Food Safety* (Washington, D.C.: Woodrow Wilson International Center for Scholars, September 2008), pp. 17–18; Keisuke Suganuma, "Zanryu Noyaku Mondai no Taisaku ni Torikumu Chugoku no Yasai Sanchi #1", [China's vegetable production bases dealing with pesticide-residue problems #1], *Yasai Joho*, 22 (January 2006): 23.

17  F. Gale, and J. C. Buzby, "Imports from China and food safety issues", *Economic Information Bulletin*, 52 (July 2009): 2.

18  L. Bai, et al., "Food safety assurance systems in China", *Food Control*, 18(5) (May 2007): 481.
19  Kawahara, "Chugoku no shokuhin anzen mondai", p. 37; Gale and Buzby, "Imports from China and food safety issues", p. 2.
20  D. Hu, T. Reardon, S. Rozelle, P. Timmer, and H. Wang, "The emergence of supermarkets with Chinese characteristics: Challenges and opportunities for China's agricultural development", *Development Policy Review*, 22(5) (2004): 557.
21  M. Sato, "Chugoku no noyaku jijo to shoku no anzen", [Pesticides in China and food safety], p. 57.
22  S. Takata, "Chugoku no GAP (Tekisei Nogyo Kanri) to Shoku no Anzen Ishiki", [China's GAP and consciousness of food safety in China], *Nihon Sangyo Keizai Gakkai Sangyo Keizai Kenkyu*, 10 (March 2010): 58; "Good Agricultural Practice (GAP)" in "Small Producers in Export Horticulture: A Guide to Best Practice".
23  J. Huang, Y. Wu, H. Zhi, and S. Rozelle, "Small holder incomes, food safety and producing, and marketing China's fruit", *Review of Agricultural Economics*, 30(3) (2008): 477.
24  L. Bai, et al., "Food safety assurance systems in China", p. 481.
25  T. Ishikawa, "Chugoku shokuhin anzen hosei no shin kyokumen", [A new phase of China's food safety legal system], *Rippo to Chosa*, 302 (March 2010): 60.
26  D. Thompson, and Hu Ying, "Food safety in China: New strategies", *Global Health Government I*, 2 (Fall 2007): 5.
27  Oshima, "Chugoku no Nogyo/Shokuhin Sangyo", p. 20; Ellis and Turner, *Sowing the Seeds*, p. 17.
28  Ellis and Turner, *Sowing the Seeds*, p. 17.
29  W. Tam, and D. L. Yang, "Food safety and the development of regulatory institutions in China", in Dali L. Yang, ed., *Discontented Miracle: Growth, Conflict, and Institutional Adaptations in China* (Singapore: World Scientific Publishing Company, 2007), p. 184.
30  X. Lu, "A Chinese perspective: Business ethics in China now and in the future," *Journal of Business Ethics*, 86 (2009): 457.
31  A. V. Roth, Andy A. Tsay, Madeleine E. Pullman, and John V. Gray, "Unraveling the food supply chain: Strategic insights from China and the 2007 recalls", *The Journal of Supply Chain Management: A Global Review of Purchasing and Supply*, 44 (January 2008): 31.
32  Japan External Trade Organization, _Chugoku ni okeru Nosanbutsu· shokuhin no Anzen Kakuho ni Kansuru Seisaku to Jittai Chosa_ [Policies and fact-finding survey concerning securing safety of agricultural products and food in China] (Tokyo: Japan External Trade Organization, 2008), p. 36.
33  Kawahara, "Chugoku no shokuhin anzen mondai", p. 39.
34  "China faces a new worry: Heavy metals in the food", *The Wall Street Journal*, 2 July 2007, http://online.wsj.com/article/SB118333755837554826.html (Accessed on 24 October 2017).
35  Gale and Buzby, "Imports from China and food safety issues", pp. 2–3.
36  Ibid, p. 4.
37  Yuuko Akiyoshi, and Takako Mashiko, "Shoku no anzen ni okeru seisakuteki torikumi ni kansuru ichi kousatsu Nihon, Amerika, EU, Chugoku no jirei ni tsuite", [A study on food safety approach with reference to Japan, USA, EU, and China].
38  L. Bai, et al., "Food safety assurance systems in China", p. 481.
39  Gale and Buzby, "Imports from China and food safety issues", p. 23; Emako Miyoshi, "Chugoku Shokuhin wo Meguru Risuku Komyunikeishon no Kouchiku wo Mezashite", [The establishment of risk communication for Chinese-made foods], *Discussion Papers in Contemporary China Studies Osaka University Forum on China No. 2009–4* (15 October 2009): 20.
40  Gale and Buzby, "Imports from China and food safety issues", p. 3.

41 P.K. Ip, "The challenge of developing a business ethics in China", *Journal of Business Ethics*, 88 (2009): 216.
42 L. Bai, et al., "Food safety assurance systems in China", p. 481.
43 Ellis and Turner, *Sowing the Seeds*, p. 18.
44 R. Shiina, "Korede Gyoza wa makuhiki?" [Is this the end of the Gyoza incident?], *Seiron*, 436 (July 2008): 85.
45 J. Schönmann, "Greed for profit: China being poisoned by its food industry", *Spiegel Online*, 18 December 2007, www.spiegel.de/international/world/greed-for-profit-china-being-poisoned-by-its-food-industry-says-author-a-523988.html (Accessed on 24 October 2017).
46 Tam and Yang, "Food safety and the development of regulatory institutions", p. 163.
47 F. Dong, and H.H. Jensen, "The challenge of conforming to sanitary and phytosanitary measures for China's agricultural exports", *MATRIC Working Paper* 04-MWP 8 (March 2004): 2, 4.
48 Y. Yamada, "Dou Natteruno? Gyoza Jiken to Chugoku no 'Rouso'", [What's happening? Gyoza incident and China's 'labor union'], *RENGO*, 21(1) (April 2008): 5.
49 Miyoshi, "Chugoku Shokuhin wo Meguru Risuku Komyunikeishon", p. 13.
50 R. Mouri, "Shoku no Gurobarizeishon to Nihon no Chugoku karano Kaihatsu Yunyu," [Globalization of food and Japan's development import from China], *Nihon Fukushi Daigaku Keizai Ronshu*, 36 (March 2008): 25.
51 C. Chen, J. Yang, and C. Findlay, "Measuring the effect of food safety standards on China's agricultural exports", *Review of World Economics*, 144(1) (2008): 86.
52 Z. Wang, H.Yuan, and F. Gale, "Costs of adopting a hazard analysis critical control point system: Case study of a Chinese poultry processing firm", *Review of Agricultural Economics*, 31(3) (Fall 2009): 574; Gale and Buzby, "Imports from China and food safety issues", p. 19.
53 M. Sato, "Chugoku no Noyaku Jijou to Shoku no Anzen", [Conditions in pesticides in China and food safety], p. 60.
54 K. Oshima, "Chugoku Nogyo/Shokuhin Sangyo no Hatten to Shokuhin Anzen Mondai", [Development of Chinese agriculture/food industry and food safety problems], *Chugoku Keizai Kenkyu*, 6(2) (September 2009): 26.
55 Oshima, "Chugoku no Nogyo/Shokuhin Sangyo", p. 23.
56 K. Suganuma, "Zanryu Noyaku Mondai no Taisaku ni Torikumu Chugoku no Yasai Sanchi #2", [China's vegetable production bases dealing with pesticide-residue problems #2], *Yasai Joho*, 23 (February 2006): 26.
57 T. Narita, "Chugokusan Tainichi Yushutsuryo Gensho to Chugoku Yasai Yushutsu Kigyo no Jigyo Saihen", [Decline of export volume of China products to Japan and reconstruction of business of Chinese vegetable export companies], *Nogyo Shijo Kenkyu*, 18(4) (2010): 44.
58 Wang, Yuan, and Gale, "Costs of adopting a hazard analysis critical control point system", p. 575.
59 K. Oshima, *Chugoku Yasai to Nihon no Shokutaku* [China's Vegetables and Japan's Dining Tables] (Tokyo: Ashi Shobo, 2007), p. 145.
60 Ibid, p. 154.
61 Shoku no Kagaku Henshubu, "Chugoku 'san no modai' to Nihon eno eikyo", p. 28.
62 Japan External Trade Organization, "Chugoku ni okeru Nosanbutsu", pp. 15–18, 23.
63 U.S. Congress, "Food from China: Can we import safely?", *Subcommittee on Oversight and Investigations Staff Trip Report* (4 October 2007): 7; X. Pei, A. Tandon, A. Alldrick, L. Giorgi, W. Huang, and R. Yang, "The China melamine milk scandal and its implications for food safety regulation", *Food Policy*, 36 (2011): 419.
64 "Chugoku, Shoku no anzen kakuho to hinshitsu kojo kyoka e", p. 25.
65 X. Lu, "A Chinese perspective: Business ethics in China now and in the future", *Journal of Business Ethics*, 86 (2009): 455.

66  Y. Baba, "'Shoku no anzen' ga kaeru Chugoku no fudo bizinesu", ['Food safety' changes China's food business], *Toa*, 482 (August 2007): 10.
67  Akiyoshi and Mashiko, "Shoku no anzen ni okeru seisakuteki torikumi", p. 8.
68  F. Kamata, "Chugoku ni okeru Shokuhin no Anzensei Kakuho ni taisuru Torikumi", [Efforts to secure food safety in China], *Gaikoku no Rippo*, 235 (March 2008): 170–171.
69  Mouri, "Shoku no Gurobarizeishon", p. 14.

# 5 Deadly alchemists

## Implications of the illicit pharmaceutical industry in China for human and health security

*Victor Teo and Sungwon Yoon*

## Introduction

Pharmaceutical drugs are essential for the maintenance of good health and longevity. Unlike food, drugs are often consumed only when human beings are taken ill. When drugs are counterfeited, the lethal risks run high for consumers. Up until the 1980s, counterfeit drugs were not much of a problem, but advances in technology (cloning of drugs or products that approximate the appearance of real drugs and reproduction of the packaging including the security mechanisms of the authentic drugs packaging), logistics (high speed volume delivery) and communications (the facilitation of ordering fake drugs and payment systems over the internet) have rendered the fake drug industry a serious but silent public health crisis today.

Amidst globalization, the prevalence of counterfeit medicines appears to be rising rapidly. It has been estimated that counterfeit incidents increased 122% for the period from 2005 to 2010.[1] The U.S. Food and Drug Administration (FDA) estimates that counterfeit medicines comprise approximately 10% of the global market, and in parts of Africa and Asia, this figure appears to be greater.[2] Reports from other intergovernmental and professional organizations have also highlighted the increasing challenges associated with counterfeit medicines.[3,4,5] Importantly, China is a dominant source of a counterfeit incident accounting for 27.6% of the total 1,510 incidents in 2013, according to the Pharmaceutical Security Institute.[6] This suggests that China accounts for a larger share of this criminal enterprise.

To date, the definition of "counterfeit" remains imprecise. In general, counterfeit drugs may refer to a drug that lacks an important ingredient or contains an unnecessary one, or maybe even harmful ones. It may also be a product mislabelled, expired or worse: a product born of a mixture of various unacceptable ingredients. Legally speaking, the idea of a "counterfeit" refers to the misappropriation of the techniques and technology of manufacturing. In accordance with *Black's Law Dictionary*, the term "counterfeit drug" may be used to describe a drug made by someone other than the genuine manufacturer, by copying or imitating an original product without authority or right, with a view to deceive or defraud, and then marketing the copied or forged drug as the original.[7] In reality, however, a counterfeit drug is defined differently across different jurisdictions.[8]

According to the World Health Organization (WHO), a counterfeit medicine is one which:

is deliberately and fraudulently mislabeled with respect to identity and/ or source. Counterfeiting can apply to both branded and generic products and counterfeit products may include products with the correct ingredients or with the wrong ingredients, without active ingredients, with insufficient active ingredients or with fake packaging.[9]

Even though there are different national definitions of what constitutes fake medicine or drugs, there is a general common sense agreement that anything not manufactured by the original or authorized manufacturer and less than pristine or up to standard medicine would be unacceptable to most people.

In China, the definition of counterfeit medicine is established by the Pharmaceutical Administration Law of the People's Republic of China (PRC) (2001).[10] There are calls that the definition be revised or improved.[11] In particular, Article 48 stipulates that the production (including preparation, which also applies to the following) and sale of fake medicines are prohibited. A fake medicine has at least one of the following characteristics:

1) Its components are different from those prescribed by state pharmaceutical standards.
2) A non-medical substance is passed off as a medicine, or one medicine is passed off as another.

Additionally, the statute considers that a medicine shall be handled as fake medicine in any of the following cases:

1) Where the use of the medicine has been prohibited by the pharmaceutical supervisory and administrative department under the State Council.
2) Where the medicine is produced, and imported without an approval dictated according to this Law, or the medicine is sold without being inspected as dictated according to the Law.
3) Where the medicine has deteriorated.
4) Where the medicine has been contaminated.
5) Where the medicine has been produced with pharmaceutical materials without obtaining the dictated registration document of approval for the materials.
6) Where the indications or the functions marked on the labels of the pharmaceuticals do not fall within the prescribed scope.

Article 49 stipulates that the production and sale of medicines of inferior quality, referring to the medicines whose components do not conform in quantity to that required by state pharmaceutical standards, are prohibited. A medicine shall be handled as medicine of inferior quality in any of the following cases:

1) An expiration date is not indicated or is altered.
2) A registration number is not indicated or is altered.
3) The medicine has passed its expiration date.
4) The packages and containers which have direct contact with pharmaceuticals have not obtained approval.

5) The medicine has been added presumptuously with colour or preservative additives, spice, disguising odour or supplementary materials.
6) The medicine fails to meet the prescribed standards in other respects.

In 2011, Article 141 of the *PRC Criminal Law* was amended to include the death penalty and now reads:

> Whoever produces or sells fake medicines which are sufficiently able to seriously endanger human health is to be sentenced to not more than three years of fixed-term imprisonment or crimination detention and may in addition or exclusively be sentenced to a fine of not less than 50 percent and not more than 200 percent of the sale amount; when causing serious harm to human health, is to be sentenced to not less than three years and not more than ten years of fixed-term imprisonment and may in addition be sentenced to a fine of not less than 50 percent and not more than 200 percent of the sale amount; when causing death or particular harm to human health, is to be sentenced to not less than ten years of fixed-term imprisonment, life imprisonment, or death penalty and may in addition be sentenced to a fine of not less than 50 percent and not more than 200 percent of the sale amount or confiscation of property.[12]

As a departure point, Chinese authorities have revised the law to increase the penalty and the asset forfeiture amount. The clarification of the definition of what constitute fake medicine, and the corresponding punishment, contextualizes our discussion of what goes on in this illicit industry in China in the following section.

## Characterizing the illicit pharmaceutical drug industry in China

China's research and development-based Pharmaceutical Association estimates that about 8% of China's over-the-counter drugs are counterfeit.[13] In 2002, the Drug Administration of China seized counterfeit drugs valued at US$57 million and closed 1,300 factories.[14] A survey of recent incidents would attest to the seriousness of the threat of this industry. Nine people in in Guangdong died as a result of using fake drugs made by a Chinese pharmaceutical company in northeastern China's Heilongjiang province. This occurred at Sun Yatsen University No. 3 Affiliated Hospital, and the victims suffered acute kidney failure after receiving injections of Armillarisin A – a medicine used for liver, gall bladder and gastric ailments. Police arrested 14 people from the company in Heilongjiang Qiqihar.[15] Subsequently, the Ministry of Supervision found 21 people liable for the deaths of 11 people in Guangzhou.[16] In 2007, Chinese investigators found more than 60 hospitals and pharmacies in northeastern China have been using fake blood protein in patient drips, particularly for victims suffering from shock and burns and during open-heart surgery. In the province of Jilin itself, 18 hospitals and more than 30 pharmacies sold or were selling false batches of albumin, and it was suggested by the officials that these outright fakes were generating about 300% profit.[17]

In December 2010, the State Food and Drug Agency published an update outlining the "ten classic cases" of enforcement that were tackled in the year. The variety of the cases were impressive, and outlined the work undertaken by the SFDA provincial offices in Beijing (internet sales of fake medicine), Zhejiang (manufacture of Gefitinib), Shanghai (sales of counterfeit Botox Type A), Guangdong and Shenzhen (sales of counterfeit branded medicine), Hubei (manufacture of fake medicine), Jilin (manufacture of 70 types of counterfeit medicine and the boxes/containers, storage, distribution, and sales worth ¥70.1 million), Liaoning (manufacture of counterfeit popular Chinese health supplement), and Jiangsu and Wuxi (manufacture of counterfeit medicine).[18]

The following year, the Chinese SFDA broke up more than 1,800 business that made or sold counterfeit medicine worth ¥3.35 billion (US$530 million) over a span of two years. Thirteen government departments with more than one million law enforcement officers combat the sale of 5,000 illegal pharmaceutical products.[19] In May 2011, police seized more than 6.9 million Viagra pills and a large amount of raw materials in Guangzhou and Zhongshan city in Guangdong (see Figure 5.1). They captured 51 machines, 1,200 moulds and packaging boxes, and 3.9 million bottles from 49 different locations and sites.[20] Police and inspectors from the Food

*Figure 5.1* Signboard advertising Viagra for sale. A significant percentage of Viagra in China is fake

and Drug Administration in Nanjing raided 30 adult stores, but they were unable to distinguish whether the Viagra were real or not as the counterfeiters had copied certain core techniques of the manufacturer Pfizer in terms of packaging.

In February 2012, Shandong Jinan policy found 1,500 boxes of Yu Ding retro gradation plasm, Gefitinib Tablet, and Imatinib Mesylate Capsules – all cancer drugs – alongside eight manufacturing platforms that had operations spanning 14 provinces with net worth over ¥ 11 million. In April 2012, the Guangzhou Police broke up counterfeit group which was manufacturing Gardasil (加德士). They arrested one person who sold the box of the medicine to a wholesaler for ¥4,000, and the wholesaler resold the box with the counterfeit drug at ¥10,000 to a beauty parlour. The beauty parlour then resold the same to a retail customer for ¥23,800.[21]

Two months later in June 2012, Tianjin police found a gang which imported fake pharmaceutical drugs from India, Hong Kong and other places and resold the drugs over the internet.[22] The persistence and rapid expansion of the industry lies in the tremendous profit to be gained from this industry. With labour, plain water and packaging that costs as little as ¥5, counterfeiters manufactured breast cancer medicine that can be resold at ¥8,500 to the end user.[23] In the same year, police in China arrested more than 1,900 people and seized ¥1.16 billion (US$182 million) worth of counterfeit drugs and related goods amid a government crackdown in the world's fastest-growing pharmaceuticals market (see Figure 5.2).[24] Chinese police announced in July 2012 that in a nationwide operation, they seized millions of pills that were clones of well-known brands that were used to treat diabetes, hypertension, skin problems and cancer, worth ¥1.16 billion.[25] From June to December 2013,

*Figure 5.2* Chinese customs officials seized over one million capsules of fake pharmaceutical products in Ningbo City, Zhejiang province, China in 2012

China launched a nationwide crackdown on fake medicine. The Ministry of Public Security shut down 140 illegal websites and online pharmacies in 29 provinces and major cities, seizing nine tonnes of raw materials worth ¥2.2 billion.[26]

In 2016, 20 suspects were detained in China's eastern provinces, and almost 20,000 boxes of fake drugs and several tons of raw materials were seized by police in Huzhou, Zhejiang. The distribution means of the drugs were through China's most popular Wechat social media platform, with a network of 30 provinces for the total value of about ¥100 million. The drugs were sold as exclusive parallel imports, and included diet drugs and painkillers.[27] Additionally, police also seized more than 88,000 counterfeit Viagra and 95,000 other doses of fake aphrodisiacs after breaking up a ring based in Dongguan, Guangdong. Another 1.42 million unfinished doses of fake drugs were seized in the case by the Guangdong Public Security Bureau that involved in 230 different kinds of fake medicines with a retail value of ¥37 million.[28] There is a reportedly popular saying in China regarding the country's illicit pharmaceutical industry: The counterfeit-drug rings are earning the profit of selling heroin, but without the risk.

This is best exemplified what happened in Hainan Island. By November 2017, the Hainan Island's Province Food and Drug Agency had detained over 77 suspects in a fake drug sales network. The seized products involved 1.29 million pills in 83 types of drugs, valued at ¥200 million, to be distributed to 24 other provinces in China and regionally across Asia. Investigations revealed that the drugs were mainly manufactured in Guangxi Zhuang Autonomous Region.[29]

In 2018, a Chinese gang based in Shenzhen was convicted of selling fake drugs in China from 2014 to 2016. They used a Hong Kong-based and registered company and website to sell drugs unlicensed on the mainland at extremely inflated prices. In particular, they bought one cancer treatment drug for ¥7,500 (US$1,150) and resold it for ¥175,000, and some of the profits were passed onto doctors in hospitals in Beijing, Shanghai and Hunan once they introduced new customers, in the short time they operated, they made over ¥4.3 million. This episode is indicative of how a company with a Hong Kong cover was able to provide the legitimacy for the gang to approach hospitals and doctors with impunity, and also raises the question if the weakest link in the medical supply chain is the greedy medical doctors who take kickback at hospitals.[30]

## The mechanics of the industry[31]

Like most counterfeit industries that offer goods for sale, counterfeit drugs have their own manufacturing process and marketing strategies. However, unlike counterfeit consumer goods such as cloned iPhones or clothing, etc., this category of goods is neither welcomed nor tolerated by either consumers and authorities. The manufacture, marketing and sales are usually done in secret, and the consumption is almost invariably unwitting. Almost without exception, this category of illicit activity is seen as a crime by most Chinese people. The only possible exception is when some citizens who are too poor to have adequate access to legitimate healthcare and/ or insurance knowingly import generic medicine from abroad, or in more severe cases manufacture their own medicine using the ingredients. It was reported in 2016

*Figure 5.3* Idealized stages of the value chain of one method of production in China's illicit pharmaceutical industry

that many Chinese are buying India-produced Geftinat, or another drug, AZD9291, otherwise known as Osimertinib, from Hong Kong because the drugs then had yet to be approved. Some poorer Chinese were even buying the active ingredients to make their own mixtures.[32] Only this category of consumers exhibit a knowledge and voluntary consent for the purchase and consumption of fake drugs.

Overall, the stages of this industry could be described in Figure 5.3, which looks similar to many other manufacturing cycles in reality. There are different manpower requirements and capital investments at each stage. There are instances when the manufacturer openly starts up a brand of medicine and advertise openly that their medicine cures certain ailments, particularly the serious terminal illness (e.g. cancer) without any scientific basis. This is what happened in Shandong Jinan, where a fake medicine manufacturer was brought down after a sting operation. There were four people arrested, and police estimated they made over ¥30 million marketing their medicine. Each box of their medicine probably cost less than ¥20.[33]

If the criminal entrepreneurs wanted to "clone" existing medicine instead of inventing outright "new" ones, then the basic stem is to simply ensure they could copy the packaging and produce pills or solutions to emulate the real thing. The initial stage of the value chain usually involves the consolidation of raw materials needed to manufacture these drugs. At this stage, the criminals usually try to obtain samples of the real products to decide on the raw materials required. The manufacturing of pills or solutions is simple enough even for most home industries. This stage involves manufacturing with weakened or substituted ingredients[34] Alternatively, some illicit entreprenuers simply dispense with the need to even put in approximate active ingredients.

Convictions have shown that the pills could be made out of chalk or processed flour, with colouring to boot. Solutions are either just water or saline with the appropriate colouring and, if necessary, flavour enhancer. In 2011, along with Viagra, counterfeiters are targeting cancer drugs because of huge profit margins. Cancer drugs were then the eighth most popular counterfeit drugs, according to the Pharmaceutical Security Institute.[35]

One of the most critical "inputs" for the fake pharmaceutical industry is the collection of authentic used medical packaging so that they can be "recycled".[36] From the narratives collected from those involved in the industry, the more "complete" and "new" the packaging, the higher the sales involved. The collectors are often the garbage collectors or workers in Chinese hospitals where genuine products are used. They could resell the boxes for anywhere between ¥300–1,500 depending on the price of the end product.[37] Naturally, the higher the end product is priced, the more valuable is the box. Collectors of the packaging resell it to the consolidator who could either be the "manufacturer" of the fake drug himself or just a wholesaler of the boxes. Depending on the locality, there could be tiers of business reselling these "genuine" boxes. There have been reports that often, the collectors are so successful in accumulating these boxes that they manage to collect sets with running serial numbers. With sets like these, the resale value becomes even higher. A cleaner in the hospital makes about ¥700–1,000 a month depending on locality. Selling of such boxes becomes a phenomenally attractive way to improve their economic status.

The wholesaler of pharmaceutical boxes consolidates through their network of hospital cleaners (or their relatives) and in turn distributes the boxes to the manufacturers. The wholesalers of these boxes could be the manufacturers themselves. Depending on their "morality" or intent, these manufacturers might either try to repack the empty packaging with domestic "cloned" versions of the drug(s) (quality varying), or just fill the packaging with something that resembles the real thing without any real medicinal value (e.g. ingredients like flour). In the worst cases, many of the drugs are made in places with extreme unsanitary conditions, and consumption of these drugs brings adverse effects to the consumers. There are, of course, those who try to duplicate the real medicine (i.e. cloning the real medicine) by replicating the ingredients and process of manufacture. Rightly or wrongly, all these actions are categorized under counterfeiting medicine in the eyes of the law.

The marketing of the fake drugs is probably the most critical juncture. In order to sell the fake drugs, the distributors would have to market the drugs at a rate that offers a slight discount in relation to the real prices to end users, i.e. 10–20% discount. Too steep a discount would usually raise suspicions. Depending on the kind of drugs they are selling, the wholesalers would have different channels of distribution. From the profiles of criminal cases, they have known to work either in collaboration with hospital or clinic staff via direct use (e.g. in the case of Shanghai Ruian eye clinic, a joint collaboration between a Hong Kong company and a local Shanghai hospital, the clinic stuff was buying in fake medicine to be administered on the patients)[38] or via prescription (getting the patients to buy from certain pharmacies or drugstores). For cosmetics and lifestyle drugs such as Viagra or birth control pills, they will be sold at a discount (often dressed as bulk discount) to outlets to be resold to retailers such as convenience stalls, "adult" equipment stores (sex shops) or general provision shops. In Shanghai, one of the most outrageous cases is the sale of fake Botox to cosmetic surgery clinics. Many of the retailers or clinics often do not even know they have sold fake medicines, not to mention the consumers.

One of the biggest boons to the industry is modern communications. There is a mass effort to market these drugs as "bulk" discount items on internet websites and market places such as the Taobao, a Chinese version of eBay. There are also efforts to use multi-level marketing to sell prescription drugs through social media like chat forums, Weibo or Weixin under different discussion groups. The distributors are also known to employ direct salespersons such as cleaners or attendants in hospitals or the elderly who sit around the dispensary dishing out name cards to patients and suggesting individual or bulk purchase discounts. They might even collect the identity details of the patients and do direct marketing via telephone, as many elderly are still not conversant with the internet. The transactions are then closed using bank deposits, electronic transfers and Chinese version of Paypal: Zhifubao and Weixin payment.

Alternatively, the counterfeit drugs could enter the legitimate supply chain at various stages: at the factories, warehouses, pharmacy, hospitals or clinics, usually through the bribing of corrupt bureaucrats, businessmen, or company employees or officials at drug depots, distribution centres, pharmacies in hospitals and clinics. Due to the underpaid nature of public hospital workers, the lax and difficulty of enforcement and most importantly the lack of ethics amongst many practitioners, China's public health system is tainted by corruption.

This is probably the most insidious aspect of the industry: The patients who have not opted to buy drugs on the internet or discounts but instead relied on the traditional trusted "sources" such as pharmacies and hospitals also risk the chance of acquiring fake drugs without the slightest inclination. Education, legislation and due diligence over the internet may reduce the retailing of these harmful products, but if the counterfeit products enter the legitimate "trusted" supply, then it would be almost impossible to weed out these products without great effort. On the Chinese websites, there are many sad and angry accounts of people who were the victims of this industry. Most serious in this is the issue of pharmaceutical bribery. It has been reported that close to 100 doctors in Shanghai were investigated by Shanghai Food and Drug Agency. In 2000 alone, it is estimated that the doctors and pharmacists who brought fake drugs pocketed ¥490,000 (US$59,000) each.[39] Doctors at major hospitals in big cities such as Beijing and Shanghai were recommending patients buy drugs from a company in Hong Kong that were in fact peddling branded drugs that the Chinese government have yet to approve.

These drugs of course turn out to be fake, but it was not clear if the doctors had knowledge of this and were complicit in ways other than recommending unapproved drugs to the patients.[40] Chinese medical workers, particularly doctors are therefore susceptibly to be bribed by pharmaceutical companies to recommend one drug over the other, and this is becoming extremely problematic.[41]

On the supply side, it is even more problematic. Unlike other counterfeit industries, the actors in manufacturing fake pharmaceutical products maintain an extremely low profile. From the case files of those convicted of participation in the drug trade, there is evidence that many of the manufacturing rings are "family-based" operations. The heinous nature of this action meant that very often they will only work with people they can trust. The nature of many of these operations is not particularly high-tech. For those particular aspects that counterfeiters have problems with, for example, printing of the boxes, they will outsource the job. The informal way that these illicit industry actors are organized often means that the operations can be moved at the moment's notice, and can swiftly change to meet the changing demands or more likely react to the threats from exposure or police.

Because of the huge profits involved, many of the actors are able to recruit advisors and workers to their operation. At every stage, people who participate in this industry benefit immeasurably. Individuals ranging from cleaners and garbage collectors to the people who collect the packaging to the "drugs" manufacturer to the distributor and sales person, this industry benefits almost everyone in the chain financially – with the end consumer as the biggest loser. In short, China's counterfeit medicine rings have reportedly grown into full-fledged underworld networks, with the help of unethical and corrupt businessmen, medical professionals and new technology. This has a huge impact on the public health system and the state in terms of escalating health-care costs.

This is something that is even admitted by the Chinese government itself. China's State Food and Drug Administration (SFDA) officials stated that some rings have fully integrated systems for production, internet promotion and courier distribution of fake medicine. The *Economic Information Daily* alleged that medical workers and people with medical backgrounds were implicated in counterfeit drug probes in Beijing, Hangzhou (Zhejiang province), Guangdong province, and Shandong province. The mastermind of the previously mentioned case is a post-doctoral fellow who returned to China after spending years in the United States. Ding Haiyi, a naturalized U.S. citizen and a Jiangsu native who graduated from one of the top medical schools in China, was convicted by the Hangzhou Intermediate Court in November 2009 as part of one of the largest fake medical schemes in China.[42] Reportedly, his scheme with four collaborators was estimated to worth ¥30 million.[43] Officials and investigators apparently found detailed paperwork describing exactly which doctors and hospitals have been bribed, the amounts paid and the quantity of drugs dispensed.[44]

## Health and human security implications

The concept of "human security" is a relatively recent phenomenon in international relations theory. This concept shifts our understanding of security from its traditional focus on nation-states to the level of human beings as potential casualties. The threat comes from a wide variety of sources – not just physical harm from military confrontation – but is located in wider framework of emotional and physical suffering and harm from environmental, migratory, social dislocation and disparities, criminal and other sources. The interpretation is not as "objective" as traditional theorists might wish it to be, but nonetheless the concept of human security cannot be construed as an abstract concept.[45]

Perhaps the clearest articulation of the human security concept comes from United Nations Development Programme though the establishment of the United Nations Development Index (UNDI) –the central premise of this index is that human beings rather than states must be at the centre of any thinking on development policy.[46] The narratives of human security over time shifted from the emphasis on security of nation-states to ordinary people, and mandates that security and foreign policies construed must address the "legitimate concerns of ordinary people who sought security in their lives".[47] There is therefore no question here that drug safety becomes an all-important aspect of human security in China. While there are many points for discussion from the depiction of the illicit pharmaceutical industry in China, health and human security implications reign supreme. Beyond that, once the pharmaceutical supply is tainted, the confidence in the entire health system would nose-dive.

### *Direct human health risks*

Needless to say, there is tremendous impact in terms of the loss of lives due to these fake drugs. Reports from developed countries indicate that the most frequently counterfeited medicines are new and thus expensive lifestyle medicine: drugs like antihistamines, hormones and steroids are being counterfeited; whereas in developing countries, it is the drugs that have to do with life-threatening situations such as malaria, tuberculosis and HIV/AIDS.[48] In China, it would appear that both categories suffer severely from counterfeiting, from Viagra to cancer drugs: As long as there is a profit to be made, it will be counterfeited.

Undoubtedly, the consumption of counterfeit medicine poses significant human health risks. Most of all, counterfeit drugs may contain toxic doses of harmful ingredients and therefore people may not recover from the illness or they may end up getting sicker. The WHO has calculated that each year, 700,000 worldwide deaths are attributed to counterfeit medicine for malaria and tuberculosis.[49] Over the last few years in China, there have been increased reports regarding drugs that are being associated with severe illness such as cancer. It would appear that the counterfeiters are targeting drugs that are the most expensive and price inelastic, i.e. for people with life-threatening illnesses. The real problem is that many patients with life-threatening illnesses buy these drugs on a regular basis thinking they are getting the correct treatment whereas in fact they are spending a fortune without any real meaningful return. In particular, the reports indicate that many Chinese patients seeking treatment for cancer or diabetes often die without realizing that they have been consuming the counterfeit medicines.

In addition to mass poisoning and treatment failure for chronic conditions and cancer, the counterfeit medicine encouraged the emergence of new, drug-resistant strains of viruses, parasites and bacteria. As counterfeit medicines contain low doses of active ingredient, these products cause low circulating levels of the drug in the patient, which in turn selectively favours the growth of drug-resistant organisms. Although it is difficult to estimate the burden of drug resistance caused by counterfeit medicine due to dearth of data, drug resistance threatens efforts to contain pathogens and other infectious diseases.

### *Costs to the healthcare system*

China's medicine registration and pricing system, together with the market reforms, have not adequately developed to contribute to the establishment of a mature and healthy pharmaceutical system. The medicinal distribution system is ineffective, and there are many illegal practices. In short, China does not have a system in place to ensure that basic and safe medicine remains accessible to the people – rich or poor. For the uninsured, access to health-care today costs 40 times more than it did in the early 1980s, but 58% is financed by individual out-of-pocket payments.[50] The official count of rural people in the low-income spectrum in 2002 is 60 million, or 6.2% of the total rural population. Thus, the combined total of absolute rural poor and low-income rural dwellers in 2002 was 88.2 million people representing 9.2% of the rural population.[51] There is no official estimate for the urban poor, but various studies have put the figure to be around 200 million – or one-fifth of China's population.

Compounding this problem is China's ageing population. By 2015, there were about 220 million over-60s, and within 40 years, the number might increase to 500 million people.[52] In 2018, the number has risen to 241 million people aged 60 or older, around 17.3% of the total population.[53] China's dependency ratio for retirees could rise as high as 44% by 2050.[54] Assuming natural demographic increases to 1.5 billion or so people, it is expected that more than one-third of the population will turn 60 at some point in the future. It will take China two decades for the proportion of the elderly population to double from 10% to 20% (between 2017 and 2037). Japan took 23 years; it was 61 years for Germany and 64 years for Sweden.[55]

Whilst there is no quantified estimate available, if a significant number of the ageing population coincides with the segment that falls below the poverty line, then the multiplier effect of the counterfeit drugs would become more evident. This is a particular problem that, together with food and water safety, sits irreconcilably with President Xi Jinping's Chinese Dream.

Today, there is a sense that many Chinese consumers are losing faith in the health-care system that is in place in China, especially after experiences with falsified drugs. The crazy "rush" by mainlanders to come to Hong Kong to buy medicine is indicative of this trend. A study in China suggests that patients view the loosely regulated private health-care system poorly, seeing it as rife with fake doctors and fake drugs.[56] People might also turn to traditional medicine and alternative systems of "healing", and this again would have ripple on implications for China.

The existence of counterfeit medicine also undermines the public health-care system in other ways. First, resources that could be used for strengthening the health-care system are used to combat the counterfeit drugs, and this is by no means cheap. According the State Food and Drug Enforcement (SFDA), over one million enforcement officers took part in the operations in second half of 2012 to target the manufacture, distribution and sales of counterfeit medicine. While no cost estimates are currently available, this represents the substantial loss of resources including the human and legal cost resulting from the prosecution and enforcement.[57] Such resources could be channelled to improve access to health-care and increased efficiency in care delivery systems. Second, counterfeit medicine places a greater strain on already heavily burdened Chinese health-care system. The use of counterfeit drugs can lead to greater sickness and even to death, imposing further financial burden on the system. Last, there are criminal liability and ethical implications for health-care workers and institutions. In instances where hospitals and clinics dispensed fake medicine (even without the management's knowledge), these health-care institutions will have tremendous legal and ethical responsibility. How does one reconcile with the fact that people are admitted to hospitals for their ailments only to have been killed by fake drugs? This is not just a public health or a food safety issue, but also a national security one. Should this be the responsibility of the state, the hospital authorities or the people who manufactured the drugs or those that that partook in the trade? Who should bear the legal responsibility? The criminality of the counterfeit drugs cannot be understated.

*A regional and global security challenge*

The issue pertaining to counterfeit medicines is not simply a national problem, but a grave global problem. Even if China does not produce counterfeit medicine, it could still import these medicines. However, today China remains as much a problem as an exporter as it does an importer. A total of 5,012,617 capsules of assorted counterfeit medicines – including amoxicillin, ampicillin, cloxacillin, ampiclox and other products – were seized in December 2003 in Myanmar after being smuggled in from India and China.[58] In 2004, a pharmacist in Texas in the United States was convicted of buying over 1,000 fake Cialis tablets and 4,500 fake Viagra tablets from an agent in China to resell in his pharmacy.[59] In 2007, the National Agency for Food and Drug Administration and Control of Nigeria issued a press release that the seized counterfeit anti-malarial pills (labelled "Made in India") were in fact produced in China.[60]

In 2008, a contaminated blood thinner found in the drug Heparin killed 11 people in the United States, and the U.S. FDA identified 12 drug companies that supplied this contaminated Heparin to 11 countries. Heparin is usually used in kidney dialysis and heart surgery. The source of the contamination comes from a cheap fake additive introduced during the manufacturing process. Heparin is made from the mucous membranes of the intestines of slaughtered pigs that, in China, are often cooked in unregulated family workshops. The contaminant – identified as oversulfated chondroitin sulfate, a cheaper substance slipped through the usual testing – was recognized only after more sophisticated tests were undertaken.[61] This incident caused the deaths of 150 Americans and 350 medical events in patients who consumed tainted Chinese supplies of blood thinning medicine, prompting a sea change in the thinking in the United States and China over the control of the supply chain of Heparin.[62] Subsequently, China's SFDA ordered local agencies to increase supervision of the production of Heparin. It would appear that the factories involved were unlicensed and unregulated, as they were considered chemical and not drug makers.[63]

In May 2011, the police found 6.9 million capsules in Guangdong, China. The investigation revealed that the counterfeit Viagra was being readied for export to the Middle East. There have been reports of death (usually heart failure) associated with counterfeit Viagra in Southeast Asia (Singapore, Malaysia, Myanmar, Laos and Thailand) and also in the Middle East. According to the public data available, 27.6% of counterfeit incident reports indicated China to be the source country of the counterfeits, while Asian and Latin American regions – as well as middle-income markets – reported the most incidents of fraudulent drugs.[64] The pattern of consumption and distribution continued in 2018, with China and India reported to be the main manufacturing hubs and the Southeast Asian nations of Myanmar, Vietnam and Thailand as transit hubs, with seaports like Singapore and Malaysia and Thailand acting as global shipping ports. The World Customs Organization estimate about 50–60% of fake drugs are shipped.[65]

The industry is not only hurting China's image abroad, but impeding China's ability to do something good such as developmental aid and health assistance in Africa. China has had a very successful history of combating malaria, and Chinese People's Liberation Army (PLA) scientists had discovered antimalarial drug known as artemisinin in 1967, but Swiss pharmaceutical giant Novartis bought the patent in 1990s and developed the drug. Fake drugs today erode China's efforts to help combat malaria in Africa – even China has been at the forefront of these efforts since the time of the Cultural Revolution. Beijing has set up at least 30 anti-malaria centres across Africa, but those efforts have been largely undermined by sale of illicit drugs from China, amongst other factors, in 2013.[66]

The transnational nature of this threat cannot be underestimated. While China's state capacity to control the industry is gradually increasing, it is still overwhelmed by the sheer volume of the production of these drugs. The real threat, however, is when these drugs get exported beyond its borders to countries with little capacity to mount a vigorous anti-fake medicine campaign to restore the medicinal supply system. This is particularly true in places like sub-Saharan Africa[67] and parts of Southeast Asia. Beyond that, this phenomenon is no longer a China problem, giving that the counterfeiting of drugs is found in many other countries. Due to the absence of an overarching authority in this area, as well as the overwhelming and illicit nature of the trade, the profits from this crime are increasingly being co-opted by organized crime groups and terrorist entities looking to fund their illicit and unrelated activities. Evidence suggests that provision of illicit income to organized crime and unbridled flow of fake pharmaceuticals into global markets help support burgeoning crime syndicates around the world.[68] As such, counterfeit medicines are not only a challenge to the integrity of public health systems worldwide, but also a threat to a national and international security. How do we tackle a problem that may well be a problem of global public health and international security?

## Conclusion: enhancing the governance system in China

How can China strengthen the governance of the pharmaceutical industry and improve drug safety? What measure should be in place to contain the problems associated with counterfeit medicines in China and elsewhere? It is important to recognize that counterfeit medicine is a global problem that requires collaborative activities at local, regional, national and international levels. Therefore, the Chinese government should not only formulate a comprehensive policy to address the potential threats in domestic counterfeit markets, but also foster development of strategies to promote international coordination.

As the prevalence of the fake drugs has become more widespread, extensive public and international pressure and anger over this category of fake goods have prompted the Chinese government to take this threat very seriously. The government faces a dilemma. On the one hand, the government wants to encourage domestic enterprises to be able to build up their research and development expertise to provide cheaper alternative versions of the drugs in order to prevent the health-care system from being held "hostage" by foreign pharmaceutical companies for cost and national security considerations. On the other hand, the government has to act to prevent fake and substandard drugs from entering its medical supply, and therefore has to rein in and lift production standards. The former calls for liberalization and promotion of domestic industries to speed up pharmaceutical R&D, but the latter calls for greater caution and increase cooperation with foreign drug companies.

In order to enhance China's overcapacity to increase governance of this rampant fake drug industry, the Chinese government has taken steps to increase regulatory framework. The legislation that forms the backbone of combating fake drugs is the 1984 "Drug Administration Law of the PRC" (amended 2001) and "Implemental Statutes for Drug Administration Law" issued in September 2002. Collectively, these two pieces of legislation increased the penalties for the production and sales of counterfeit drugs, increased the range of offences considered to be counterfeiting and most importantly, added to its arsenal of penalties the ability to strip a manufacturer of its license to produce drugs. Other administrative regulations were added, including "Drug Supervision and Administrative Penalty Procedure", "Drug Import and Export Administration Measures" and "Drug Distribution Supervision Measures". In 2009, China's Supreme People's Court and Supreme People's Procuratorate issued a Judicial Interpretation for handling criminal cases of counterfeit drug manufacture of distribution.

In 2009, the China Food and Drug Administration Bureau announced that the China State Council approved the establishment of an inter-ministry task force to combat counterfeit drugs. The inter-ministry task force model of enforcement is extremely useful, and collectively, it is definitely a step forward in tackling fake drugs. The task force closed counterfeit drug websites, took down advertisements, targeted and disrupted the logistical routes of some of these counterfeiters. China's State Food and Drug Administration (SFDA) closed over 74 websites that sold drugs, and the SFDA apparently had only licensed about ten websites to see drugs online to individuals.[69]

### *Extending and enlarging the powers to confiscate the "proceeds of crime"*

Despite years of crackdown, however, the problem of fake drugs persisted. This category of product cannot be explained by increasing demand alone, just like counterfeit bags or watches, as consumption is never tolerated or much less desired by anyone – including the counterfeiters themselves. Demand only dictates the kind of drugs that are produced in different localities worldwide. In developed countries, it is often the lifestyle drugs that are in demand, such as Viagra or Botox, and the fake industry rises to meet this demand. In developing countries, such as sub-Saharan Africa, where malaria is a real threat, anti-malarial drugs are being produced and sold. This is a supply-driven industry, fuelled by greed, and works best when trade is done in secret. Despite years of combat against the fake drugs industry, the illicit drugs trade is still rampant. This is particularly true in China. As noted earlier, the saying is that this is an industry that has the profitability of illegal drug trade without the corresponding penalties, despite an increase in penalty (capital punishment included) for drug counterfeiting by the Chinese government in 2011.[70]

The Ministry of Public Security offers as much as ¥50,000 to anyone who contributes to uncovering fake medicine rings and operations, yet the situation continues to be of concern. To understand why this industry thrives, one needs not look too far. It is akin to the drugs industry in poor countries. The profits involved in this industry are so great that it far exceeds the deterrent of the capital sentence. Like corruption offences in China, the patriarch of the family who is often well unto his years might take responsibility, leaving the rest of his accomplices such as friends and family to go scot-free. For many of those involved in drugs or white-collar breach of trust or corruption, the attractiveness of making large amounts of money that might benefit the entire clan or family for generations in a short time[71] outweighs the prospects of facing death resulting from these sentences.[72,73] Consequently, as long as there is a chance for profit, the motivation will remain.

One possible way out is to consider increasing the legal penalties of these crimes. For instance, China should consider establishing an agency to seize proceeds and profits from people engaged in this industry. The current law (Article 141 of the Criminal Law) stipulates seizures up to 200% of the profit or confiscation of property. The devil is, however, in the details. Even with the 2011 amendment to the criminal code, it has yet to deal with a drastic blow to the supply side. The penalties for seizure are still not draconian enough to sufficiently deter the crime. It is reported that people making fake drugs usually face paltry fines.[74] For someone who trafficks or deals with a small amount over a long time, if he or she is caught, the penalty will not be severe.

The courts must be empowered to ensure that confiscation orders are issued in relation to anyone who benefits from criminal conduct through participation in this industry, so that property (car, factories or leases) obtained through unlawful conduct (or which is intended to be used in the industry) is forfeited. This means that anyone who lends property (e.g. vehicles or warehouses) to these criminal entrepreneurs would have that property confiscated, and this does not limit to those people who are directly involved. It would send an extremely powerful message to people who consider entering this industry for profit, and anyone aiding them. As long as the family of those suspected cannot explain where the source of wealth comes from, their assets should be considered "proceeds of crime". Once the idea that "one or two persons could own up to take responsibility for the crime while the rest of the family benefits remain intact" is destroyed, this enforcement would perhaps become more effective.

### Treating packaging as medical waste

Disposal of genuine packaging of medicine is something mundane, but extremely important in the fight against fake medicine. One way forward might be for the packaging to be treated like medical waste. This, however, is to a large extent still reliant on the cleaning staff in hospitals and clinics – who are amongst the least well-paid personnel in the public health system. It is highly doubtful that the threat of losing their jobs would deter the cleaners from reselling the packaging for high profit. Therefore, it should only be the job of medical staff (nurses/doctors) to administer medicine rather than being left to "helpers" or "cleaners" to administer these drugs. Additionally, hospitals could allocate individual responsibility to the staff for signing out the medicine, and it would be his or her responsibility for the staff to log back the packaging and/or bottles. In doing so, if the packaging is to be treated like equipment as opposed to waste, it should not go missing. District offices could employ daily or weekly onsite inspectors to see to the public (or witnessed) destruction of these packaging/boxes through incineration.

The principle should be to treat this packaging as "equipment" or "cash", and have a system to ensure that they would be able to ascertain or track the packaging to someone in the clinic/hospital at any one time. There may be no better method than this, unless the manufacturers can design the packaging/bottles in a way they are self-destructed upon use. Like guns taken off the streets, the original packaging should be tracked all the way to the incinerator. Admittedly, even supposedly "destroyed firearms" often find their way back onto the streets, as ultimately there is no foolproof way. While this might seem costly at first, if the pharmaceutical companies take into account the negative impact that the fake medicine industry has on their business in terms of reputation, trust and operations, innovative packaging would serve their interests.

### Packaging security

Packaging security is one potential area where manufacturers and the authorities can collaborate to prevent fraudulent and fake medicines from entering the legitimate pharmaceutical supply system. This is particularly important in China, since most of the counterfeit drugs are for serious illness such as chemotherapy solutions for cancer or pills for cardiovascular disease, and counterfeiting involves hospital cleaners reselling the boxes to counterfeiters. Other large-scale counterfeiters print their own boxes of foreign medicine, often with gross errors on them (e.g. spelling mistakes), but Chinese consumers are unable to recognize the difference because many do not read English.

At the global level, there is currently no worldwide standard to prevent fraud – even though admittedly most of the large-scale pharmaceutical manufacturers are considering more sophisticated multi-level packaging which requires both overt and covert technologies.[75] Overt technology allows packaging to be authenticated using visual representations, without requiring expert knowledge or sophisticated devices, for instance holographic stickers (with hidden text or diagrams) or colour-shift inks. Covert techniques might include infrared and ultraviolent detection, micro-text and microscopic tagging – all of which are invisible to the naked eye. Pfizer and GlaxoSmithKline have introduced radio frequency identification (RFID) tags to Viagra and Trizivir packaging.[76]

Packaging security should ensure not only that the medicine cannot be switched out or replaced, but that the packaging and bottling can only be used once. For instance, there are factories that utilized scratch-off codes (e.g. after purchase) for authentication via the internet or telephone or QR (quick response) codes that could be scanned before consumption. Once scanned, the code will be rendered useless and if the bottle is recycled, then the QR codes would not work. There could also be matching codes for each bottle of medicine. Only when both numbers are entered would the bottle be considered "used". Again, this method is not foolproof because what is important is in the bottles/packaging.

### Holistic governance through enhancement of regulation

Rather than simply focusing on the packaging or individual measures, the Chinese government should move to tighten regulations on all companies in the pharmaceutical industry. First, the government should tighten the regulation and licensing of all players at various levels within the industry without exception: from suppliers of raw materials to those in charge of producing pharmaceutical products and ultimately who supply the packaging and marketing. Second, the process and standards required of obtaining a license to partake in the manufacturing for the various stages must be made more rigorous and conform to international standards, thereby raising the value of the license in the eyes of the vendors. If possible, China's Drug and Food Agency should try to establish certain bench-mark for quality (e.g. ISO9000 management program) for these vendors before allowing them to obtain a license. This means that once a vendor loses one's license to operate, it should not be easily replaceable (i.e. offending vendors are unlikely to continue their business, as relatives or friends are not qualified to reg-ister the business under his name). Having strict guidelines may be a challenge initially, but would actually penalize vendors from deviating from good practices required by the industry. This will reduce the production of substandard medicine and prevent cases of negligence that may pose a public health threat. For instance, if China had regulated the suppliers of pig intestines used to make Heparin, then the case of Heparin contamination that killed 150 people in the United States might have been prevented.[77]

One might argue that licensing would not reduce the fake medicine industry, as regulation is akin to regulation in immigration cases. Implementing a tougher visa regime will only make things harder for people who abide by the law, as illegal immigrants might not want to contend with the visa regime. In the same light, people who are intent on manufacturing fake medicine will not pay atten-tion to any regulation imposed. This may be true, but once the players within the legitimate industry are licensed and adopt the best practices, it will help reduce loopholes and secure the supply chain. This would have the effect of diminishing the opportunities that unscrupulous businesses might have to taint or infiltrate the legitimate drug supply. Given that the counterfeit drug industry is supply-led, such an approach may be an important step. This will also make things easier for the state to target off-license retailers, those unauthorized advertisement and multi-level marketing of fake drugs.

The real problem with China, however, is that its public services are reactive in nature. By extension, the law is always legislated in reaction to issues and crises that crop up, rather than to prevent problems from cropping up. China's legal infrastructure is still a long way from being able to combat counterfeiting as it is still lacking transparency, effectiveness and consistency.[78] It is the extent and the profitability of the counterfeiting that constrain the legislation. This has roots in the public policy domain, and is linked to China's wish for a vibrant and strong domestic drugs sector to be built.

### *Boosting the capability of domestic pharmaceutical companies*

Looking at access issues might be important here. The prospects of counterfeit medicine will not be eradicated even if say the supply sources are nationalized. Many countries wish to enter pharmaceutical R & D owing to national security reasons. The basis of this is to ensure that the country is not held hostage to MNCs such as Pfizer, Glaxo Smith Kline when it comes to access to medicine in terms of both supply and prices. China is in this situation. Foreign pharmaceutical execu-tives have often groused about the long time it takes for drugs to be approved in China, and very often, domestic versions of the drugs will appear very quickly before the arrival of foreign patents and filings of pharmaceutical products to ensure that the companies will not have a monopoly to the medicine concerned.[79] Other reasons include red tape and China's FDA being understaffed.

The problem with this domestic cloning, even with tacit authority approval or endorsement, is that it would mean that domestic drug companies will never gain the technical and R&D skills required of (or comparable to) foreign pharmaceutical companies. This reinforces a lack of respect for intellectual property rights and ethics, and encourages a culture of profiteering. Until these two trends are addressed, it would be difficult for China to build suitable Chinese R&D expertise and pharmaceutical companies suited for the needs of a rapidly modernizing country. Of particular interest here would be biotech and pharmaceutical expertise, which are strategic industries that would enable China to ween off dependence on the influence of big foreign pharmaceutical companies and keep the price of health-care low for its citizens.

In 2006, the Chinese government's powerful National Development and Reform Commission (NDRC) highlighted that biotech and pharmaceutical development as one of the China's key pillars of development. The idea is to increase the amount of money spent by private and public corporations in pharmaceutical research and development. The current climate of cloning and counterfeiting in China unfortunately does not recognize and reward innovative drugs. For one, the industry in China has too many producers and the competition is extremely stiff. But the biggest problem is the standards by the domestic firms licensed to produce drugs are appalling.

In 2005, Hangzhou-based Zhejiang Pukang Biotechnology Company produced a problematic Hepatitis A vaccine which accounts for 60% of the Chinese market. This drug killed a child and made several hundred children sick.[80] In April 2006, an injection of Armillarisin, a drug produced by Heilongjiang Pharmaceutical Giant, killed nine people and injured 50 others. In July 2006, another drug, clindamycin injection, produced by Anhui Huayuan Biotechnology killed four people in Beijing, Harbin and Hangzhou.[81] The fact of the matter is that even large statesanctioned pharmaceutical companies have problems. Can one reasonably expect that Chinese domestic pharmaceutical R&D could improve the extent of replacing or substituting foreign firms?

The economic impact of this messy situation with counterfeit products thrown in makes things is even worse. The WHO and FDA estimate that the sales of counterfeit drugs present between US$32 billion and US$35 billion annually, that is US$88 to US$96 million dollars in sales each day, with Asia accounting for the largest share of the pie.[82] Most analysts agree that China and India are the two largest producers. Under such circumstances, a crisis of confidence in the pharmaceutical system and diminished motivation for domestic firms to engage in R&D are likely to persist, since drug manufacturers are unable to protect their research from the prying threats.

There is no answer except for international collaboration. China must allow for more collaboration, education and exchange for those working in the sector. Such an exchange would allow for more international good practices to be inculcated in China, and hopefully corresponding ethical considerations. China must open up to possible collaborations with world bodies like the WHO and the UN.

*Towards true international collaboration*

While national regulatory authorities are responsible for assuring drug quality in their respective countries, the international trade, multi-national manufacturing systems and modern pharmaceutical distribution chains often make it difficult for national law enforcement agencies to combat counterfeit medicines. Today, the chance that problems pertaining to counterfeit drugs in one country affect that country alone is slim, since illegally manufactured drugs travel along global illicit supply chains. The interconnectedness of illicit manufacturing systems takes advantage of an increasingly globalized drug market posing a threat to global health and security. Despite the recognized dangers, to date, no global governance structure exists to effectively respond to this serious form of pharmaceutical crime. Therefore, coordinated and collective actions and systems of global governance are required to address the problem. This means renewed partnerships and international cooperation across individual countries and key international organizations such as WHO, UNODC (United Nations Office on Drugs and Crime) and WCO (World Customs Organization) are essential in combating the counterfeit medicine.

In an effort to counter the counterfeit medicines, the WHO initiated programs for the prevention and detection of the import, export and smuggling of counterfeit drugs since 1988.[83] More recently, more than 200 member states of the WHO agreed to develop instruments to more accurately measure the burden of substandard and falsified drugs in 2012. Subsequently, in the same year, the WHO formed a 'coordinated, continuous and ongoing global surveillance and monitoring system'.[84] The system makes use of a rapid alert form like a spreadsheet to allow investigators in multiple countries to complete cases involving illegitimate drugs and send the forms to the WHO. However, building surveillance systems is challenging in many ways since the reporting systems mostly rely on motivated and knowledgeable patients. Additionally, reporting bias across regions, inadequate laboratory capacity and lack of comprehensive data surveillance sources across regions and countries make the detection and accurate reporting difficult. All these limitations underscore the need to improve global capacity building, such as developing robust surveillance tools and setting up laboratories for quality testing particularly in low and middle-income countries.

While guidelines for surveillance and drug regulation is key to achieving global governance of counterfeit medicines, the problem may not be solved without law enforcement. The illicit pharmaceutical industry is a global business that employs clandestine manufacturing and distribution channels. Consequently, the nature of crimes constrains the national law enforcement authorities from prosecuting and punishing offenders. It is therefore important to establish protocols for international cooperation on investigations and extradition. In response, Interpol, an international organization that facilitates police cooperation around the world, defines pharmaceutical crime as 'counterfeiting and falsification of medical products, their packaging and associated documentation as well as the theft, fraud illicit diversion, smuggling, trafficking and the illegal trade of medical products and the money laundering associated with it'. Interpol has been a key factor in large global seizures of suspect drugs, and has recently initiated anti-pharmaceutical crime programme in collaboration with global pharmaceutical manufacturers.[85] Interpol was also involved in raising awareness about falsified drugs through media campaigns.[86,87] However, it appears that the investigative activities are on an ad-hoc basis rather than in any systematic and sustained way.

In short, national and international response to counterfeit drugs to date is limited by the lack of national infrastructure and regulations, absence of international convention and weak legal framework for confronting the counterfeit pharmaceutical industry. It is therefore important that collective actions against counterfeit medicine address both regulatory and systemic governance challenges through legal, technical and financial mechanisms. Additionally, strengthening national capacities is likely to have the most enduring value, in conjunction with an international convention.

## Notes

1 WHO, "Growing threat from counterfeit medicines", *Bulletin of World Health Organization*, 88(4) (2010): 247–248.
2 R. Cockburn, P. N. Newton, K. Agyarko, D. Akunyili and N.J. White, "The global threat of counterfeit drugs: Why industry and governments must communicate the dangers", *Plos Medicine* (2005). https://journals.plos.org/plosmedicine/article?id=10.1371/journal.pmed.0020100
3 Institute of Medicine, "Countering the problem of falsified and substandard drugs", 2013, www.iom.edu/Reports/2013/Countering-the-Problem-of-Falsified-and-Substandard-Drugs.aspx
4 United Nations Office on Drugs and Crime, "Trafficking in fraudulent medicines", www.unodc.org/unodc/en/fraudulentmedicines/introduction.html
5 A. Attaran, D. Barry, S.H. Basheer, R. Bate, D. Benton, J. Chauvin, L. Garrett, I. Kickbusch, J.C. Kohler, K. Midha, P.N. Newton, S. Nishtar, P. Orhii, and M. McKee, "How to achieve international action on falsified and substandard medicines", *BMJ*, 345 (2012): e7381.
6 T. Mackey, B.A. Liang, P. York, and T. Kubic, "Counterfeit drug penetration into global legitimate medical supply Chinas: A global assessment", *American Journal of Tropical Medicine and Hygiene*, 92 (Suppl 6, 3 June 2015): 59–67, www.ncbi.nlm.nih.gov/pmc/articles/PMC4455087/
7 WHO, *Combating Counterfeit Drugs: A Concept Paper for Effective International Cooperation* (Geneva: WHO, 2006).
8 Institute of Medicine, *Countering the Problem of Falsified and Substandard Medicine* (Washington, DC: National Academy of Sciences, 2013).
9 WHO, Does quality of medicines matter?, http://www.who.int/medicines/services/counterfeit/faqs/QACounterfeit-October2009.pdf
10 Law Regulating Pharmaceutical Products, "Full Version at the State Food and Drug Administration Website", 2001, www.sda.gov.cn/WS01/CL0064/23396.html
11 樊迪,《药品管理法》中假药定义的不足及完善建议 [Fan Di, *Regulation of Pharmacuetical Products – The Incomprehensiveness of legal definition of Fake Medicine and some suggestions*], China Pharmaceutical University, http://journal.9med.net/html/qikan/zgyx/szgygy/20101212/ysgl/20100317090712841_516791.html
12 See *Article 141 of Criminal Law of the People's Republic of China*, www.fmprc.gov.cn/ce/cgvienna/eng/dbtyw/jdwt/crimelaw/t209043.htm

13 WHO, "Counterfeit Medicine: An update on estimates", www.who.int/medicines/services/counterfeit/impact/TheNewEstimatesCounterfeit.pdf. 15 November 2006.

14 *WHO Fact Sheet No. 275*, 11 November 2003.

15 "Death toll over fake drug rises to 9 in China", *China Daily*, 22 May 2006.

16 K.Huang, "21 held liable for Qiqihar drugs scandal", *South China Morning Post*, 20 July 2006.

17 "Chinese hospital used fake drips", *BBC News*, 11 June 2007, http://news.bbc.co.uk/2/hi/asia-pacific/6742293.stm

18 Xinhua News Agency, 国家食品药品监管局公布今年十大典型假药案 (National Food and Drug Agency Announces this year's ten counterfeit drugs classic cases), *Xinhua News Agency*, 21 December 2010, http://news.xinhuanet.com/health/2010-12/21/c_12903946.htm

19 "China busts counterfeit drug racket", *The USA Daily*, 29 December 2011.

20 Xaixion Zheng, "Police nab 15 in crackdown on fake Viagra", Chinadaily, 26 May 2011, www.chinadaily.com.cn/china/2011-05/26/content_12582340.htm

21 "湖北一團夥維生素粉末掺入藥渣制成20余種假藥", *Xinhua News Agency*, 27 May 2013, http://big5.xinhuanet.com/gate/big5/news.xinhuanet.com/health/2013-05/27/c_124767378.htm#

22 China Network, Anti-cancer fake drugs are on sale, 20 March 2013, http://finance.china.com.cn/roll/20130320/1338990.shtml

23 5元成本抗癌假冒针剂卖8500元 利润率超贩毒, 23 February 2013, http://news.qq.com/a/20130223/000110.htm

24 N. Khan, "China police arrest more than 1900 people in fake drug hunt", *The Business Times*, 5 August 2012.

25 "China arrests 1900 in crackdown on fake drugs", *BBC News*, 6 August 2012.

26 "China detains 1300 people suspected of making, selling fake drugs: Media", *Reuters*, 15 December 2013.

27 C. Liu, "Chinese police bust fake drug ring that sold to clients on Wechat", 12 May 2016, https://thenanfang.com/topics/fake-stuff/

28 C. Zheng, "Counterfeit Viagra, other fake drugs seized", *China Daily*, 19 January 2016.

29 "China police bust cross-border fake drug network", *Xinhua News Agency*, 15 December 2017.

30 K.Huang, "Gang jailed for manufacturing, selling fake medicine to Chinese hospitals", *South China Morning Post*, 12 January 2018, www.scmp.com/news/china/society/article/2127968/chinese-fake-medicine-manufacturing-gang-jailed

31 This section benefitted from a close survey of Chinese court cases as well as from information gathered from conversations with colleagues and interested parties in China.

32 C. Campbell, "Chinese cancer patients are illicitly importing and preparing their own drugs", *Times Magazine*, 1 September 2016, http://time.com/4475469/china-health-drugs-cancer-taobao-internet-azd9291-astrazeneca/

33 This case was reported on CCTV, and is archived as "山东济南警方破获两起特大制售假药案" (Shandong Jinan Police Broke two major fake medicine ring) at www.tudou.com/programs/view/4cVzqK_m_zA/?spm=a2h0k.8191414.0.0

34 L.Y. Wu, H.F. Lee, and J. China, "Fake drugs have Chinese ingredients", *The Taipei Times*, 10 March, 2017, www.taipeitimes.com/News/front/archives/2017/03/10/2003666478

35 J. Whalen, and B. Faucon, "Counterfeit cancer medicines multiply", *WSJ*, 31 December 2012, https://www.wsj.com/articles/SB10001424127887323320404578211492452353034.

36 The information is gleaned from conversations with colleagues in Guangdong who have knowledge of this industry. An independent source for corroboration is the police investigation. Footage (date unknown) of the Guangdong Satellite TV news station shows that police investigation into a ¥2billion industry. The report confirms that the

police too agree that the recycled boxes is one of the most fundamental ingredients of the industry. In the report, one empty packaging can fetch ¥300, http://v.youku.com/v_show/id_XMzI0MTczNjI0.html?from=s1.8-1-1.2&spm=a2h0k.8191407.0.0

37 Another report by Guangdong Satellite TV shows confirms the process described here. The report suggests like other reports that this particular scam is worth ¥2 billion dollars, and the hospital cleaners form an important part of the supply chain: http://v.youku.com/v_show/id_XMzI0NDM4Mzgw.html?from=s1.8-1-1.2&spm=a2h0k.8191407.0.0

38 This incident was reported by CCTV News on the 2nd Oct 2010. The news footage is archived here at www.tudou.com/programs/view/0GznT-hlwNQ/?spm=a2h0k.8191414.0.0

39 The Asiabiotech, "Is China capable of eradicating fake drug market?", *Trends & Prospects*, 19(5): 2001 https://www.asiabiotech.com/05/0519/0488_0489.pdf

40 K. Huang, "Gang jailed for manufacturing, selling fake medicine to Chinese hospitals", *South China Morning Post*, 12 January 2018, www.scmp.com/news/china/society/article/2127968/chinese-fake-medicine-manufacturing-gang-jailed

41 "Bribery claims infect drug companies' dealings in China", *The Financial Times*, 23 September 2013, www.ft.com/content/93990558-2156-11e3-a92a-00144feab7de

42 美籍博士后"裁"在抗癌药上, 25 October 2010, http://tj.legaldaily.com.cn/content/2010-10/25/content_2327447.htm

43 Ibid.

44 The Asiabiotech, "Is China capable of eradicating fake drug market?", *Trends & Prospects*, 19(5): 2001 https://www.asiabiotech.com/05/0519/0488_0489.pdf

45 66th General Assembly Plenary, 112th Meeting, "Human security more than an abstract concept", www.un.org/News/Press/docs/2012/ga11246.doc.htm

46 See *United Nations Development Index*, http://hdr.undp.org/en/statistics/

47 United Nations Development Program (UNDP), "Redefining security: The human dimension", *Current History*, 94 (1994): 229–236, p. 229.

48 WHO Media Center, *Fact Sheet No. 275*, November 2003.

49 World Health Professions Alliance, "Background document on Counterfeit Medicines in Asia", prepared for participants at the WHPA Regional Workshop on counterfeit medical products, 30 June–1 July 2011, www.whpa.org/background_document_counterfeit_medicines_in_asia.pdf

50 S. Tang, J. Sun, G. Wu, and W. Chen, "Pharmaceutical policy in China: Issues and problems", *WHO Archives*, http://archives.who.int/tbs/ChinesePharmaceuticalPolicy/English_Background_Documents/summarypapers/PPChinaIssuesProblemsShenglan.doc

51 Asian Development Bank, *Poverty Profile of the People's Republic of China*, May 2004, p. 5; available at ADB website www.adb.org/sites/default/files/pub/2004/poverty-profile-prc.pdf

52 The situation is now so grime that in Beijing, there are now about 215 public nursing homes and 186 private homes, or roughly 3 beds for every 100 seniors. See "China's Ageing Population: 100-year waiting list for Beijing nursing home", *The Telegraph*, 16 January 2013, www.telegraph.co.uk/news/worldnews/asia/china/9805834/Chinas-ageing-population-100-year-waiting-list-for-Beijing-nursing-home.html

53 X. Zhou, S. Zheng, and J. Ma, "Putin, North Korea and a US trade war – Li Keqiang's press conference to close Two Sessions as it unfolded", *South China Morning Post*, 20 March 2018, www.scmp.com/news/china/policies-politics/article/2137907/live-premier-li-keqiang-addresses-media-close-landmark?aid=197778625&sc_src=email_2185779&sc_llid=4996&sc_lid=150002713&sc_uid=xTtmohAUni&utm_source=emarsys&utm_medium=email&utm_campaign=GME-O-NPC-Feb18&utm_content=hk-180320

54 K. Rapoza, "China's aging population becoming more of a problem", *Forbes*, 21 February 2017, www.forbes.com/sites/kenrapoza/2017/02/21/chinas-aging-population-becoming-more-of-a-problem/#12bf7f3a140f

55  Ibid.
56  M.K. Lim, H. Yang, T. Zhang, W. Feng, Z. Zhou, "Public perceptions of private health care in socialist China", *Health Affairs*, 236 (2004): 222–234.
57  E.A. Blackstone, J.P Fuhr, and S. Pociask, "The health and economic effects of counterfeit drugs", *American Health & Drug Benefits*, 7(4) (2014): 216–224.
58  Myanmar Information Committee, *Yangon Information Sheet No. C-2891 (I)*, 2004.
59  "Pharmacist convicted of purchasing Chinese counterfeit drugs", 25 May 2006, www.justice.gov/archive/criminal/cybercrime/press-releases/2006/georgeConvict.htm
60  "Chinese passing off fake drugs as 'Made in India'", *The Times of India*, 9 June 2009, http://timesofindia.indiatimes.com/business/india-business/Chinese-passing-off-fake-drugs-as-Made-in-India/articleshow/4633377.cms
61  G. Harris, *U.S. Identifies Tainted Herapin in 11 Countries*, 22 April 2008, www.nytimes.com/2008/04/22/health/policy/22fda.html?pagewanted=all&_r=0
62  L. Rosania, "Heparin crisis 2008: A tipping point for increased FDA enforcement in the pharma sector?", *Food and Drug Law Journal*, 65(3) (2010): 480–501.
63  D. Barboza, "China orders new oversight of Heparin, with tainted batches tied to U.S. deaths", *The New York Times*, 22 March 2008.
64  T.K. Mackey, B.A. Liang, P. York, and T. Kubic, "Counterfeit drug penetration into global legitimate medicine supply chains: A global assessment", *American Journal of Tropical Medicine and Hygiene*, 92 (supple 2015): 59–67.
65  A. Boyd, "Fake pharma thrives on the Mekong", *Asia Times*, 9 November 2017, www.atimes.com/article/fake-pharma-thrives-mekong/
66  K. McLaughlin, "Fake drugs from China: What's stopping a cure for malaria in Africa?", *The Atlantic*, 11 June 2013.
67  Ibid.
68  G. Satchwell, "A sick business: Counterfeit medicines and organized crime", *The Stockholm Network*, 2004.
69  "China names and shames fake drug websites", *Reuters*, 10 December 2008.
70  N. Khan, "China police arrest more than 1900 people in fake drug hunt", *The Business Times*, 5 August 2012.
71  "China vows to tacke family corruption – Even state media can't hide its skepticism", *The Washington Post*, 29 April 2016, www.washingtonpost.com/news/worldviews/wp/2016/04/29/china-vows-to-tackle-family-corruption-but-even-state-media-cant-hide-its-skepticism/?utm_term=.51bea671b094
72  J. Zhu, "Do severe penalties deter corruption? A game-theoretica analysis of the Chinese case", *China Review*, 12(2) (Fall 2012): 1–32.
73  Dr Victor Teo's personal conversations with Chinese Prosecutors and Judges.
74  K. Lewis, "China's counterfeit medicine trade booming", *Canadian Medical Association Journal*, 181(10) (10 November 2009).
75  "Tackling pharmaceutical counterfeits: beyond packaging", www.pharmaceutical-technology.com/features/featuretackling-pharmaceutical-counterfeits-beyond-packaging/
76  Ibid.
77  G. Harris, "U.S. identifies tainted Herapin in 11 countries", 22 April 2008, www.nytimes.com/2008/04/22/health/policy/22fda.html?pagewanted=all&_r=0
78  J. L. Bikoff, D. K. Heasley, V. Sherman, and J. Stipelman, "Fake it 'til we make it: Regulating dangerous counterfeit goods", *Journal of Intellectual Property Law and Practice*, 10(4) (2015).
79  Dr Victor Teo's personal conversation with colleagues in China who are knowledgeable with patent and licensing approval in the PRC.
80  H. Jia, "Poor enforcement could jeopardize China's drug innovation policy", *Nature Biotechnology*, 24(10) (October 2006): 1182–1183.
81  Ibid.
82  World Health Professions Alliance.

83 WHO, *Combating Counterfeit Drugs: A Concept Paper for Effective International Cooperation* (Geneva: WHO, 2006).
84 WHO, *New Global Mechanism to Combat Substandard/Spurious/Falsely-Labelled/Falsified/Counterfeit Medical Products* (Geneva: WHO, 2012).
85 INTERPOL, "Interpol and pharmaceutical industry launch global initiative to combat fake medicines", 12 March 2013, www.interpol.int/News-and-media/News/2013/PR031
86 INTERPOL, "Pharmaceutical crime: A major threat to public health", 2012, www.interpol.int/Crime-areas/Pharmaceutical-crime/Pharmaceutical-crime
87 INTERPOL, "Interpol launches global campaign against fake medicines with powerful African voices", 20 October 2011, www.interpol.int/News-and-media/News/2011/PR090

# 6  The smuggling of animal parts in Chinese medicine

## The pangolin trade between China and Southeast Asia

*Koh Keng-We*

Southeast Asia has long been an important trading partner for China, both as a source of forest, marine, and mineral products from within the region, and as a transhipment centre for commodities from the Indian Ocean rim. Animal products and animal parts in particular have constituted an important segment of this trade, both historically and in the present. From shark fins to tortoise shells, ivory, bear parts and the meat and scales of the pangolin, these animals and animal parts have long been used in traditional Chinese medicine and consumed as tonic and exotic food by the affluent, being associated with various nutritional and curative powers in Chinese *materia medica*. The collection, cultivation, and consumption of these animals and their body parts have had a long history in Asia.

Yet, the last few decades have seen the rapid growth in the collecting and trade in these animals, to the extent that many of them are threatened with extinction. The rapid economic growth in China and other parts of Asia since the early 1990s has greatly increased the demand for exotic animal products and parts in these countries, especially in China, and the trade in them. This has led to the rapid depletion of these animals, both in China and outside, threatening them with extinction, and putting their environments at varying degrees of risk. The last two decades in particular have seen various concerns being raised by environmentalists about the trade in various animals and animal parts in terms of their scale and handling, and their impact on the endangered populations of these animals and their environments. The profits from the high demand for these animals and animal parts have undermined legal and institutional attempts to limit and ban these trades.

The pangolin is a good example of a previously prevalent species in different parts of southern China and Southeast Asia endangered by this escalation in consumption, especially in China. It has also become one of the most commonly smuggled animals in the illicit trade in animals/animal parts between Southeast Asia and China. The failure of the determined efforts by non-governmental organizations (NGOs), animal rights groups, zoologists and governments to ban the trade in pangolins and pangolin meat and scales raises important questions not only about the efficacy of the measures, but also the nature of the problem.

Efforts at curbing the trade in animals and animal parts have focused on a variety of means, through legal sanctions against these products in the countries of collection and export, efforts at education, education and control in the relevant collecting habitats and environments, stricter policing at customs in Southeast Asian and East Asian countries (not only supplying and destination countries, but also transit ones), and advertising campaigns against their consumption in countries like China, Vietnam and Korea, and within Southeast Asia itself.[1] Despite all the Southeast Asian states signing on to CITES, the Convention for International Trade in Endangered Species, since 1990, massive smuggling in pangolins continues to take place, as evidenced by interceptions of large-scale shipments by customs, forestry and wildlife officials and agencies in the region. Much remains to be done to control or stop the trade in pangolins and pangolin parts.[2]

This chapter does not purport to offer any permanent solution to the problems just highlighted. It is an exploratory study of the illegal trade in pangolins between Southeast Asia and China in terms of its structures, methods and flows, and its implications for the people involved in the trade. It also attempts to locate the trade within its historical contexts, especially of China-Southeast Asia exchanges and flows. It is by understanding the changing interests and perspectives of the consumers, trappers, processers and carriers of the trade, as well as the policing agencies, within the context of broader cultural, economic and political changes in the global and regional environments, that we can obtain a better understanding of these smuggling trades and their underlying dynamics, and hopefully find a better way of tackling the problem.

For the supply side, research on the hunting, collecting and trading of pangolins and other endangered animals and animal parts has highlighted how they are part of broader economic strategies of livelihood for communities in different parts of Southeast Asia. They are also part of broader commercial networks connecting Southeast Asia to China, licit and illicit. Perhaps, recent studies about borders and border control, smuggling networks and informal economies might contribute towards a better understanding of these channels and strategies, and possibly their policing and control.[3]

The failure of legislative measures, international networks and cooperation, and policing broaches the question of whether the approach to the problem is focusing on the right segments of the supply-demand chain – namely, the consumers and the people whose livelihoods are most dependent on this trade. The failure of efforts at policing and "education" at the level of the producing and transit regions suggests that whilst these measures are necessary, greater attention should be spent understanding the demand side of the equation.

This is a need to understand the culture of consumption in China and East Asian societies surrounding the medicinal and nutritional benefits of pangolin meat and pangolin scales, and the economy surrounding the supply of these and other animal and herbal produce in the traditional medicinal and nutritional industries. We can ask if "shaming" campaigns based on removing the "status" element of pangolin consumption actually understand the deeper cultural and historical background to this consumption in East Asian countries, especially in terms of the medical knowledge and traditions in these areas. Can we just dismiss this knowledge as ignorance and myth, in the very same way Western medicine has treated alternative medicinal traditions?[4]

Furthermore, is the persistence in the scale of the trade a result of cultural predilections, or the greed of the people trying to profit from this demand? If this consumption is not new, how have present patterns of consumption differed from the earlier periods in terms of scale and supply? Is the problem really in culture and the efficacy and foundations of alternative medicinal traditions, or in market and technological forces fuelling the rapidly expanding scale of international trade? Does the spike (on a level hitherto unseen) in the hunting and selling of these animals and animal parts over the past two to three decades reflect demand, or is supply attempting to drive demand?

Ultimately, a more holistic, in-depth, and long-term approach is needed. Essential to this will not only be the contextualization of this commerce within the long-term structures of regional-international trade and recent developments since the economic reforms in China, both licit and illicit, but also a broader multidisciplinary approach to the problem that involves the fauna and environment experts, NGOs dedicated to wildlife conservation and the state, as well as social scientists and historians studying cultural conceptions of health and food, and experts in traditional medicinal practices and knowledge.

## The pangolin

There are four major species of pangolin in Asia, the *Mani crassicaudata* (Indian pangolin), the *Manis pentadactyla* (Chinese pangolin), the *Manis javanica* (Sunda pangolin), and the *Manis culionensis* (Philippines pangolin), out of a total of eight in the world.[5] The *Manis culionensis* only recently became recognized as a species on its own, being previously classified under *Manis javanica*. The *Manis javanica*, or the Malayan/Sunda pangolins, are found throughout Indonesia, from the major islands of Sumatra, Java and Kalimantan to smaller islands such as Mentawai, Bangka, Bali, Nias and other parts of the archipelago.[6] Of the four Asian species, three (*javanica*, *pentadactyla* and *culionensis*) are found in Southeast Asia, one in southern China (in the past), and one in India.[7]

They were essentially nocturnal animals that are semi-arboreal. They feed on ants and termites, and thus could be found in habitats where there were such food sources. They tend to curl up like a ball when threatened, with their scales serving as protection. Whilst probably effective against some other animals, this only made them all the more easy to be hunted by humans.

They have been long regarded in China as important sources of parts for traditional Chinese medicine, from their scales to their meat.[8] Their skins had also been hunted for use in the making of leather products both locally and in other parts of the world. Historically, it has been the *Manis pentadactyla* and *Manis javanica* which have been hunted in large numbers for their scales, meat and skin, with the first two also sought for medicinal and nutritional purposes, and the last also sought for distinctive leather products.[9]

Pangolins had been hunted for centuries on a subsistence level in southern China and other parts of Southeast Asia. Whilst the local pangolin populations in China and mainland Southeast Asia had been tapped to feed local demand, the expansion of the demand, together with the dwindling of the supply in China and neighbouring mainland Southeast Asia, has led to the trade in pangolins and pangolin meant or scales extending further afield, to island Southeast Asia, India and even to Africa.[10]

The large-scale commercial collecting and hunting can be traced to the last few decades.[11] Anecdotal accounts of pangolin export to mainland China can be traced back to 1925.[12] Harrison and Loh[13] had reported more than 60 tonnes of pangolin scales being exported between 1958 and 1964 from Sarawak, Malaysia. Yet, the seemingly rapid growth in its trade since the 1990s, coupled with the processes of deforestation in their habitats, has led to grave concern about its future.[14]

Since 2009, most of the pangolin trade in Asia has been driven by the demand in China for scales and meat to be used in traditional Chinese medicine.[15] Wu, writing in 2007, estimated that demand in China ranged between 100,000 and 135,000 pangolins.[16] Since the exhaustion of the supplies in southern China, pangolins had been imported from other Association of Southeast Asian Nations (ASEAN) countries since the 1990s, affecting the pangolin population in these countries.

The pangolin species were included in Appendix II of the CITES (Convention on International Trade in Endangered Species of Wild Fauna and Flora) since 1975.[17] A zero-quota ban was implemented in 2000, after a failure to move the pangolin to Appendix I.[18] Hence, any trade in the countries which had signed the CITES would have been illegal, although many countries were still not fulfilling the obligations or having the necessary laws in place. This would have covered most, if not all, of the Southeast Asian and East Asian countries.

Yet, despite the ban, 30,000 pangolins were seized in East and Southeast Asia between 2000 and 2007. Most of the pangolins that were detained or confiscated were bound for China via Vietnam or Thailand. Most of the pangolins observed in this trade had originated from Malaysia and Indonesia.[19] With the thinning or even extinction of the pangolin populations in China and other range countries, procurers have gone further afield, which has seen the growing importance of Malaysia, Indonesia and – more recently, after 2009 – India.[20] Large shipments continue to be intercepted today, with high profile cases in the Philippines, Indonesia, Malaysia and Vietnam.[21]

The confiscations and seizures probably constitute only the tip of the iceberg. The bulk of the pangolin trade remains undetected, and more intensive research has only been gradually begun to be conducted into the pangolin trade. As late as 2008, it was acknowledged that very little was known about the Pangolin populations, biology, ecology and their conservation, despite general agreement among experts regarding their rapid decline since the 1960s.[22]

A study conducted by Chin and Pantel[23] with respect to the pangolin trade emphasized that it was still "widespread" in Malaysia, with the population declining over the previous five years, with the extinction of the pangolin looming in the horizon, due to the continued high prices and demand.

In parts of Vietnam surveyed, the rapid escalation in trade and decline in the pangolin population was said to have begun from 1990, although it was said to have to have been declining in the decades before that.[24] Whilst a variety of environmental factors might have accounted for the declining populations of pangolins, it was the increased commercial demand and the hunting of the pangolins that seem to have taken their greatest toll.[25]

## Demand

The pangolin has had a long history of demand in the China-Southeast Asia or the East Asia-Southeast Asia trade. The geographical patterns of demand for pangolins and pangolin parts have varied over time, as have the major subject or purpose of the demand, and the sources of the supply.

The present demand for pangolin is mainly in China, but also in other East Asian and Southeast Asian countries influenced by Chinese culture, such as Korea, Taiwan and Vietnam. The scales of the pangolin are used for traditional medicine, and the meat is consumed as part of cultural beliefs pertaining to health and virility in these regions. Pangolins were often also consumed locally in Malaysia and other parts of Southeast Asia on a subsistence level, as part of traditional dietary beliefs.[26] It is also consumed in Indonesia, with Pangolin foetus soup being believed to increase the virility of men.

In China, the demand has been largely in southern provinces, where the consumption of wild meat has been more most prevalent. Nevertheless, the pangolin trade extends beyond southern China to northern China, as well. A study of the pangolin market in key cities in southern China between December 2007 and January 2008, namely in Kunming, Nanning, Fuzhou, Guangzhou and Haikou, highlighted the scale and scope of the illicit trade in pangolin meat in restaurants and markets, and in pangolin scales in different types of traditional Chinese medicine markets.[27]

Despite a ban on the sale of pangolins and pangolin parts, the study showed that almost 20% of the 50 restaurants surveyed in these cities sold pangolin meat at the rate of about ¥1,200 or US$175 per kg, with two of 25 markets surveyed selling pangolin meat at ¥700–800 per kg. Whilst only five out of 40 traditional Chinese medicine (TCM) wholesale centres surveyed (with 20 from Kunming and 20 from Guangzhou) sold pangolin scales at ¥900 (US$130) per kg, up to 163 of the 200 TCM retail outlets surveyed sold pangolin scales at an average price of ¥1082 per kg.[28,29]

Markets selling pangolin meat were found only among those surveyed in Nanning. Of the nine restaurants found to be serving pangolin meat in these cities, four each were from Nanning and Haikou, with one from Fuzhou. The TCM wholesale outlets selling pangolin scales were found only in Kunming and Guangzhou, numbering two or three, or constituting 10% and 15% of the outlets surveyed in these cities. The number of TCM retail outlets selling pangolin scales were more widespread, constituting more than 90% of the outlets surveyed in Nanning, Fuzhou, Guangzhou and Haikou. Kunming, however, had only 12% of the retail outlets selling pangolin scales, suggested that most of the scales sold by the wholesale outlets were for export, whilst Guangzhou was not only a supplier but also a market for the pangolin scales.

The 2005–2008 survey on the pangolin trade in China showed the rapid increase in the price of live pangolins and pangolin scales since 1990 and 1980, respectively. From ¥80 per kg in the early 1990s, it had reached ¥240 by the middle of the decade, and ¥690 towards the end. The prices seem to show a wide fluctuation. The prices of pangolin in the survey ranged from ¥800 per kg and ¥1,500 (US$220) per kg. The highest price attained in 2008 was about 20 times the price in the 1990s. For pangolin scales, the prices had ranged between ¥900 per kg and ¥1,200 per kg, which were about 100 times the prices reported from surveys in the early 1980s.[30]

A survey of Chinese internet sites show how the prices have continued to rise, despite the pangolin being listed as a prohibited commodity. Sites like 中国药材市场 have put the prices over ¥3,000 per kg in markets like 安徽亳州 and 河南禹州.[31] The price increases since the 1980s could actually reflect not just the high demand, but also the growing scarcity of local supplies in southern China and Vietnam or the effectiveness of regulation and enforcement.

Despite the lack of adequate statistics on the pangolin trade, several public confiscations of pangolin shipments since 2009 highlight the persistently large scale of the trade. A report on Project Pangolin had estimated that between 41,000 and 60,000 pangolins might have been killed for the illegal trade in 2011 alone. "Medicinal use" pangolin farms were also believed to have been stimulating this trade.[32]

Whilst cultural concepts of health and nutrition have been often been cited as the main impetus for the rapidly escalating demand in the last two to three decades, the coincidence of the latter with the economic liberalization in China and the rapid economic growth and affluence in the country since the 1980s, especially between the 1990s and the present, suggest that culture is but a background factor. The changing attitudes and patterns of consumption arising from economic growth and the forces of market capitalism are equally, if not more, important, in pushing both demand for and supply of pangolin meat and scales.

## *Supply*

Pangolins are said to be very susceptible to over-hunting, due to the nature of their defence mechanism when threatened. They also do not seem to breed well in captivity, and reproduce very slowly, although efforts are being made to improve knowledge and methods in the rearing of pangolins.[33] The subsistence hunting of pangolins and their involvement in the trans-Asian trade seems to have been taking place long before, but the last few decades had seen a rapid escalation of hunting and trading. As such, the pangolins traded are all from the wild.[34]

The trade in pangolins has been banned since 2000,[35] but reports in the press, government agency reports and information from the confiscation of such shipments, even today, suggest that the trade is far from eradicated, and still very active in East Asia and Southeast Asia. All the pangolins that are traded are from the wild. They are known to be rather difficult to keep and breed in captivity.[36]

The exhaustion of the pangolin population in southern China and Vietnam has led to pangolin traders venturing further afield in Southeast Asia and to India in the search for pangolin sources. With the growing distance of shipping, pangolins were increasingly being killed and frozen before shipping, with scales even being shipped separately from the meant. They were often declared as frozen fish and shipped in large quantities.[37] Strategies include mixing the pangolin with other cargo, or deliberately mislabelling them.

The WCMC-UNEP CITES trade database for the years 1990–2007 shows how most of the pangolin parts traded before 2000 had consisted mainly of scales and skins. The greater part of the skins were exported to Japan and Mexico via Singapore and used in the production of leather goods. Scales, on the other hand, were exported to China and Hong Kong to be used in traditional medicines.

Both skins and scales were exported to Singapore before being re-exported to Mexico and Japan for skins, and China and Hong Kong for scales. Some of the skin exports to Japan were re-exported to Mexico, the United States and even back to Singapore.[38] Data collected from locals in peninsular Malaysia by TRAFFIC Southeast Asia in 2008[39] suggested that most of the pangolins capture was "opportunistic" (consisting of 69%) rather than deliberate targeted capture (33%). Most of the pangolins were captured in palm oil plantations, forests (primary and secondary) and rubber estates, followed by other habitats. They were often captured through various ways of 'tracking, spotlighting, hunting with dogs and trapping'.[40]

Traders interviewed in 2008 suggested that Indonesian and Malaysian pangolins had constituted the largest group in the pangolin trade to East Asia. Some of the largest confiscations and seizures of Asian pangolins have occurred in Indonesia.[41] The pangolin trade in Indonesia had been rising since the 1990s. The volume of the trade has outstripped those of other endangered species in Indonesia. The high prices of the pangolins have been a major stimulant behind the scale of the trade. Pangolin hunting has worked its way into the livelihoods of the villages in different parts of Indonesia. Traditional farmers in the villages have become "opportunistic pangolin hunters", with a collector being able to buy a 10-kg pangolin from a hunter for the price of a young cow between 2004 and 2006. There seems to have a drastic fall in pangolin prices between 2007 and 2008, but the trade continues.[42]

The *Manis javanica* pangolin was traded from Malaysia legally between 1998 and 2003, primarily for their skin and scales, with Mexico and Japan as the main destinations, followed by the United States and Singapore.[43] The pangolin skin trade from Malaysia, ironically, saw a sharp spike in 2000, the year in which the pangolin trade was banned. The growing trade in scales had already been documented in 1998, with a hike in 1996. The figures derived from reported confiscations (in the press and the CITES management authorities in Singapore) show that the pangolin trade continued between 2000 and 2007 despite the ban, with more than 30,000 pangolins confiscated across the region during that period.

In Malaysia, pangolins were sold at an average price of MYR95 per kg (US$27 at 2008 rates), with prices fluctuating between MYR30 per kg (US$9) to MYR330 per kg (US$100). The average price had risen from MYR0.80 per kg (US$0.24) in the 1970s, to ¥5 to ¥15 (US$1.51–4.55) in the mid-1980s, and ¥40–50 per kg (US$12–15) in the 1990s when pangolin numbers were still high, and demand was low. The price varied according to market demand, the agent and location, as well as the climate or season in the consuming countries, and the various enforcement activities. Most of the informants remembered the high variation of the prices. The price increases in Malaysia by kilogram were ¥80 to ¥100 to ¥120 (US$36), and finally great jump to ¥750.

There were important parallels between the pangolin hunters, collectors and traders in Malaysia and Indonesia. Regional and international traders mediated between destination markets in East Asia and elsewhere, and collection regions in Southeast Asia.[44] The growing distance between collection sites and markets also meant that the pangolins were often killed and frozen before shipping, compared to earlier trade which tended to ship them live.

In Malaysia, most of the pangolin collectors were farmers and plantation workers in the oil palm and rubber estates, as well as hunters. The "Orang Asli" and Malays, and Indonesians, were especially involved in the capturing of pangolins.[45] Whilst the majority were part-time collectors, exploiting opportunity, there were "skilled and serious collectors" who deliberately searched for pangolin, either in groups or alone, especially when prices were high. When prices were low in the late 1990s, not much hunting or collecting took place. All of the collectors maintained that they had to sell the pangolins immediately after capture[46] and faced high risks of getting caught with the pangolin and the fear of losing profit on the pangolin, given that they lose weight over time. These collectors attempted to maintain a lower profile to avoid detection from the authorities.

In the schema of Chin and Patel,[47] the traders or agents and middlemen were those 'who owned businesses such as grocery shops, licensed wildlife traders', and were involved in the pangolin trade as a sideline. However, the volatile prices the spot checks and enforcement activities by the Department of Forestry presented formidable risks for the people involved. Nevertheless, they had good networks of collectors in different locations. Malays and Orang Asli also acted as agents for these middlemen. All the traders emphasized the importance of the China international market, and they were sent live via Thailand or other Southeast Asian countries, depending on expedience. Some east coast Malaysian ports include Kuantan, Terengganu and Sungei Golok.[48]

The pangolin trade in Malaysia involved a hierarchy of agents who made profit from the different transactions passing the pangolin along, making profits of between MYR20 (US$6) and MYR30 (US$10) per kg. Business competition meant they were always ready to undercut each other and collectors came to be very selective towards the larger traders. Pangolins, according to the traders, were shipped first to Thailand, where the traders will supply the pangolin to China, before they were shipped via other traders in Thailand, Laos, Vietnam and Myanmar, with traders stationed in these areas to ensure the safety of their shipments to China, with some now being sent by sea or air freight. The transit processes through island and mainland Southeast Asia highlight the importance in this flow as well.[49]

It was a largely similar case in Indonesia. In the early period, pangolins were traded in Indonesia only for their skin, to be used to produce leather products such as wallets and bags.[50] By 2008, there was no longer any demand for skin and two of the pangolin "collectors" interviewed in the TRAFFIC-LIPI survey claimed to have accumulated 300–400 skins. By the early 2000s, the international demand for pangolins from Indonesia had shifted to their scales, and Sopyan[51] argued that the demand had expanded to include meat and internal organs, which continues to the present.

This suggested that demand for pangolins in Indonesia from China for TCM was not on a substantial scale until after 2000. The pangolins were shipped, both live and dead, although with the growing distance, the former was becoming increasingly rare. In the case of the latter, they were stored in wooden boxes before their slaughter by cutting the throat. The scales were then removed from the body beginning from the tail by boiling in 90-degree water for 2–5 minutes. A slit was then made in the abdomen after the removal of the scales, so as to remove the internal organs, which were washed and wrapped individually inside plastic bags before being restored in the bodies of the pangolins. The pangolins were then placed inside plastic bags and stored in freezers, to be shipped out of the country once full.[52] The scales were dried for up to three hours under the sun, and then packed into large bags before being shipped to Jakarta in trucks.[53]

The pangolin traders often operated under the cover of legal businesses, from enterprises related to wildlife collection/captive breeding, to ''small businesses such as bakery, grocery, home decoration, and constructions suppliers'. The pangolins, and other prohibited animals, were often labelled as various non-protected species, or mixed in with them. Private vehicles depicted as carrying other products, and even buses, were used in this trade. Most importantly, bribes were used to pay officials to allow the movement of such species.[54]

Estimates of the pangolins processed in different slaughterhouses in southern Sumatra over a three-month period allowed Sopyan[55] to posit that a total of 8–11 tonnes of pangolins were exported each month (with 7 kg as the average weight of one pangolin).[56] The Palembang slaughterhouses processed pangolins from around the region, such as Java, Lampung, Bangka, Belitung, Sekayu, Baturaja, Muba, Lahat, Seililin (southern Sumatra) and various regencies in Jambi. They were hunted throughout Sumatra and the surrounding islands, then exported out of Indonesia via Medan and Palembang.[57]

It seemed that there was a higher proportion of females collected in southern Sumatra between November 2007 and January 2008 (i.e. two-thirds of the numbers). Exporters from Palembang reported the ability to send out one shipment of pangolins from Indonesia every one to two months. TRAFFIC had actually observed the preparations of two shipments for export, with the first one yielding 25 tonnes (December 2006) and the second 8 tonnes (November 2007).

A shipment captured in Vietnam in early 2009 had yielded a total of 24 tonnes with both shipments coming from Indonesia.

Sopyan also argued that the pangolin trade consisted of five organizational levels connected the pangolin hunters to the different levels of collectors and to the exporter.[58] The people hunting the animals were not only farmers living around plantations, but also people from outside the villages, the latter often hunting pangolins through opportunity, and belonging to the lower social class, obtained loans from collectors to cover their daily living expenses. The collectors are divided into different levels.

Those closest to the hunters buy the pangolins from these hunters at the 'village, sub-district or regency levels'. They were usually Chinese shopkeepers in these villages and on the local level. They were connected in turn to an extensive network of collectors at higher levels (e.g. regency and provincial) who sometimes financed their purchases. It was the latter who were connected to broader international networks. They were also the ones who invest in the processing of the pangolins for export, or what Sopyan called the 'slaughterhouses'.[59]

The Riau-Lingga archipelago was also another region where pangolins, 'abundantly and easily found', have been increasingly hunted between 2005 and 2008 by the local population. They were sold to small collectors in the region, who then ship them to Singkep and to Jambi in eastern Sumatra, where bigger buyers purchased them for Singapore and shipped them there, via Batam, to sell in the Singapore markets. The price difference of a live pangolin between the level of the hunter and the big collectors was about three times (between IDR15,000–20,000 per kg or US$1.60–2.10 and IDR50,000—100,000 or US$5.25–10.50). Dry bauxite hills and rubber plantations formed the habitat. Pangolin trading was rather "new" in the region, and the pangolins caught (between 3 and 7 kg) will provide an income of IDR 45,000–60,000 IR $4.60–6.30) per animal. This was a substantial amount of money given the minimal cost of living was IRP30,000 (US$3.10) per day.[60]

The geography of the region, with the many islands and the open sea, as well as 1,000 small ports alongside the 22 official international harbours, has historically presented a challenge to states wishing to regulate the movement of commodities, people and ideas in island Southeast Asia. Smuggling and piracy had long constituted challenges to states in the maritime region. The overlaps between the pangolin trade and the trade in other commodities further complicate the problem. Just as the pangolins were often shipped as fish products, the trade was often undertaken at sea and camouflaged as fishing. Enforcement was only possible through a good intelligence network and cooperation across borders between countries like Malaysia, Singapore and the Philippines.

Hunters and buyers within Southeast Asia were also transcending borders. On 26 March 2011, a Singapore-Malaysian news service reported that five poachers had been caught hunting pangolins at the Marang Tembat Forest reserve in Kuala Terengganu by rangers from the Wildlife Department. One came from Cambodia and four were Vietnamese. Spotted as they were leaving the forest reserve, a search of their car yielded pangolin scales, timber pieces and parang and axe, respectively.[61] Confiscated shipments of pangolin were often seized alongside other prohibited animal products.

It is clear from the patterns described that the search for overseas supplies of pangolin meat and scales tapped on existing trade networks and channels, often involving other commodities. The mapping of these networks, and the web of advance, credit and finance underlying them, and further investigations into how the pangolin trade ties into different sectors of China-Southeast Asia commerce, including its relationship with the trade in other commodities, will allow us to better understand the dynamics of this trade at local, regional and trans-regional levels. Such knowledge will be crucial in devising strategies to control and limit the trade in pangolins and pangolin parts.

## State of research/issues

In the first workshop on the trade and conservation of Pangolins native to South and Southeast Asia in 2009, most of the presenters lamented the relative dearth of research into the habitat, biology, environmental impact and possibilities of captive rearing for the pangolins. Since then, much has been done to promote research, advertising and international/inter-agency cooperation in curbing the hunting, trading and consumption of pangolins and pangolin parts.

The IUCN reported in 2009 that no statistics were available on the pangolin populations in the world. They were said to be difficult to observe due to their "secretive, solitary, and nocturnal habits". There is a general perception that populations were declining rapidly, especially in Asia.[62] Chin and Pantel[63] lament that the 'volumes, values, and uses of wildlife in trade are still poorly documented', especially the Sunda Pangolin *Manis javanica*, the only native pangolin species in Malaysia.

Statistics on the trade have also been fragmentary, based on the collation of reports of confiscations by custom authorities in different parts of Southeast Asia, and various recent field surveys in Malaysia, Indonesia, Vietnam and Cambodia, which were regional in focus. Yet these statistics alone, and assuming the worst, suggests that the problem is becoming all the more serious. Even people involved in the trade directly or indirectly, as shown in the study by Chin and Pantel[64] conducted with respect to the pangolin trade in Malaysia, regarded the animal to be in danger of extinction, due to the consumption of the past few decades, and the continued high prices and demand.

A host of non-government organizations like TRAFFIC, World Wildlife Fund and Wildlife Enforcement Network have begun to pay greater attention to the trafficking of pangolins and work with governments in East Asia and Southeast Asia to institute laws, measures, arrangements and education campaigns to combat the pangolin trade. Alongside these agencies, more specialized groups like pangolin.org have been formed to collate information with a more specific focus on the pangolin.

Much research remains to be done on various aspects of the pangolin trade and the biological habitats of the pangolin. Between 2005 and 2008, various key surveys and research were conducted on the pangolin populations, habitats and trade in different parts of Southeast Asia as well as China. NGOs like TRAF-FIC worked with national research, environmental and scientific organizations to conduct research in key supply, transit and consumer areas. Other global wildlife organizations have built databases for the populations and trade in various endangered animals. Yet statistics are far from complete and accurate about the illicit nature of this trade.

At the same time, more intensive field surveys are being done to collect ethnographic and local data. In March 2008, TRAFFIC worked with LIPI (the Indonesian Institute of Sciences) to mount a 10-day survey in southern Sumatra (Ketenong Village, Lebong Regency, Bengkulu).[65] They had investigated 17 pangolin dens to obtain a better idea of their living environments.

In 2007, a study to investigate the habitat of the pangolins and their capture and trade had been conducted by Chin and Pantel,[66] which has sought to investigate the habitat and the populations of the Sunda Pangolin in Malaysia, as well as the trade dynamics, and to shed light on current issues and situations concerning the trade. In fact, that study was to be the first one to be conducted on the trade in the Sunda Pangolin.

These studies have been excellent for their combination of field surveys with various forms of available statistical data, such as the UNEP-WCMC database, press reports and Departments of Wildlife and National Parks Peninsula Malaysia (Perhilitan) annual reports, as well as customs records of seizures. Perhaps what Semiadi et al.[67] have suggested in terms of allowing a quote for the pangolin trade instead of the zero-quota system might be more successful in curtailing the trade and also in allowing greater supervision, especially in the abuses within the system.

Research is also increasingly being conducted into the habitats of the pangolins and their life habits, as well as the habits and responses of pangolins in captivity, not only to allow better rehabilitation of captured pangolins, but also to investigate possibilities of rearing pangolins to feed the demand in scales and meat. The major challenge facing students, activists and policy-makers with regard to the current and future state of knowledge on the pangolin trade remains the continued expansion of the scale and scope of field research, with respect not only to the scale, the structure, organization and habits of the trade, but also the extent of the impact of pangolin hunting and the reduction in its populations on the environment.

More importantly, more research needs to be done on the consumption end in China. Rather than simply denying the medicinal significance of pangolin meat and scales, and educating populations in these areas about these myths, there is a greater need to understand the basis of consumption and demand for these parts in southern China and areas with concepts of health and food similar to the Chinese. The cultural demand had been there for centuries. Yet, it was the last few decades since the economic liberation and rapid growth of China that has seen a surge in demand and supply. The economic conditions fuelling this growth in trade, especially in the way it is entangled with cultural perceptions and traditional medicinal knowledge and practice in China and among the Chinese overseas, merits greater attention.

## Conclusion: future challenges

In February 2012, a Pangolin Specialist Group (PangolinSG) was formed by the IUCN SSC (International Union for the Conservation of Nature Species Survival Commission), as one of more than 120 IUCN SSC specialist groups to collate and coordinate online and global resources, initiatives and news pertaining to pangolin trade, habitats and research, so as to promote interest in the plight of the pangolin.[68] It has pushed for the celebration of World Pangolin Day, on the third Saturday of February, and campaigned for greater public awareness of the plight of the pangolin worldwide on various research and public media platforms.[69]

From 24 to 27 June 2013, the first global conference ("Scaling up Pangolin Conservation") on the pangolin and its conservation was held in Singapore by the PangolinSG and the Wildlife Reserves Singapore Conservation Fund to continue the push for better understanding and regulation of the trade, as well as research on the pangolin and its conservation. The workshops and conferences on the conservation of the pangolin in East Asia and Southeast Asia, held in 2009 and 2013, respectively, highlighted the need for a holistic approach to the reduction and cessation of the pangolin trade, whilst lamenting the failure of laws and enforcement measures in stemming the trade. Despite the growing reports of seizures, it is difficult to ascertain whether they represented the turning of the tide in the pangolin trade, the growing efficiency of the enforcement agencies, sometimes in conjunction with NGOs, or, conversely, the growing scale of the trade.

Activists, scholars and officials have lamented the failure of the whole slew of laws enacted by respective Southeast Asian and East Asian governments to ban this trade and the trades in other animals and plants since the 1970s.[70] Some have even speculated on whether it might be a good idea to legalized a controlled trade, whilst others had argued for still greater penalties and the upgrading of these of the status of the pangolins in the CITES appendix list.

In the case of Indonesia, the campaigns to promote public awareness did not seem to have been successful,[71] and enforcement did not seem to have been particularly successful, either, with researcher Sopyan[72] being able to conduct interviews even among those involved in the trade in one way or another. In other parts of Southeast Asia, there has been growing inter-departmental and government-NGO collaboration in the supervising, surveillance and enforcement of pangolin trade bans, but again with varying degrees of success.

A group of Indonesian scholars, Semiadi et al.,[73] argued that the economic problems of the local people were the main driving force pushing them to the pangolin trade. The hierarchy of traders and collectors in Indonesia, for example, financed this trade by providing advances to these more impoverished people in return for the catching of the pangolins. This resembled the older patterns of regional-international trade that had long characterized Southeast Asian-Chinese commercial interactions.

The government and non-governmental agencies have made important progress in enacting legislation against the trade in pangolins and other endangered animals, and expanding knowledge and awareness about these trades. They have been relatively successful in organizing co-operative ventures to investigate the extent, structure and impact of the trade, as well as the biological and ecological dimensions of the pangolin species, and their importance to their respective environments. In spite of the limited success in enforcement, government agencies, NGOs and scientific organizations (especially with respect to wildlife and biological/ecological sciences) have continued to expand their cooperation and to educate the public about the extent of the problem and the environmental problems and challenges that the extinction of the pangolins and other animals might pose to their immediate habitats, and to the global environment.

Yet, as many members of these agencies have highlighted, it was socio-economic and cultural forces which accounted for the expansion and continued resilience of this trade despite the manifold measures adopted in the last two decades since the listing of pangolins in CITES as a List II species and the imposition of a zero-quota in 2000. The cultures of consumption in the destination markets, the transformation of these cultures by the rapid economic expansion and affluence it brought about in China and other parts of East and Southeast Asia, and the rationales for the hunting of the pangolins in the supply regions all deserve greater attention.[74]

In 2015, a Pangolin Range States Meeting was held in Da Nang, Vietnam hosted by the governments of Vietnam and the United States. Just a year earlier, in 2014, A global conservation plan entitled "Scaling up Pangolin Conservation" was another recent development in these transnational frameworks created to push for protection of pangolins worldwide.[75] In late June 2017, in another meeting of the Pangolin Specialist Group in Singapore, a regional strategy for the conservation of the Sunda pangolin in Southeast Asia was created for the first time. It was part of a concerted effort to develop detailed frameworks for tying national plans which had been gradually developed over the years with more regional initiatives.[76]

The 2017 workshop also highlighted the urgency to engage and work closely with local communities in or around the habitats of Sunda pangolins, and the need for further research to better comprehend the forces and motivations underlying the consumption of the pangolin and its parts, to devise new strategies to promote more sustainable modes of consumption.

Ultimately, it is by both understanding the socio-economic and cultural factors shaping demand in China and other East Asian and Southeast Asian countries, as well as the variables affecting supply, such as the hunting and collecting of these animals and parts, the impact of these activities on their local and regional environments, as well as the trade networks that facilitate these flows, that we can better tackle the challenge of protecting the pangolin from extinction.

## Notes

1  R. Conniff, "Poaching Pangolins: An obscure creature faces uncertain future", *Yale Environment 360*, 19 September 2013, http://e360.yale.edu/feature/poaching_pangolins_ an_obscure_creature_faces_uncertain_future/2692/
2  The multifaceted nature of the problem requires a multi-dimensional approach, dealing with questions of cultural understandings and epistemologies of health in different traditions of medicine and lifestyles, new economies of mass consumption and the

commercial and collecting networks to meet these demands, and the politics of border zones. Those approaches also covered not only the globalization of environmentalism as a new ideology in Asia, but also the growth of the state in these frontier zones. Yet, state control did not necessarily mean an end of the trades in these animal and animal part projects.

3  E. Tagliacozzo, "Border permeability and the state in Southeast Asia: Contraband and regional security", *Contemporary Southeast Asia* (2001): 254–274. W. Van Schendel, "Geographies of knowing, geographies of ignorance: Jumping scale in Southeast Asia", *Environment and Planning D*, 20(6) (2002): 647–668.

4  D.W.S. Challender, "Asian Pangolins: Increasing affluence driving hunting pressure", *TRAFFIC Bulletin*, 23(3) (2011): 92–93.

5  S.Y. Chin, and S. Pantel, "Pangolin capture and trade in Malaysia", in *Proceedings of the Workshop on Trade and Conservation of Pangolins Native to South and Southeast Asia*. 30 June to 2 July 2008, Singapore Zoo, Singapore, TRAFFIC Southeast Asia, 2009, p. 143. See also "Pangolin Facts", http://pangolins.org/amazing-pangolin-facts/

6  E. Sopyan, "Malayan Pangolin Manis javanica Trade in Sumatra, Indonesia", in *Proceedings of the Workshop on Trade and Conservation of Pangolins Native to South and Southeast Asia*. 30 June to 2 July 2008, Singapore Zoo, Singapore, TRAFFIC Southeast Asia, 2009, p. 134.

7  S.Y. Chin, and S. Pantel, "Pangolin capture and trade in Malaysia", p. 144.

8  See the different editions of 本草纲目 originally compiled by 李时珍, as well as other historical works on Chinese medicine and healing through the centuries. 李时珍 is commonly regarded as one of the most important figures in the history of traditional Chinese medicine and medicine in China. His famous compendium, the 本草纲目, compiled during the late Ming dynasty, included the pangolin and pangolin scales, and the ailments they can be used for. The pangolin is listed in the compendium and other historical works on Chinese medicine and *materia medica* as 穿山甲 and 鲮鲤 respectively. See 李时珍(1653), 重订草木冈本 and 李时珍(1872), 草木冈本. 53 卷 3图卷.

9  S.Y. Chin, and S. Pantel, "Pangolin capture and trade in Malaysia", p. 144.

10  R. Conniff, "Poaching Pangolins."

11  C.R. Shepherd, "Overview of pangolin trade in Southeast Asia", in *Proceedings of the Workshop on Trade and Conservation of Pangolins Native to South and Southeast Asia*. 30 June to 2 July 2008, Singapore Zoo, Singapore, TRAFFIC Southeast Asia, 2009, p. 7.

12  See G. Semiadi, et al., "Sunda Pangolin Manis javanica conservation in Indonesia: Status & problems", in *Proceedings of the Workshop on Trade and Conservation of Pangolins Native to South and Southeast Asia*. 30 June to 2 July 2008, Singapore Zoo, Singapore, TRAFFIC Southeast Asia, 2009.

13  T. Harrisson, "A future for Borneo's wildlife?", *Oryx*, 8(2) (1965): 99–104.

14  "Asian pangolins being wiped out". *Newswatch*. http://newswatch.nationalgeographic.com/2009/07/13/asian_pangolins_being_wiped_out/

15  S.B. Wu, G.Z. Ma, M. Tang, H. Chen, and N.F. Liu, "中国穿山甲资源现状及保护对策。" [The status and conservation strategy of pangolin resource in China], *Journal of Natural Resource* (2002); S.B. Wu, M.A. Guangxi, T. Mei, H. Chen, Z. Xu, and N. Liu, "大雾岭保护区穿山甲冬季生境选择", [The population and density of Pangolin in Dawuling Natural Reserve and the number of pangolin resource in Guangdong Province], *Acta Theriologica Sinica*, 22(4) (2003).

16  吴 (2007: 175) lists seven major species of pangolin, some based on regional origin and habitats, and limits the arguments for tested medical efficacy (both in terms of historical *materia medica* and modern medicinal testing) of pangolin parts (namely the meat and the scales) to the China variety.

17  C.R. Shepherd, "Overview of pangolin trade in Southeast Asia", p. 7.
18  CITES CoP 11, 2000.
19  S.Y. Chin, and S. Pantel, "Pangolin capture and trade in Malaysia", p. 143.
20  C.R. Shepherd, "Overview of pangolin trade in Southeast Asia", p. 7; S.Y. Chin, and S. Pantel, "Pangolin capture and trade in Malaysia", p. 143.
21  "Empat WN China Ditangkap di Bandara Soetta". Poskotanews. *www.poskotanews.com/2013/01/04/empat-wn-china-ditangkap-di-bandara-soetta/*; "Trenggiling senilai Rp 9miliar gagal diselundupkan". www.poskotanews.com/2012/10/10/trenggiling-senilai-rp-9-miliar-gagal-diselundupkan/; "Ratusan ekor trenggiling gagal diselundupkan". Poskota News www.poskotanews.com/2012/05/02/ratusan-ekor-trenggiling-gagal-diselundupkan/
22  C.R. Shepherd, "Overview of pangolin trade in Southeast Asia", p. 6.
23  S.Y. Chin, and S. Pantel, "Pangolin capture and trade in Malaysia".
24  "Manis Javanica." *The IUCN Red List of Threatened Species.* www.iucnredlist.org/details/full/12763/0 (Population).
25  C.R. Shepherd, "Overview of pangolin trade in Southeast Asia".
26  S.Y. Chin, and S. Pantel, "Pangolin capture and trade in Malaysia", p. 143.
27  L. Xu, "The Pangolin trade in China", in *Proceedings of the Workshop on Trade and Conservation of Pangolins Native to South and Southeast Asia.* 30 June to 2 July 2008, Singapore Zoo, Singapore, TRAFFIC Southeast Asia, 2009.
28  Ibid, pp. 189, 191.
29  In the markets and restaurants surveyed, the pangolin meat was not displayed, with customers having to give several days advance notice. The pangolin scales were also only shown on request in the wholesale centres, but they were openly sold in the retail outlets. See ibid.
30  Ibid., p. 191.
31  "穿山甲"。《中国药材市场》。www.zgycsc.com/price/html/nid/1326.html
32  "94 Pangolins Seized in Malaysia". http://pangolins.org/2012/05/14/94-pangolins-seized-in-malaysia/
33  C.W. Yang, et al., "History and dietary husbandry of pangolins in captivity", *Zoo Biology*, 26(3) (2007): 223–230.
34  C.R. Shepherd, "Overview of pangolin trade in Southeast Asia", p. 7.
35  S.Y. Chin, and S. Pantel, "Pangolin capture and trade in Malaysia", p. 143; C.R. Shepherd, "Overview of pangolin trade in Southeast Asia"; E. Sopyan, "Malayan Pangolin Manis javanica trade in Sumatra, Indonesia".
36  C.W. Yang, et al., "History and dietary husbandry of pangolins in captivity".
37  C.R. Shepherd, "Overview of pangolin trade in Southeast Asia", p. 8.
38  S.Y. Chin, and S. Pantel, "Pangolin capture and trade in Malaysia", p. 147.
39  The data for their survey was collected through interviews and surveys (202 respondents answering to a semi-structured interview). Of the 202 respondents, 175 were involved in the pangolin trade, or at least aware of it (Chin & Pantel 2009, p. 143).
40  S.Y. Chin, and S. Pantel, "Pangolin capture and trade in Malaysia", p. 143.
41  C.R. Shepherd, "Overview of pangolin trade in Southeast Asia", p. 7.
42  E. Sopyan, "Malayan Pangolin Manis javanica Trade in Sumatra, Indonesia", p. 134.
43  S.Y. Chin, and S. Pantel, "Pangolin capture and trade in Malaysia", pp. 145–146.
44  C.R. Shepherd, "Overview of pangolin trade in Southeast Asia", pp. 7–8.
45  Pangolins from Malaysia were captured through tracking, spotlighting, hunting with dogs and trapping, with tracking being the most commonly cited method. There did not seem to be any seasonal variation in capturing pangolins, as they were captured throughout the year, with most collectors capturing pangolins regardless of their size or age (Chin & Pantel 2009, p. 150).
46  S.Y. Chin, and S. Pantel, "Pangolin capture and trade in Malaysia", p. 152.
47  Ibid, p. 152.
48  Ibid, p. 152.

49  Ibid, p. 153.
50  E. Sopyan, "Malayan Pangolin Manis javanica trade in Sumatra, Indonesia", p. 136.
51  Ibid, p. 136.
52  Ibid, p. 137.
53  Ibid, pp. 137–138, provides detailed photos of different stages of the processing.
54  Ibid, p. 139, see pictures for the preparation, packing and shipping of the pangolins for the trade.
55  Ibid, p. 140.
56  This included Palembang, Bengkulu, Rejang Rebong Regency, Bengkulu, Kuto Baru Sub-district, Darma Seraya Regency in west Sumatra, regencies in Riau and W. Sumatra, and the Musi Rawas region near Palembang (Sopyan 2009, p. 140).
57  E. Sopyan, "Malayan Pangolin Manis javanica Trade in Sumatra, Indonesia", p. 141.
58  Ibid, p. 140.
59  Ibid.
60  G. Semiadi, et al., "Sunda Pangolin Manis javanica conservation in Indonesia: Status & problems".
61  "Malaysia: Five foreign pangolin hunters nabbed", *The Star/Asia News Network.*. www.asiaone.com/News/AsiaOne+News/Crime/Story/A1Story20110326-270211.html
62  "Test your pangolin knowledge with 25 amazing Pangolin facts", no. 4. http://pangolins.org/amazing-pangolin-facts/
63  S.Y. Chin, and S. Pantel, "Pangolin capture and trade in Malaysia", p. 143.
64  Ibid.
65  E. Sopyan, "Malayan Pangolin Manis javanica trade in Sumatra, Indonesia", p. 135.
66  S.Y. Chin, and S. Pantel, "Pangolin capture and trade in Malaysia", p. 144.
67  G. Semiadi, et al., "Sunda Pangolin Manis javanica Conservation in Indonesia: Status & Problems".
68  "About". *The IUCN SSC Pangolin Specialist Group*. https://www.pangolinsg.org/about/
69  "The end of the IUCN quadrennium 2012–2016 and a look towards 2017–2020", *IUCN SSN Pangolin Specialist Group*, www.pangolinsg.org/2016/12/21/the-end-of-the-iucn-quadrennium-2012-2016-and-a-look-towards-2017–2020/ (Accessed on 30 October 2017).
70  See G. Semiadi, et al., pp. 12–13, for example.
71  Ibid.
72  E. Sopyan, "Malayan Pangolin Manis javanica trade in Sumatra, Indonesia".
73  G. Semiadi, et al., "Sunda Pangolin Manis javanica Conservation in Indonesia: Status & Problems".
74  L. Zhang, et al., "Wildlife trade, consumption and conservation awareness in southwest China", *Biodiversity and Conservation*, 17(6) (2008): 1493–1516.
75  *Celebrating World Pangolin Day and Five Years of the IUCN SSC Pangolin Specialist Group*, www.pangolinsg.org/2017/02/18/celebrating-world-pangolin-day-and-five-years-of-the-iucn-ssc-pangolin-specialist-group/ (Accessed on 9 November 2017).
76  "Experts make first ever Regional Conservation Strategy for Sunda Pangolin", *IUCN SSC Pangolin Specialist Group*, www.pangolinsg.org/2017/07/09/experts-make-first-ever-regional-conservation-strategy-for-sunda-pangolin/ (Accessed on 9 November 2017).

# 7 Profits downstream, unsustainability upstream

## Illegal logging and Siamese rosewood trade in the Greater Mekong Basin (GMB)

*Keokam Kraisoraphong*

## Introduction

The high demand for timber products under the now visible Chinese investments within the Greater Mekong Basin (GMB) continues to fuel illegal logging, and with it the illicit activities associated with timber trades among the Mekong countries. This has been even more true for high-value hardwoods, of which China is a particularly important market and for which there is significant illegal trade.[1] To feed the surge in demand from its market of increasing wealth and purchasing power, China's imports of rosewood logs from the Mekong countries rose to just under half of its total rosewood log import in 2011 – despite the logging and trade bans in these countries to protect the endangered rosewood species.[2] The listing of Siamese rosewood (*Dalbergia cochinchinensis*) to the Convention on International Trade in Endangered Species of Wild Fauna and Flora (CITES) Appendix II[3] in 2013 – as a species in need of strict trade and export control – reflects the dire situation, and the expectation that the CITES mechanism would effectively help regulate illegal logging of Siamese rosewood being traded internationally. CITES enactment notwithstanding, China's 2014 rosewood logs import reached an all-time high – with imports from the Mekong countries continuing to account for 50% by volume and 70% by value.[4] The slight drop in China's 2015 rosewood imports occurred only when the decades of overharvesting in the GMB made it necessary to shift to sources in West Africa,[5] where similar illicit practices have also been transferred.

Studies of China's role and manner of investments in countries with forest governance and regulatory problems argue that whilst the Mekong states do have their interests in the Chinese and 'China-linked' investment into the Mekong region – the investments are based more on the dynamics of global capitalism and accumulation.[6] From the perspective beyond a spatial container view of states, the studies point out that 'economic organization and production in both China and the Mekong countries is being shaped by the broader competitive pressures involved in the transnational capitalist dynamics, and through corporate-controlled global commodity and production networks'.[7] The Environmental Investigation Agency (EIA)[8] indicates that the nature of timber extraction and sourcing, which are driven by Chinese traders in each region, follows the same pattern – with the range states finally seeking international protection through CITES. In the case of

rosewood trade, the tremendous potential profits have rendered national regulations ineffective and thus led to the listing of eight rosewood species.[9] However,
efforts to protect the remaining rosewood stock remain to be challenged by the
emergence of transnational organized crime syndicates to exploit the profitability
related to its trade.[10] Among the Mekong countries, the sourcing of illegal rosewood is operated by organized crime networks of Chinese and Vietnamese traders, whilst in West Africa, rosewood has become a conflict timber and revenues
from the illegal rosewood trade have benefited their main separatist movement
in armed conflict.[11] For reasons that illegal logging within the GMB 'perpetuates
corruption, undermines livelihoods, fuels social conflict, deprives governments
of revenue and erodes countries' natural resource bases', they are activities with
significant implications for achieving sustainable development.[12] To meet China's
insatiable demand for rosewood, the species are being stripped across the globe
from 'the Mekong region, India, Madagascar, Central America and Africa'.[13] At
the rate that China's domestic consumer market absorbs its illegal timber imports,
without any counter action, China would become 'the chief driver of illegal logging worldwide'.[14]

Drawing from findings of the various research studies on illegal logging within
the Mekong region, this chapter examines the governance failure reflected in
Mekong countries' response – or lack thereof – to the unsustainable rosewood
extraction together with its illicit sourcing pattern. Related issues are further discussed in three parts. Following this introduction, the first section begins by a
brief review of the illicit timber trade among the Mekong countries: on the one
hand, the demand for rosewood as determined by the lucrative and rapidly growing market of China, and on the other hand, the supply induced by the tremendous
profit potential from illegal rosewood trade under ineffective national regulations.
The second section focuses on the case of Siamese rosewood and the protection through its CITES listing since 2013. It also examines the challenges facing
CITES effective implementation in this case. Before the conclusion, the third section draws from a number of concepts which explain illegal logging and its related
trade – as well as the key components of the framework on international institutions and national policies to discuss the extent of CITES influence on compliance among the Mekong nations and China – given the climate of corruption and
conflict under the criminal networks of illicit rosewood trade. It also attempts to
identify the conditions necessary for compliance, which could lead to the potential success of efforts to preserve the remaining Siamese rosewood stock in the
Mekong region and protect the rosewood species from being driven to extinction
by the currently thriving illicit rosewood trade.

## Illegal logging and the illicit trade of rosewood in the Mekong region: demand and supply

Severe deforestation among the Mekong countries in the past three decades has
been highly driven by illegal logging,[15] which involves timber trade associated with
the broader problem of malpractice and crime. Illegal logging includes 'logging

outside concession boundaries, cutting more timber than stipulated in concession contracts, logging in protected areas and felling protected tree species'.[16] Whilst driven by global demand, illegal logging occurs 'only in conjunction with local corruption'.[17] Such is witnessed among the Mekong countries, where despite the series of measures for logging controls and timber trade restrictions imposed, illegal harvest and trade in stolen timber prevail under poor governance.[18]

The policy shifts among the majority of the Mekong countries towards market-oriented economy in the late 1980s, followed by the massive over-exploitation of forest resources during the 1980s and 1990s, led to the imposition of domestic logging controls.[19] The Bali Declaration agreed at the East Asia ministerial meeting on Forest Law Enforcement and Governance (FLEG) in 2001 marked the first time governments from the region, including China, came together to address the threat posed by widespread illegal logging. In support of East Asia FLEG, Cambodia, Laos, Thailand and Vietnam committed to taking action against illegal logging and trade in illegally sourced timber. All four countries then agreed to the Vientiane Action Programme under the Association of Southeast Asian Nations (ASEAN) banner in 2004 – setting the target to eradicate unsustainable forest management practices by 2010. Towards the end of 2007, ASEAN pushed further in the Singapore Declaration on Climate Change, Energy and the Environment for the strengthening of forest law enforcement and governance to combat illegal logging and other harmful practices. By October 2016, the 38th ASEAN Ministry of Agriculture and Forestry (AMAF) put forth the policy framework on forestry cooperation to develop a regional framework for mutual recognition of timber legality system and to strengthen joint strategies in seeking greater market access and promoting ASEAN forest products that are sourced legally.

These commitments notwithstanding, illegal logging and timber smuggling continues to thrive under each Mekong country's willingness to exploit the forest resources of its neighbours. Though in breach of national regulations, Thailand and Vietnam have been the regional timber processing centres, which source their raw timber supplies from Cambodia and Laos.[20] China, on the other hand, has become a destination for significant volumes of timber export from Laos, at the same time that Chinese firms are logging in Cambodia and Myanmar.[21] With the exception of Siamese rosewood, the flows of timber trade among the Mekong countries from a demand-and-supply perspective places China, Vietnam, and Thailand more on the demand side and Cambodia, Laos and Myanmar as the source of supply.

### *Demand for illegal timber: Siamese rosewood* (Dalbergia cochinchinensis Pierre)

China topped the list of countries reporting the greatest annual gain in forest area during 2010–2015,[22] with the highest afforestation rate of any country in the world.[23] With its increase in forest cover over the past 30 years of 9%,[24] China's forest cover today constitutes over 20% of its total land area.[25] The increase occurred following timber harvest control from natural forests together with replanting under

China's Natural Forest Protection Program, which was initiated in the early 2000s in response to the massive flooding of the major river basins in 1998.[26]

Whilst China's total wood consumption is estimated to reach 457–477 million cubic metres by 2020,[27] its own supply can meet only at best 50% of its demand.[28] In 2007, China's domestic timber supply of 202 million cubic metres had left a consumption gap of over 100 million cubic metres.[29] This gap increased to 150 million cubic metres in 2011, and by 2015, the International Timber Trade Organization (ITTO) reported China's timber consumption gap to have reached over 180 million cubic metres.[30]

To feed its growing demand for timber products, China has resorted to imports, which reached an all-time high in 2016 of close to 290 million cubic metres – a 7% increase from its 2015 imports.[31] China's wood-processing industry's bulk of timber imports include round logs, sawn timber wood chips and pulp for paper manufacturing. At the same time that China is one of the world's largest importers, consumers and exporters of wood-based products, 15% of its imports are estimated to be illegal[32] – making it the world's largest destination for illegally logged timber.[33] The countries through which these illegal timber supplies are secured are known to be 'at high risk for poor governance and corrupt institutions which are associated with high levels of illegal logging and broader land clearing'.[34] China's commendable reforestation effort is thus viewed to have been achieved partly by its export of deforestation – at the expense of other countries.[35]

Whilst China's domestic wood consumption is driven by its construction sector, its industrial demand was fuelled by the export demand, which grew rapidly in the 2000s from the United States, Europe and Japan.[36] Its wood product exports of the highest values were wood furniture, followed by paper, plywood and wood panel.[37] The decrease in China's wood product exports over recent years despite the continued growth in its consumption gap, however, indicates that more of the imported timber is being consumed domestically within China.[38]

Among its timber imports, China has a global dominance of trade on the rosewood species, which are predominantly for domestic consumption, and for which China heavily depends on imports because its demand far exceeds its domestic supply.[39] The surge in demand for rosewood has been a result of the increase in China's wealthy consumers' purchasing power and their tastes for high-end Ming and Qing dynasty reproduction furniture which is made from rosewood, collectively referred to as *hongmu*.[40] Rosewood timber displays a range of brown to reddish-black colourings – and with this quality they are highly prized for decorative purposes and for their use in luxury wood products ranging from furniture, musical instruments, ornaments and veneer.[41]

The growth in the market for replica *hongmu* had driven China's demand for rosewood timber from 66,000 cubic metres in 2005 to 565,000 cubic metres in 2011. – with the most notable six-fold increase over two years, between 2009 and 2011 – equivalent to a value of at least US$700 million.[42] Overall, rosewood prices typically rise 25% per year. The price quoted in 2017 for rosewood sold in China was US$50,000 per cubic metres.[43] However, for certain types of rosewood, such as the locally known *huanghuali*, market prices have increased six-fold to US$190,000 per tonne in a matter of two years. As finished products, the price of high-end individual pieces of rosewood furniture made with exquisite craftsmanship can be as high as US$1 million, whereas a set of furniture made from the most highly prized rosewoods could cost up to US$320,000.[44]

Of the total rosewood imports to China between 2000 and 2009, almost 70% were from the Mekong region. Between 2000 and 2013, rosewood timber imported to China totalled 3.5 million cubic metres – nearly half of which was from the Mekong region[45] – making the Mekong region the largest source of rosewood logs for China – despite its diversified sourcing to African countries in 2013.

With its *hongmu* furniture trading companies increased by 40% in 2010, China's rosewood log imports from the Mekong region partly mirrors the locations of its rosewood furniture industry: Shanghai ports and land borders in Yunnan and Guangxi around the border towns of Ruilii near Myanmar, Fangchenggang near Vietnam and Mohan near Laos, whilst the main entry point is by sea into Guangdong province where Zhongshan is the main centre, manufacturing 60% of China's rosewood furniture production.[46]

### Rosewood supply from the Mekong countries

Rosewood refers to the tree species largely from the *Dalbergia* genus – which provides extremely durable, richly hued brown to reddish-black timbers – highly valued for luxury wood products, particularly high-end furniture targeted for the Chinese market. The important rosewood-producing tree species native to the Mekong region include Siamese rosewood (*Dalbergia cochinchinensis Pierre*) and Burmese rosewood (*Dalbergia bariensis Pierre*). Both rosewood species provide the most valuable wood in the Mekong region's timber trade and have thus been the main target for the region's illegal loggers and timber traders. Of the 33 official rosewood species, Siamese rosewood is the most valuable and most highly threatened.[47] Found in Cambodia, Laos, Thailand and Vietnam, it has been classified as the species endangered and vulnerable to extinction on the Union for Conservation of Nature (IUCN) Red-List of Threatened Species as it is 'critically endangered in Cambodia, vulnerable in Vietnam, a high priority species for conservation in Thailand and Laos'.[48]

In response, the range states put in place their national regulations to prohibit the harvest and trade of rosewood across the region. Yet, illegal rosewood logging persists in connection to the several hundred million dollars' annual worth of its illicit trade. Predominantly destined for China's rosewood market, rosewood trade from the Mekong countries has been facilitated by weak international trade regulations and poor governance within the range states. Raw rosewood prices from the Mekong region have been and continues to be driven by a combination of rising demand, market speculation and growing scarcity.

### Illegal logging and key rosewood species of the Mekong countries

Among the five Mekong countries, Vietnam and Thailand have both heavily exploited their once rich forest resources. The continued development of their domestic timber processing sectors have only been possible through the sourcing

*Figure 7.1* Map of Mekong countries

of raw timber supplies of their neighbouring states – Laos, Cambodia and Myanmar (Figure 7.1) – where rapid deforestation has more recently shifted.[49] However, in the case of Siamese rosewood, Thailand currently has the largest remaining stock, which continues to be highly threatened by well-equipped and armed smugglers of the supply chain destined for the Chinese market.

*Myanmar*, which shares its border with China's Yunnan province, once had an estimated forest cover of 48% of its land area – but recent estimate indicates a reduction to only 24%. China's timber imports from Myanmar since the late 1990s – the majority of which are illegally logged and traded – have been on the rise, from the imported amount of 300,000 cubic metres in 1997 to an estimated 1.6 million cubic metres in 2005. Not surprisingly, Myanmar's forest cover loss of 18% between 1990 and 2005 is considered be one of the world's worst deforestation rates,[50] with the example of illegal timber exports from Kachin state resulting in the area's deforestation at its worst.[51] However, when the environmental and social costs of rampant illegal logging in northern Myanmar was internationally publicized, the governments of China and Myanmar signed an agreement which in effect closed the Yunnan border to timber trade in 2006, causing illegal log imports over the northern Myanmar and Yunnan border to temporarily decline by 70%.[52] But by mid-2012, illegal log exports over the Yunnan border rose again – to an annual volume of almost 500,000 cubic metres.[53] As timber traders from the provincial capital of Yunnan, Kunming, continue to move deeper into Myanmar to secure their timber supplies, at the ongoing depletion rate, it is predicted that Myanmar's northern forests will be exhausted of wood supplies within a decade.[54] At the core of China's wood trade, Myanmar continues to be the source in the Mekong region to provide China with substantial flows of illicit timber.

Two rosewood timber species found in Myanmar are most commonly sourced by Chinese traders: tamalan and paduak. Between 2000 and 2013, rosewood at a total of 624,000 cubic metres – worth US$737 million – was imported from Myanmar to China.[55] Of this total trade volume, almost one-third occurred in 2013 alone. At 237,000 cubic metres worth US$324 million, rosewood imports from Myanmar to China in 2013 rose threefold from that in 2012, in both volume and value.[56] This trend continued into 2014 – making Myanmar the largest rosewood supplier to China worldwide – with the value of rosewood imports from Myanmar into China between January and April already reaching more than 72% of the 2013 total.[57] Despite Myanmar's national log export ban, which came into effect on 1 April 2014, rosewood imports from Myanmar to China reached a value of US$52 million by June of the same year.[58] Based on Myanmar's Ministry of Environmental Conservation and Forest (MOEAF) data – which suggest that Myanmar's forest has a standing stock of approximately 1.2 million cubic tons (1,699,200 cubic metres) tamalan and 1 million cubic tons (1,4416,000 cubic metres) paduak – the Environmental Investigation Agency (EIA) estimates the commercial extinction of the species could be within 3–13 years.[59]

*Cambodia* experienced severe forest degradation resulting from bombing, burning, spraying of herbicides and illegal logging since the late 1960s.[60] As of 1970, its forest cover still accounted for 70% of its total land area.[61] But during 1990–2005, Cambodia lost 19.3% of its total forest cover, and 58% of its primary forest, to commercial logging, agricultural expansion and shifting cultivation for harvesting of charcoal and fuel wood.[62] By 2013, Cambodia's forest cover was reduced to 43% as a result of illegal logging and land conversion for commercial agriculture during 2000–2012.[63] Notably, up to 90% of Cambodia's timber supply for domestic as well as for export are currently obtained through economic land concessions (ELCs), which refers to land clearing activities in large-scale agricultural leases. ELCs are known to often serve as a cover for accessing valuable timber. Once land concession is granted for agricultural purposes, the timber could be clear-cut and sold as part of the process to convert land for agricultural plantations. Revenues generated from the timber obtained from forest clearing in such cases have also served as a source of finance for the agribusiness project receiving the concession.[64] In some cases, ELCs are used to launder timber that has been harvested elsewhere. At an increase of 16.7% from 2011, ELCs leased to private companies as of late 2013 accounted for 73% of Cambodia's arable land.[65] Illicit rosewood trade in Cambodia is also known to occur through illegal logging in protected areas in connection with ELCs.[66] Although this negative publicity ensued, up to 70% of recently allocated ELCs continue to be in protected areas, and illegal logging continues to thrive.[67]

Cambodia's 2002 Forestry Law, the moratorium on logging and the 2013 ban – which prohibits the collection, storage and processing for either domestic use or export of Siamese rosewood known as *Krah Nuong* in Cambodian[68] – have not been able to curb its illicit trade. Currently, mature rosewood trees are rare outside of strictly protected areas, and their populations face severe depletion as a result of forestland conversion, logging and illegal poaching.[69] Beginning in mid-2009, timber imports from Cambodia to China saw a dramatic increase. According to the Cambodian government 2011 statistics, China is the destination for 85% of Cambodian's total timber export, and within this trade volume, the proportion of China's demand for rosewood timber had become increasingly significant.[70] According to Global Witness,[71] over the last decade, rosewood accounted for 20% (110,202 cubic metres) of Cambodia's approximately 541,138 cubic metres logs and sawnwood exported to China. By the first nine months of 2014, the percentage of rosewood in the total log imports from Cambodia to China (54,094 cubic metres) had surged to 97% (52,405 cubic metres). This exceeded the 2005–2013 import average by 901% – and exceeded the 2013 total import by 152%. In 2014, between January and September alone, China's rosewood imports from Cambodia stood at 55,748 cubic metres.[72]

Cambodia is also the third largest timber supplier to Vietnam – with the majority of logs and sawnwood import from Cambodia to Vietnam consisting of rosewood species. Of the total sawnwood import in 2013, rosewood comprised 45% in volume, and 86% in value. By 2015, rosewood comprised 82% of total volume, and 95% in value. The sharp increase in the volume of log and sawnwood imported from Cambodia to Vietnam was largely as a result of Vietnam's 2014 deregulation in the trade of logs and sawnwood from Cambodia – and partly due to Laos's and Myanmar's policy restrictions on the export of timber materials.[73]

The illicit rosewood trade in Cambodia is also known to involve violence related to logging in protected areas and in connection to land concession. Those who seek to expose the trade – environmentalist activists and journalists alike – have been threatened by the collusion of powerful interests, including the police, and some have been killed.[74] Illegal rosewood logging and smuggling along Cambodia's western border with Thailand has been particularly violent. An estimate by Cambodian officials indicates that by 2011, illegal cross-border logging of rosewood from Laos involved up to 70–90% of Cambodian villagers in Siem Pang district, where checkpoints are relatively isolated and formal regulations are weakly implemented.[75]

*Laos*, when compared to any of its neighbouring states – Vietnam, Cambodia and Thailand – has retained more of its forest cover, due partly to its low population of 5.6 million as well as its relatively low economic growth. Nevertheless, Laos has been experiencing continued decline in forest cover – from what accounted for approximately 70% of its land areas during the 1970s to the less than 40% today.[76] Despite having lost close to 300,000 hectares of its forest in 2105,[77] Laos has been particularly targeted as the source country for illegally logged timber.[78] Siamese rosewood is found in the southern and central provinces of Laos, where rosewood logs extracted by farmers are sold by the kilogram along the roadside.[79] As of 2003, Laos's total number of *Dalbergia cochinchinensis* seed trees registered stood at just 46 – all of which were in protected conservation natural forestland.[80]

Despite the 2008 Prime Ministerial Order No-17/PM, which prohibits the harvesting of all domestic *Dalbergia* species, and its reinforcement by the 2011 Prime Minister's Order No 010/PM, by 2012, the natural populations of Siamese rosewood in Laos were confirmed by field surveys to be under severe threat and with no mature trees standing.[81] In Laos, access to logging quotas is usually associated with infrastructure and plantation projects. Commercial contractors for forest cutting are predominantly Chinese companies involved in a host of projects whereby forests are clear-cut to harvest the logs whilst creating an area for dam construction or plantations for rubber and palm oil.[82] Rosewood extracted is often laundered through the quotas for the project site.[83] This is also reflected in the relatively different roles of Vietnam and Thailand in Laos's process of illicit timber trade.

Thai-owned companies are important financiers of logging operations in Laos through rural development and dam projects, such as Nam Theun II, Nam Nguem III and Xe Kaman III, where Thai traders obtain Siamese rosewood from Laos.[84] Vietnam's furniture industry, on the other hand, relies heavily on Laos's log supply transported to Vietnamese ports via Laos's porous border with Vietnam, facilitated by military connections between both sides.[85] Vietnamese and Chinese traders play a significant role in sourcing rosewood from Laos – whereby sourced rosewoods are trucked to Vietnam to be containerized and shipped to China for up to tenfold return.[86] Increasing amounts of Laotian logs sold on the international market have also used Vietnam as a laundering hub.[87] Whilst 80,000 cubic metres of rosewood logs from Laos was exported directly to China in 2011, the bulk of the illegal rosewood timber is controlled by Vietnamese traders and transported across the border to be processed in Vietnam – or mostly to be transported onwards to China.[88] Regardless of the route, more than doubled rosewood imports from Laos made their way to China in 2014.[89] Even after the successive bans on unprocessed timber products from Laos in 2015 (No. 1360) and 2016 (PM Order 15) – rosewood trade continued in 2016. Rosewood accounted for over 90% by value and 60% by volume of Laotian logs imported to China in 2016.[90] In this same year, Laos became China's largest rosewood supplier by value and second largest by volume. On the other hand, rosewood accounted for over 30% of logs and 80% of sawnwood imported from Laos to Vietnam in 2016. With the complicity of government officials, which has been a key factor attributing to Laos's failure to enforce legal controls over the harvest and export of Siamese rosewood in Laos, an unprecedented rate of export growth is expected to continue.[91]

*Vietnam* had lost a significant part of its once rich old-growth forests that covered 43% of its territory[92] as a result of large-scale logging in the 1980s and early 1990s. The shift of government policy in the early 1990s to conserve its remaining forests effectively put in place an 80% logging quota reduction and a log export ban. Through its strenuous efforts to increase its own forest cover, Vietnam was able to achieve almost 3 million hectares of plantation forests which helped increase its forest cover to 12 million hectares in 2005.[93] By 2015, the increase in Vietnam's forest cover reached 14.7 million hectares – equivalent to an increase to 44.6% of Vietnam's total land area as compared to the 1990 forest cover of 9 million hectares.[94] On the other hand, Vietnam continues to rely on the illicit timber from its neighbours, particularly Laos and Cambodia – mainly for its rapidly expanding furniture industry, which grew tenfold since 2000.[95] This heavy reliance on timber imports is likely to continue as the Vietnamese government continues to promote the rapid expansion of an export-oriented wood-processing sector – and the industry looks to sustain its furniture export of which the target is set at US$8 billion for 2017 – an substantial increase from US$7.3 billion in 2016.[96]

According to a survey of Vietnam's five protected areas in 2010, Siamese rosewood was found in low density of 1–10 trees per hectare[97] even though commercial harvesting of Siamese rosewood is prohibited in Vietnam – and individual collection had been further prohibited since 2007.

Despite domestic control on the logging of natural forests, Vietnam has become the main exporter of Siamese rosewood within the Mekong region's flow of rosewood trade to China. This is because the majority of rosewood exports from Vietnam are rarely from Vietnamese forests. Instead, they originate in Laos, Thailand and Cambodia and are transported to Vietnam, where in many cases their origin would be obscured by new documents prepared to misdeclare their species to facilitate their export onward to China.[98] By declaring the rosewood at Chinese customs as Vietnamese, Vietnam assumes the role of a middleman between rosewood-producing countries of the Mekong region and China. The volume of Vietnam's rosewood log export to China in 2011 stood at 123,000 cubic metres, which accounted for almost half of the total Siamese rosewood exports from the Mekong countries.[99]

*Thailand* has a forest cover of about 30%, and its remaining natural forests are now protected.[100] A National Logging Ban imposed in 1989, following the 1988 severe flood, resulted in an 83% reduction of logging in natural forests,[101] and deforestation rate has been decreasing over the past three decades. On the other hand, forest area increased during 2010–2015 as a result of the expansion in timber plantations. Currently, Thailand imports timber to meet over half of its domestic demand, 20% of which is estimated to be illegally sourced.[102] Thai wood traders have sourced valuable hardwood supplies, particularly teak, from Myanmar – and sawn timber from Cambodia and Laos – the majority of which is consumed within the country. Timber supplies for manufacturing wood-based products for export to China, Europe, Japan, and the United States mostly come from domestic plantations.

Illegally logged rosewood bound for China is trafficked from Thailand through Cambodia, Laos and Vietnam. In recent years, illegal logging by the encroachment of Cambodian loggers into Thai territory along the border area has become increasingly violent, as fatal confrontations leading to occasional deaths have been reported. In 2011 alone, 14 Cambodian loggers were reported shot dead by Thai authorities, and dozens more injured.[103]

A 2011 estimate indicates that Thailand currently hosts the world's largest remaining stock of Siamese rosewood, numbering 80,000–100,000 trees – much of which is within the Dong Phayayen-Khao Yai Forest Complex.[104] This number is an alarming reduction from the 2005 estimate of 300,000 trees,[105] considering Thailand had a logging ban in place since the late 1980s[106] and prohibited logging in rosewood-rich conservation and protection forests.[107] However, the World Wide Fund for Nature (WWF) has reported that the Thai government has taken action across the value chain to stop logging – beginning with its commitment in 2015 and 2016 to invest US$1.5 million in ranger training and enforcement so that rangers are currently better equipped to prevent logging.[108] The United Nations Educational, Scientific and Cultural Organization (UNESCO) has reported a 40% decrease in the number of logging cases detected, and a reduction in rosewood seizures from the Dong Phayayen-Khao Yai Forest Complex from approximately 420,000 cubic metres in 2014 to approximately 110,000 cubic metres in 2015.[109] To further protect the timber, Thailand and others made the effort to have CITES parties agree in September 2016 to place all 300 species of rosewood under trade restriction.[110] However, rangers patrolling Thailand's eastern forests bordering Cambodia continue to face loggers who are well equipped and armed. A raid on two warehouses of poached rosewood timber on 25 January 2018 led to the confiscation of 15 tonnes of illegal rosewood logs and planks about to be smuggled out of Thailand to China and the arrest of seven men, two of them Chinese nationals.[111]

## The CITES situation: policies for Siamese rosewood protection

The Siamese rosewood species had been evaluated since 1998 using the Listing Criteria of the Convention on the International Trade in Endangered Species (CITES), by a Netherlands-led evaluation of tree species[112] – and was since found to be a species that Appendix II listings was justified to prevent it from unsustainable trade.[113] But it wasn't until 2008 that Thailand – in an effort to seek protection for the Siamese rosewood species – sought the support of other Mekong states for a CITES listing and formally proposed that rosewood be protected under CITES. Despite the species having been put under the IUCN Red-List of Threatened Species as critically endangered and a high-priority species for conservation, Laos and Cambodia at that time rejected the proposal on grounds that regional timber trade would be negatively affected by a listing. But following the Environmental Investigation Agency's (EIA) call for an urgent CITES listing in early 2012, the Department of Agriculture and the Department of Natural Parks, Wildlife and Conservation on behalf of Thailand – with the eventual co-sponsorship of Vietnam – again proposed an Appendix II listing for Siamese rosewood (*Dalbergia cochinchinensis*) at the 16th Meeting of the Conference of the Parties to CITES: (CITES CoP16) hosted by Thailand in March 2013. This time, with overwhelming support from the 177 member countries of CITES, the proposal was approved by unanimous consensus.

Being listed on Appendix II of CITES means that Siamese rosewood trade would be regulated and controlled subject to the issuance of CITES permits against agreed quota. Source countries of Siamese rosewood – the Mekong countries – are now legally required to export only controlled quantities of the species, which would be closely monitored with documentation. This is expected to ensure that the international trade of Siamese rosewood would not threaten its survival. In this way, trade regulation, monitoring and enforcement mechanisms not regularly available to national governments are thus provided by CITES, as all parties to CITES are now obliged to prohibit and seize the imports of Siamese rosewood which are not accompanied by official CITES permits issued by its country of origin.

But trade in illegally harvested Siamese rosewood persists, despite its listing on Appendix II of CITES since 2013, because Annotation 5 of the listing restricted control to logs, sawn timber and veneers only. Such control restrictions conse-quently exempted some products from CITES certification, permitting and quotas system. This became a loophole for rosewood traders who resorted to obtaining their rosewood supplies in the forms of unregulated, unmonitored semi-finished products. Such exploitation of the Annotation 5 loophole undermined the effec-tiveness of the Appendix II listing by allowing rosewood traders to continue to find supplies in the forms of semi-finished products, which has led to more furni-ture and component trade not regulated by CITES.[114]

In order to help close this loophole and strengthen Appendix II listing, Thai-land proposed the amendment of Annotation 5 to become Annotation 4 at the CITES Conference of the Parties in September 2016. CITES obligations thus now apply not only to raw materials but also to semi- or fully finished products, which include carvings and furniture.[115] It is now a legal obligation that range states issue CITES export permits for such products made with Siamese rosewood.[116]

However, significant risks of illegitimate trade in CITES-listed rosewood spe-cies remain a critical threat – such as the increasing trade of Burmese paduak *(Pterocarpus macrocarpus)* via lookalike replacement species not yet listed on CITES.[117] This involves the misdeclaration of source of species replacement – such that Vietnam has become the main Siamese rosewood exporter to the single market, China – even though the rosewood exported is rarely from Vietnamese forests.[118] Siamese rosewood is instead sourced from Laos and Thailand – where, according to the IUCN Red-List, they are considered a high-priority species for conservation, and from Cambodia where they are considered critically endan-gered.[119] Ongoing illegitimate Siamese rosewood exports by such traders' rounda-bout means reflect the core and structural problems, which continue to undermine the effectiveness of CITES deployment and implementation.[120]

## Discussions: the question of compliance, international institutions and national policies

The current situation on illegal logging and trade of Siamese rosewood offers at least two interesting issues for further discussion. First, international agreements and monitoring frameworks have provided states with the means to manage and mitigate existing problems – but with resulting limitations in their implementation.

International agreements and monitoring frameworks have enabled range states to establish rules – both proscriptive and prescriptive – so as to govern an issue area and provide compliance monitoring mechanisms (such as timber tracking and licensing systems). On the other hand, international agreements and monitoring frameworks have their limitations in that institutional operation mechanisms alone cannot successfully function if they lack the necessary allies to take ownership of the issue and compel compliance with international stipulations. Even more so, in cases of prohibitions and stipulations where it is not the state that is directly required to comply, but rather where the state is relied on to follow through and issue measures to alter people's incentives, operational success becomes even more difficult. Altering incentives may involve measures to shift consumers' demand from rosewood to other types of timber or raw material, or providing disincentives by prosecuting those who do not comply with rules and regulations. These tasks are more difficult in cases wherein the state may have no incentive, no capacity – or in fact, no mechanism in hand to carry them out – such as generating the disincentives to change people's taste or preference from rosewood.

Whilst the WWF report on halting the illegal trade of CITES species from World Heritage sites suggests greater action must be taken to curb demand through 'education, enforcement, prosecution, and legislative action',[121] the demand-driven nature – particularly by a single largest market, which thrives on its vicious rarity cycle – remains to be a major challenge for effective elimination of the illegal Siamese rosewood trade. Efforts to quantify illegal logging and its related timber trade point out that the key target of illegal logging and related timber trade is the 'highly valuable timber – often rare and endangered species that are protected under harvest and/or trade regulations'.[122] In cases like Siamese rosewood species, its rarity could drive its price up above its marginal costs, and therefore potentially lead to its depletion because the 'vicious cycle among value, rarity (scarcity) and illegality' would likely occur as a result of its related illicit activities.[123]

Given this vicious cycle, even if China is pressured to undertake progressive demand-side policies to tackle its rapidly growing illegal timber consumption, it would take much more efforts to include Siamese rosewood as the target species. In fact, current laws regulating rosewood trade within China mainly encourages the consumption of real rosewood by listing 33 species regarded as legitimate *hongmu* to protect domestic consumers from purchasing fake rosewoods.[124] Over one-third of the 33 listed species are designated as either endangered or vulnerable – and whilst many are protected species in range states, Siamese rosewood is the most valuable and most threatened.[125] Moreover, the main absorber of illegal rosewood timber imported into China is now its own domestic consumer market, which is growing at a startling rate,[126] and where the value of Siamese rosewood has been driven up even further as it is now considered a safe and lucrative investment for future price speculation.

The second issue for further discussion involves the bifurcated provisions of CITES: on the one hand, to reduce demand and eliminate illegal logging and production whilst considering the policy preferences of the demand-side state, looking towards expanding investments into the Mekong countries on all fronts. Here, the question is whether the state has the capacity to change people's incentives or taste. On the other hand, range states of the supply side are in need of investment capital. Here CITES provisions must deal with issues of whether they have the capacity to handle and eliminate illegal logging – or whilst they may, whether their concerns could be different. Range states may be less concerned with the harvesting of rosewood than with the rosewood being illegally transported across the border, or than with the subrogation of logging concessions, which could cause the state to lose its fees or royalties. In some cases, the state may not be concerned about – and even support – smuggling occurring in neighbouring countries.

The listing of Siamese rosewood in Appendix II of CITES since 2013 has been an effort from the supply side, on the part of the producer countries. But just as the ongoing illicit trade of CITES-listed rosewood species persisted despite such international protection efforts, the WWF report contends that 'the current approach to preventing illegal harvesting of CITES listed species in the World Heritage sites is not working'.[127] Here, the question of compliance and how international institutions influence states to comply is a crucial issue.

To explain why countries would comply with international agreements, such as the listing of Siamese rosewood on CITES Appendix II, and how international institutions such as CITES influence national compliance – or more specifically, how they influence sovereign behaviour – Dai offers a theoretical framework by her study on international institutions and national policies to argue that international institutions can influence national policies through alternative mechanisms, which involves non-state actors and domestic mechanisms.[128] In this regard, a number of indirect channels of influence and key components comprise *monitoring arrangements, compliance mechanisms* and the *power of weak international institutions*.[129] Based on these key components, a number of explanations may apply to the situation of CITES listed Siamese rosewood trade among the Mekong countries.

In terms of *monitoring arrangements*, international institutions can influence national policies by employing victims of noncompliance whilst empowering domestic pro-compliance constituencies to monitor and enforce national compliance. However, within the Mekong countries where the issue of Siamese rosewood trade is a low priority relative to other more urgent political agendas, the victims of noncompliance remain those already most marginalized populations who may be victimized by noncompliance but have no political leverage over the government. The possibility for interest alignment between victims of noncompliance and the state is further weakened by the transboundary value chain and criminality inherent in the rosewood trade. Not only does it undermine the state's efforts in monitoring compliance, it also perpetuates the involvement of government officials in corruption and violence. Combating the illicit rosewood trade thus becomes an issue requiring the use of force, which is beyond the capacity of any regular victims of noncompliance or pro-compliance constituencies to participate in. On the other hand, domestic pro-compliance constituencies within the Mekong region have been limited to the circle of those within the government agency tasked with the responsibility to represent the government as member countries of CITES.

The argument for *compliance mechanisms* and the *power of weak international institutions* involves the political leverage and monitoring ability of domestic constituencies and how weak international institutions can affect national compliance by empowering domestic constituencies to increase their political leverage through improving their informational status in specific ways.[130] This is believed to help change the strategic environment that governments face domestically.[131] Among the Mekong countries, ineffective national regulations have provided the breeding grounds for criminal networks of illicit rosewood trade. This makes it highly complicated for international institutions to change the strategic environment that governments of the Mekong countries face domestically. However, the role of international NGOs such as the Environmental Investigation Agency (EIA) have been critical in bringing to light the need to ensure that the international trade of Siamese rosewood does not threaten its survival. It was EIA's informational provision that prompted Thailand to propose the listing of Siamese rosewood on CITES Appendix II in 2013 – and EIA's continued uncovering of noncompliance among the range states that has led to the successful amendment of the trade annotation on the CITES listing for Siamese rosewood in 2016.

Given the existing Siamese rosewood trafficking value chain,[132] the limitations of the current approach to preventing illegal harvesting of CITES listed species lie in the lack of coordinated responses. Determining that enhanced action is needed to cut off supply from the value chain dominated by a distribution network of organized criminal groups across national boundaries,[133] WWF contends that 'coordinated action across the value chain between source, transit and consumer countries'[134] is necessary. A needed approach would be one in which together with international organizations, non-state actors/civil society play an important role in supporting states in renewed commitment and coordinated action to enhance protection and monitoring.[135] Such a coordinated approach would 'engage local communities . . . to increase ownership and make local people positive agents of change'.[136] An example along this line is WWF's call for increased collaboration between CITES and the World Heritage Foundation, so as to bridge their separate focus in the current wildlife trafficking value chain and make coordinated response possible.[137]

## Conclusion

Native to the Mekong countries, Siamese rosewood is a highly valuable timber species severely affected by illegal logging and trade. Just as there are concerns that the fate of much of the world's natural forests is in China's hands,[138] the likelihood that the rosewood species will be stripped and driven to extinction by the persistence of the illicit rosewood trade remains 'at the mercy of China's burgeoning domestic demand',[139] underpinned by a rapidly growing market and consumer purchasing power for much culturally valued rosewood reproduction furniture. This situation has, on the other hand, prompted and heightened the sense of scarcity, which in turn, drives demand to further spike as speculators turn to stockpile rosewood in anticipation of much higher prices in the future.[140] The vicious cycle among value, rarity (scarcity) and illegality[141] characterizes the illicit Siamese rosewood timber trade of the Mekong countries. But now that the rosewood stocks of the Mekong countries are near depletion, China has expanded its supply chain to West Africa and Central America with targets on half the world's countries across five continents for the relocation of its trading networks.[142]

National laws enforced by each Mekong country to ban the illegal harvest and trade of rosewood have failed to overcome the complex patronage dealings which perpetuates the illicit activities associated with its trade. The willingness among the Mekong countries to exploit its neighbours' forest resources through illegal or inadequately regulated investment has inadvertently strengthened the organized crime networks of traders and criminality inherent in the rosewood trade.

The 2013 listing of the Siamese rosewood species on CITES Appendix II reflects the range states' intent to seek support from the international agreement between governments so as to protect its rosewood stocks through legal export quantity control with close monitoring and documentation. However, the implementation of CITES faces a number of challenges. Despite amendment of the listing's Annotation 5 to Annotation 4 to close the loophole in Siamese rosewood trade, challenges remain on issues of replacement species as well as noncompliance. Critics contend that range states' violations of CITES rules and obligations could undermine CITES protection, and the relentless, ongoing illicit trade of Siamese rosewood timber is a clear indication that the current approach to preventing illegal harvesting of CITES listed species has not been effective.

A theoretical framework on international institutions and national policies offers the argument that international institutions such as CITES can influence national compliance through alternative mechanisms – referring to non-state actors and domestic mechanisms. Non-state actors are also key to WWF's coordinated approach, which perceives civil society as positive agents of change. Under this approach, states should be supported by civil society and international organizations to curb demand through education, enforcement, prosecution and legislative action. On the other hand, coordinated action across the trafficking value chain is also necessary to cut off supply.

## Notes

1  J. Saunders, *CITES Conference Marks Major Breakthrough in Battle Against Endangered Rosewood Trade*. Chatham House, 20 October 2016 (London: Chatham House, 2018), https://www.chathamhouse.org/expert/comment/cites-conference-marks-major-breakthrough-battle-against-endangered-rosewood-trade (Accessed on 31 August 2018).

2  EIA, *Appetite for Destruction: China's Trade in Illegal Timber* (London: EIA, 2012a), p. 22; and EIA, *Rosewood Robbery: The Case for Thailand to List Rosewood on CITES* (London: EIA, 2012c), p. 2. The term 'rosewood' refers to a wide variety of richly hued, extremely durable and increasingly rare timbers harvested from an array of tree species worldwide, largely from the *Dalbergia* genus.

3  CITES, "Consideration of proposals for amendment of Appendices I and II", *Sixteenth Meeting of the Conference of the Parties*. Bangkok Thailand, March 3–14, 2013.

4  N.B. Treanor, *China's Hongmu Consumption Boom* (Washington, DC: Forest Trends), p. V.

Profits downstream, unsustainability upstream 137

5 P.X. To, N.B. Treanor, and K. Canby, *Impacts of the Laos Log and Sawnwood Export Bans: Significant Reductions in the Exports to Major Markets of Vietnam and China in 2016*. Forest Trends Report Series: Forest Policy, Trade, and Finance, April 2017 (Washington, DC: Forest Trends), p. 11; and N.B. Treanor, *China's Hongmu Consumption Boom: Analysis of the Chinese Rosewood Trade and Links to Illegal Activity in Tropical Forested Countries*. Forest Trends Report Series: Forest Trade and Finance, December 2015 (Washington, DC: Forest Trends), p. 12.
6 K. Barney, "China and the Mekong region: Beyond the territorial trap", *New Mandala*, 4 March 2011, http://www.newmandala.org/china-and-the-mekong-region-beyond-the-territorial-trap/ (Accessed on 31 August 2018).
7 Ibid.
8 EIA, *Routes of Extinction: The Corruption and Violence Destroying Siamese Rosewood in the Mekong* (London: EIA, 2014), p. 22.
9 EIA, *Cycles of Destruction: Unsustainability, Illegality, and Violence in the Hongmu Trade* (London: EIA, 2016), p. 1.
10 Treanor, *China's Hongmu Consumption Boom*, p. VI.
11 Ibid.
12 A. Hoare, *Tackling Illegal Logging and the Related Trade: What Progress and Where Next?* Chatham House Report, July 2015 (London: Chatham House), p. VIII.
13 EIA, *Routes of Extinction*, p. 22.
14 Ibid, p. 23.
15 EIA, *Borderlines: Vietnam's Booming Furniture Industry and Timber Smuggling in the Mekong Region* (London: EIA, 2008), p. 2.
16 L.H. Gulbrandsen and D. Humphrey, *International Initiatives to Address Tropical Timber Logging and Trade*. A report for the Norwegian Ministry of the Environment: FNI Report 4/2006 (Lysaker: The Fridtjof Nansen Institute, 2006), p. 3.
17 R.P. Cronin, *The Environment and Development: Greater Mekong Subregion Dynamics Considered* (Washington, DC: National Defense University Press, 2011), p. 179.
18 EIA, *Borderlines*, p. 3.
19 Ibid.
20 Ibid. Timber continues to be transported from Cambodia by truck to Thailand at the same time that illegal logging in Thailand continues to occur in national parks, and in some cases are transported to Laos to disguise their origin before they are imported back to Thailand.
21 EIA, *Borderlines*, p. 3.
22 FAO, *Global Forest Resources Assessment 2015: How Are the World's Forests Changing?* 2nd ed. (Rome: Food and Agriculture Organization of the United Nations (FAO), 2015), p. 17.
23 European Timber Trade Federation, *Gateway to International Timber Trade: China*, Industry Profile, 28 June 2016.
24 L. Wellesley, *Trade in Illegal Timber: The Response in China, a Chatham House Assessment* (Research Paper, December 2014): 4.
25 European Timber Trade Federation, *Gateway to International Timber Trade: China*, www.timbertradeportal.com/countries/china
26 H. Yang, "China's Natural Protection Program: Progress and impacts", *The Forestry Chronicle*, 93(2) (2017): 113–117.
27 Xiufang and Canby, *Baseline Study 1, China: Overview of Forest Governance, Markets and Trade* (Washington, DC: Forest Trend for FLEGT, EFI, 2011), p. 5.
28 Xiufang and Canby, *Baseline Study 1*, p. 14.
29 *China Wood Monthly*, October 2010, quoted in Xiufang and Canby, *Baseline Study 1*.
30 The Timber Trade Portal, *Gateway to International Timber Trade: China Industry Profile* (updated 17 July 2018), http://www.timbertradeportal.com/countries/china (Accessed on 31 August 2018).

31 Forest Trends, *China's Forest Product Imports and Exports 2006–2016: Trade Charts and Brief Analysis* (Washington, DC: Forest Trends, July 2017), p. 1.
32 Chatham House, *Illegal Logging Portal: China*, www.illegal-logging.info/regions/china (Accessed on 28 October 2017).
33 EIA, *Appetite for Destruction*, p. 1. Source countries from which illicit timber enters China's wood processing sector include Russia, Indonesia, Laos, Myanmar, Mozambique and Madagasgar.
34 Forest Trends, *China's Forest Product Imports and Exports 2006-2016*, p. 1.
35 EIA, *Appetite for Destruction*, p. 1. Source countries from which illicit timber enters China's wood processing sector include Russia, Indonesia, Laos, Myanmar, Mozambique and Madagasgar.
36 Forest Trends, *China's Forest Product Imports and Exports 2006–2016: Trade Charts and Brief Analysis* (Washington, DC: Forest Trends, July 2017), p. 1.
37 EIA, *Appetite for Destruction: China's Trade in Illegal Timber* (London: Environmental Investigation Agency (EIA), 2012a), p. 5. The export values of China's wood products are wood furniture (US$15 billion requiring 19 million cubic metres of raw wood), followed by paper (US$9.57 billion requiring 23 million cubic metres of raw wood), plywood and wood panel (US$3.26 requiring 16.5 million cubic metres of raw wood material).
38 Forest Trends, *China's Forest Product Imports and Exports 2006–2016: Trade Charts and Brief Analysis* (Washington, DC: Forest Trends, July 2017), p. 1.
39 EIA, *Routes of Extinction*, p. 2.
40 EIA, *Appetite for Destruction*, p. 22. By definition, *hongmu* is derived from rare trees with unique qualities – as reproduction furniture, imitating ornate designs from Qing and Ming dynasties. Replica *hongmu* are constructed using dense, rich hued species, which accord with cultural tradition.
41 EIA, *Rosewood Robbery*, p. 2.
42 EIA, *Appetite for Destruction*, p. 22.
43 Dalberg, *Halting the Illegal Trade of CITES Species from World Heritage Sites: Not for Sale* (WWF Report, 2017), p. 31.
44 EIA, *Appetite for Destruction*, p. 23.
45 EIA, *Routes of Extinction*, p. 2.
46 EIA, *Appetite for Destruction*, p. 22.
47 EIA, *Routes of Extinction*, p. 3.
48 EIA, *Rosewood Robbery*, p. 2.
49 Cronin, *The Environment*, p. 178.
50 EIA, *Appetite for Destruction*, p. 12.
51 Global Witness, *A Disharmonious Trade: China and the Continued Destruction of Burma's Northern Frontier Forests* (London: Global Witness, 2009), p. 4.
52 EIA, *Appetite for Destruction*, p. 12. Instead, all timber exports deemed legal by Myanmar were to be shipped from Rangoon port under the auspices of the state-run Myanmar Timber Enterprise.
53 Ibid.
54 Ibid.
55 EIA, *Myanmar's Rosewood Crisis: Why Key Species and Forests Must Be Protected Through CITES* (London: Environmental Investigation Agency (EIA), June 2014), p. 3.
56 Ibid.
57 Ibid.
58 Ibid.
59 Ibid, p. 4.
60 Cronin, *The Environment*, p. 178.
61 Global Witness, *The Cost of Luxury: Cambodia's Illegal Trade in Precious Wood with China*, February 2015 (London: Global Witness, 2014), p. 6.
62 Cronin, *The Environment*, p. 178.
63 Global Witness, *The Cost of Luxury*, p. 6.

64  Ibid, p. 10.
65  Ibid, p. 9.
66  Ibid, p. 8.
67  Ibid, p. 9.
68  Ibid, p. 8.
69  EIA, *Routes of Extinction*, p. 3.
70  Global Witness, *The Cost of Luxury*, p. 22.
71  Ibid.
72  Ibid.
73  Forest Trends, *Vietnam's Imports of Cambodian Logs and Sawnwood from Natural Forests: 2013–2015*. Forest Trends Report Series: Forest Policy, Trade, and Finance, November 2016 (Washington, DC: Forest Trends), p. 15.
74  EIA, *Appetite for Destruction*, p. 24.
75  S. Singh, *The Socio-Economic Context of Illegal Logging and Trade of Rosewood Along the Cambodian-Lao Border* (Washington, DC: Forest Trends, 2013), p. 3.
76  EIA, *Borderlines*, p. 4.
77  Forest Trends, *In Laos, Log and Sawnwood Export Ban Implementation Appears Successful* (Washington, DC: Forest Trends, 26 April 2017), p. 2, https://www.forest-trends.org/wp-content/uploads/2017/04/doc_5546.pdf (Accessed on 5 September 2018)..
78  EIA, *Borderlines*, p. 2.
79  EIA, *Appetite for Destruction*, p. 24.
80  EIA, *Red Alert: How Fraudulent Siamese Rosewood Exports from Laos and Cambodia Are Undermining CITES Protection* (London: Environmental Investigation Agency (EIA), June 2016), p. 3.
81  EIA, *Routes of Extinction*, p. 3.
82  R.P. Cronin, "The security dimension of Transboundary natural resources management in Southeast Asia", in A. Pandya and E. Laipson, eds., *Transnational Trends: Middle Eastern and Asian Views* (Washington, DC: The Henry L. Stimson Center, 2008), pp. 228–247.
83  EIA, *Routes of Extinction*, p. 5.
84  EIA, *Borderlines*, p. 3.
85  Ibid, pp. 10–11.
86  EIA, *Routes of Extinction*, p. 5.
87  EIA, *Checkpoints: How Powerful Interest Groups Continue to Undermine Forest Governance in Laos* (London: EIA, 2012b), p. 2.
88  EIA, *Appetite for Destruction*, p. 24; and EIA, *Routes of Extinction*, p. 6.
89  Treanor, *China's Hongmu Consumption Boom*, p. 6.
90  P.X. To, N.B. Treanor, and K. Canby, *Impacts of the Laos Log and Sawnwood Export Bans*, p. 2.
91  EIA, *Routes of Extinction*, p. 5.
92  EIA, *Borderlines*, p. 6.
93  Ibid.
94  EIA, *Routes of Extinction*, p. 3.
95  EIA, *Borderlines*, p. 6.
96  EIA, *Repeat Offender: Vietnam's Persistent Trade in Illegal Timber* (London: Environmental Investigation Agency (EIA), May 2017), p. 3.
97  EIA, *Routes of Extinction*, p. 3.
98  Ibid, p. 6.
99  EIA, *Appetite for Destruction*, p. 24.
100  Chatham House, *Illegal Logging Portal: Thailand*, www.illegal-logging.info/regions/thailand
101  Cronin, *The Environment*, p. 178.
102  Chatham House, *Illegal Logging Portal: Thailand*.
103  EIA, *Rosewood Robbery*, p. 1.
104  Dalberg, *Halting the Illegal Trade of CITES Species*, p. 31.

105  EIA, *Appetite for Destruction*, p. 23.
106  EIA, *Rosewood Robbery*, p. 2.
107  EIA, *Appetite for Destruction*, p. 23.
108  Dalberg, *Halting the Illegal Trade of CITES Species*, p. 32.
109  UNESCO, *Thailand's National Report on State of Conservation: Dong Phayayen – Khao Yai Forest Complex*, 2016, http://whc.unesco.org/en/soc/3467
110  Dalberg, *Halting the Illegal Trade of CITES Species*, p. 32.
111  S. Chayutworskan, "Smugglers busted sending tonnes of rosewood to China", *Bangkok Post*, 25 January 2018.
112  EIA, *Rosewood Robbery*, p. 3.
113  Ibid, p. 9.
114  EIA, "Addressing ASEAN's regional rosewood crisis: An urgent call to action", *A Briefing for the 11th Meeting of the Association of South-East Asian Nations (ASEAN) Experts Group of CITES (CITES AEG)*. Brunei, May 5–8, 2015, p. 2.
115  EIA, *Prohibited Permits: Ongoing Illegitimate & Illegal Trade of CITES-listed Rosewoods in Asia* (London: Environmental Investigation Agency (EIA), March 2017), p. 2.
116  EIA, "Addressing ASEAN's regional rosewood crisis", p. 2.
117  EIA, *Prohibited Permits*, p. 1.
118  EIA, *Appetite for Destruction*, p. 24.
119  EIA, *Rosewood Robbery*, p. 2.
120  EIA, *Prohibited Permits*, p. 1.
121  Dalberg, *Halting the Illegal Trade of CITES Species*, p. 29.
122  J. Gan, "Quantifying illegal logging and related timber trade", *Illegal Logging and Related Timber Trade – Dimensions, Drivers, Impacts and Responses* (A Global Scientific Rapid Assessment Report, International Union of Forest Research Organizations (IUFRO) World Services, 35 (2016): 38.
123  Ibid., p. 38.
124  EIA, *Appetite for Destruction*, p. 22.
125  EIA, *Routes of Extinction*, p. 3.
126  EIA, *Appetite for Destruction*, p. 6.
127  Dalberg, *Halting the Illegal Trade of CITES Species*, p. 29.
128  X. Dai, *International Institutions and National Policies* (Cambridge: Cambridge University Press, 2007), p. 3.
129  Ibid.
130  Ibid, p. 4.
131  Ibid.
132  Dalberg, *Halting the Illegal Trade of CITES Species*, p. 29. The Siamese rosewood trafficking value chain involves 'the harvesting of species in source countries, the transportation of these goods through intermediate collation or processing destinations, and the sale of goods in consumer markets'.
133  Ibid.
134  Ibid, p. 30.
135  Ibid, p. 29.
136  Ibid, p. 30.
137  Ibid, p. 29.
138  EIA, *Appetite for Destruction*, p. 27.
139  Ibid, p. 24.
140  Ibid, p. 23.
141  Gan, "Quantifying illegal logging and related timber trade", p. 38.
142  EIA, *Cycles of Destruction*, p. 3.

# 8 Shadow banking and cross-border capital flows in China

## A macro-micro survey

*Victor Teo*

## Shadowing economy and underground banking: an introduction

Given the state, size and the development of China's economy, there is much discussion of how huge the shadow economy is. Mainland officials have acknowledged that the underground economy could be larger than the 10–20% of China's gross domestic product (GDP) that most economists assume it is. The U.S. Treasury estimates that China's underground economy is approximately 50% of size of China's legitimate economy.[1] Measuring this is a particularly onerous task, given that even the Chinese government cannot comprehend the figures of China's annual GDP growth – as the figures are often thought to be made up.[2] Premier Li Keqiang was quoted as a provincial governor that China's GDP numbers were "manmade" and therefore unreliable.[3] Given the size, nature and clout of China's shadow economy, it is vital that we understand how this might pertain to the illicit industries discussed in this volume and how this shadow banking system that services the shadow economy potentially affects the health of the overall economy, not just in China but also in relation to the global economy.

It is important to understand that both legitimate businesses and individuals as well as those who cannot conduct businesses with legitimate banks often turn to the shadow banks to answer their needs, out of either convenience, necessity or habit. Particularly in the case of illicit entrepreneurs, corrupt officials and troubled enterprises, shadow banking in China often offers the only lifeline to sustain their businesses. Both legitimate businessmen and illicit entrepreneurs also rely on shadow bankers to move huge sums across borders with ease. Torn between the need to enhance governance, improve business efficiency and protect state-owned banks and enterprises, the Chinese government views the shadow banking industry with both trepidation and anxiety. Consequently, the nature of shadow banking today is one of the most discussed topics in Chinese political narratives and mainstream media. Consequently, the rigorous study of this illicit industry is more important than ever.

This chapter discusses the illicit industry of shadow banking in the People's Republic of China (PRC) using a two-pronged strategy. The chapter first offers a macro survey of the shadow banking industry. Like all other "shadow" industries, everyone in and outside China acknowledge it exists, but no one can define its exact nature. There is a tremendous amount of difficulty in trying to understand the mechanics of the industry because of the varying number of actors. We see legitimate financial institutions undertaking unregulated (and often perceived as illegitimate) activities. There are also "middlemen" operations or regulators which are creations of the main banks themselves engaging in activities that the main banks would not do, and of course we have the genuine run-off-the-mill illegal bankers operating without licenses conducting the ordinary businesses of banks. In the latter category, there are operations that often operate honestly as legitimate banks – albeit at higher costs to ordinary folks who might on paper not be vetted as suitable clients as are the banks' normal clientele. Then there are those unsavoury characters and business operations which are often illegitimate, if not outright illegal. Through a chronological survey, this section hopes to make sense of how this industry developed and the varied nature of the activities it encompasses, even though as the section mostly tracks the shadow banking activities of direct loans and wealth management products. Throughout, the chapter will be extremely mindful of which entities and what activities are being discussed. It cannot be overemphasized that new forms of underground banking practices come to light every so often, and this section will try to capture the complexity of the industry without becoming overly technical. Data from interview fieldwork from Zhejiang and Guangdong provinces, as well as analysis of cases resulting in conviction, will help supplement the evidence in this section.

In order to obtain a better idea of how particular aspects of how the shadow banking works, the second part of the chapter will "zoom in" to focus on a "micro-activity" of the industry: that of the shadow remittance agents in southern China. These shadow bankers perform an extremely important banking function: acting as currency exchange agents as a front whilst quietly providing remittance services. Using fieldwork data collected from interviews in Guangdong province, this section discusses how these agents facilitate illicit capital flows in and out of China. The picture given is by no means complete, as most of the people the author spoke to insist on anonymity due to possible criminal and legal repercussions, as well as their desire to protect their business operations. The chapter concludes with a discussion of the macro-micro linkages and governance issues related to the illicit banking industry in China.

## Overview of shadow banking in the PRC:
## a macro-chronological survey

There are various estimates of how big the shadow banking industry is. *Caijing* magazine estimates that the shadow banking system accounts for ¥15–17 trillion, about 12–13% of formal banking assets and one-third of China's GDP.[4] IHS Global Insight estimates that there is as much as ¥1.3 trillion in private financing, an amount equivalent to the U.S. budget deficit in 2011. The Bank of

America estimates the shadow banking system to be worth ¥14.5 trillion ($2.2 trillion), and loans in the shadow sector are estimated to be 25% of all loans made in China by traditional banking sector.[5] UBS AG estimates that the shadow bankers constitute more than a quarter of the country's estimated US$3.35 trillion in non-bank lending, or about 45% of the country's GDP.[6] Moody estimates that the volume of shadow banking has increased 67%, reaching US$4.7 trillion by the end of 2012, a staggering 55% of China's GDP.[7] By 2014, Moody Investment Services estimates China's shadow banking transactions to be equal to 65% of the nation's GDP. JP Morgan estimates it to be as large as ¥36 trillion – that is, about 69% of China's gross GDP – in 2012.[8] In the same year, JP Morgan revised its estimate that the shadow banking industry is worth ¥46 trillion (some US$7.5 trillion), about 80.9% of the 2013 GDP. The Brookings Institution has compiled a summary that entailed the estimates of various institutions as follows: The International Monetary Fund (IMF) estimates that the shadow banking industry accounted for 35% of PRC's GDP in March 2014 worth ¥19.9 trillion (US$3.3 trillion); the Chinese Academy of Social Sciences (CASS) estimated in 2012 that shadow banking is worth ¥16.9 trillion (US$3 trillion US), 36% of the 2012 GDP; China International Capital Corporation (CIAC) estimated in April 2013 that the shadow banking industry is worth ¥27 trillion (US$4.4 trillion), 52% of 2012 GDP; and Standard & Poor's estimated in April 2013 that for 2012, shadow banking is worth ¥22.9 trillion (US$3.7 trillion), 44.4% of 2012 GDP.

What is certain here is that the estimates of this underground banking industry all appear disturbingly huge to most analysts, and no one has an exact idea of how much money is involved – or even the range of activities involved. The second thing we are sure of is that the institutions involved in these calculations are making them on a best-effort basis, based on their estimates of the various activities they include as shadow banking. The narrower their definition (e.g. taking into account only, say, loan and trust companies and leaving out wealth management products and pawnshops, for instance), the smaller their estimates would likely be. Third, it would be difficult to imagine that reliable data can be gathered for the thousands of micro curb-side lenders, remittance agents, peer-to-peer (P2P) lenders for the estimates. In fact, many of these shadow banking activities are only exposed after the fact – either through the failings of the shadow bankers or marketed products to make good on their promises, or the organizations and actors involved are brought down by the law. Beyond the normal run-of-the-mill finance companies that exist outside the banking services, there are also nefarious and criminal elements engaged in these services (e.g. loansharking that could be considered shadow banking), and that is something that appears not to be taken into consideration by many analyses. The data thus offered for macro analysis are therefore estimates at best, and further begs the question as to the exact size and nature of the industry.

To understand how the illicit banking industry came into existence and how it works today, an appreciation of the development of China's banking industry is required. With the institutionalization of the Four Modernizations[9] and economic reforms by Deng Xiaoping in 1978, the Chinese government realized that the antiquated banking system needed to be modernized to complement the rapidly growing economy.[10] Despite the development throughout the 1990s, China's banking sector was still relatively antiquated and detached from the global financial institutions and markets[11] – a consequence of both historical development and policy control by the central government. The Chinese Communist Party (CCP) deemed it important to maintain a tight grip over the nascent banking sector – a cautious attitude born out of a unspoken recognition that neither the regime or the state officials had a complete handle on how the modern financial system worked.[12] The CCP has had three relatively consistent goals: (i) to ensure that foreign investment and capital does not leave the country easily; (ii) to buffer the economy from the vagaries of international financial crises and speculative attacks, including large financial flows; and (iii) to protect and enhance the financial security of the country.

As China began to open up and reform its economy, its banking system was still antiquated. The inability of the banking industry to open up and adopt international practices in terms of management and day-to-day operations hampered the development of the banking industry overall. For the most part of its postwar history, the banking system in the PRC has been relatively antiquated, ill-suited to complement the fast building economy that was growing in the PRC. As banking operations grew, there have been some serious concerns in a few areas. First, the technical skills and practices within the banks, as well as the oversight mechanisms, were relatively weak and out of line with international practices. Second, as many of these banks are state-owned, they often are inefficient just as they are ineffective. Third, by the 1990s, they often operated with the aim of servicing the inefficient state-owned enterprises.

For a large part of the earlier decades since Chinese embarked on reforms, Chinese shadow banking has been seen to be associated with directed lending, i.e. most of the "underground banking" transactions are in fact straightforward lending operations.[13] By the 1990s, due to the influx of huge amounts of direct foreign investment, cheap capital became abundant, and consequently loans were made easily available. These banks provided very low interest rates for depositors. The mandatory ceiling on deposit rates deprives savers of the market return on their money was around ¥1.16 trillion in 2011, about 2.6% of GDP.[14] The banks, being government-owned, were therefore perceived as a conduit by which government channels subsidies to state-owned enterprises (SOEs) in the form of cheap loans.[15] This incestuous relationship keeps the inefficient state-owned enterprises alive, and private companies have a hard time competing against them.

Correspondingly, a large number of banks began to extend loans to individuals and entities that they were not supposed to – either through the circumvention of regulations or through third party intermediaries. For instance, Xinhua News Agency has reported that Yao, a banker from Longyan in coastal Fujian, approved more than 3,000 loans totalling ¥220 million (about US$26.6 million) in his

18-year career.[16] There are many cases reported in the Chinese press of small shadow banking outfits that run out of apartments and shops that were just lending operations. One Hong Kong businessman who ran a factory in Guangdong said that when he visited one of these banks, he saw that the whole room was stacked with cash.[17] It was estimated in 2007 that one-third of these illegal banks originate in Guangdong, and police shut down more than 40 of these operations in the provinces of Fujian, Jiangxi and Guangdong, involving ¥100 million.[18] Many of these firms either were run directly by gangs or had criminal affiliations – it is not unimaginable since even legitimate banks often rely on "collection agencies" (usually made up of gangs) to enforce the collection of loans. The author's fieldwork in Guangdong and Zhejiang suggested that it would not be practical if these credit companies did not have the ability to chase down and intimidate errant borrowers.

The proliferation of these unregulated actors making loans is, of course, accompanied by an increase in problematic borrowers. Over the years, as the inefficient SOEs have accumulated more debt than they can service, an increasing number of these companies were unable to service the loans. The availability of cheap capital meant that over the last two decades or so, or at least until 2009, the banking sector has been plagued by bad debt – loans that are being dispensed with no hope of ever being recovered.[19] By March 2013, the bad debt of China's commercial banks has reached ¥524.3 billion (US$84.8 billion). Shang Fulin, then China Securities Regulatory Commission chief, said in 2013 that bad debt and hidden risks would multiply as the Chinese economy slows down.[20] The range of borrowers range from genuine enterprises striving to survive, to corrupt officials borrowing to run private projects in schemes[21] that they were handling for local governments, to individuals borrowing to run huge Ponzi schemes. Everyone who had access to cheap credit was using it, and often this was at the expense of the central and State government functions. This view is not uniform, as there are others who maintained that shadow banking products are not toxic or fearsome, and need not necessary be regulated out of existence. These analysts argue that placed in the global context, Chinese shadow banking has not reached epic proportions, and appears small since China is a net lender to the world, with little distribution of shadow banking assets beyond its shores, so the shadow banking sector has no direct systemic influence.[22] In their view, the risk the industry poses is manageable as long as a safety net is put in place along with an exit mechanism for failed institutions and contagion from Non-performing loans are pre-empted.[23]

Despite the central bank's intervention, regulations are, of course, routinely ignored. By 2009, urged to reform and improve their performance, and also growing increasingly aware of their own mortality, banks began to develop different strategies to cope. Chinese banks began to routinely extend or restructure loans to borrowers, or sell them onwards to third parties, rather than admit that they have a problem on their books. This tactic is hardly new, and is widespread in the West, with one consequence being the U.S. subprime financial crisis. In the PRC, there was a culture of "rolling things over" when they become due, and in doing this, the bank renewed the debt or pushed the deadline of loans. In this respect, the shadow banking system can renew or push out the repayment system and provide temporary credit to facilitate rollovers or provide temporary credit to facilitate interest payments.[24]

Thus, we have a new situation as an immeasurable number of banks and financial institutions became involved in the creation and selling of wealth management products (WMPs). They partner with a wide variety of actors, both regulated and unregulated, in the financial system. The unregulated actors range from those whose existence and functions are completely outlawed to the off-shoot institutions whose existence are sponsored and endorsed (knowingly or unknowingly) by the Chinese government-linked banks or SOEs. In between these range of entities are institutions and small organizations whose existence and mandates are neither outlawed nor endorsed by the government. The various wealth management products to Chinese consumers are now widely cited as shadow banking products.

The China Banking Regulatory Commission (CBRC) has tried to rein in these sales by forbidding bank sales of trust products, but in reality, trust companies continue to sell their wares. The People's Bank of China intervened 17 June 2013, simultaneously raising interest rates and at the same time injecting liquidity into institutions that would be most affected by the liquidity tightening.[25]

Chinese leaders have been coming under pressure to implement and institute banking reforms. Yet, in face of the global slowdown caused by recurring series of financial crises over the years, they have to choose between curbing excessive credit (that has led to overinvestment in infrastructural projects and capacity) and allowing loans for cash-starved enterprises to stay afloat and to manage risks from global volatility by themselves. As one underground banker told the author, as long as financial entrepreneurs stay in ahead of legislation and innovate, there will always be a "grey" area that lies beyond those who stay beyond the state's regulation.[26]

## Underground banking today: context and characteristics

The short survey presented in this chapter provides a succinct chronological overview of how shadow banking developed in China. Yet, the section still does not tell us exactly what shadow banking is or specify the range of activities that are involved[27] Shadow banking has the general characteristic of being 'wide-ranging and sometimes complex forms of activities that takes outside the traditional banking activities of deposit and lending'.[28] The World Bank defines shadow banking as 'comprising a set of activities, markets, contracts, and institutions that operate partially (or fully) outside the traditional commercial banking sector, and as such are either lightly regulated or not regulated at all'.[29] The IMF's *Global Financial Stability Report* defines shadow banking as credit intermediation involving entitles or activities by non-banks; this approximates the definition of the Financial Stability Board (FSB), which broadly describes Shadow

Banking as 'credit intermediation involving entities and activities outside the regular banking system'.[30]

In the case of China, the IMF further defines shadow banking as financial intermediation outside the regulated banking system, and establishes this to be one-fourth of total financial intermediation worldwide.[31] The IMF also specifies that shadow banking tends to flourish when tight banking regulations combine with ample liquidity and when it serves to facilitate the development of the rest of the financial system.[32] China is considered as the exceptional case of exponential growth in the fraternity of emerging economies. The People's Bank of China (PBOC) defines shadow banking as 'credit intermediation involving entities and activities outside the regular system' that services to provide 'liquidity and credit transformation' and 'which could potentially' be a source of systemic risk or regulatory arbitrage'.[33]

For many authors writing on "shadow banking", the aforementioned activities, whilst not strictly legal (or mandated by law), are "problematic" because they are often risky, flouting conventional and international standards on sound banking practices. In particular, most of the current writings on shadow banking conventionally focus on the following activities: trust products and wealth management products (WMPs), and other off-balance-sheet loan-like claims held by commercial banks.[34] In other words, shadow banking is often defined only to involve the vast amount of unregulated financial transactions such as non-bank loans and credit facilities, mortgage-backed securities and repurchase transactions among individuals, businesses, banks and various other institutions (both financial and otherwise) which occur outside the supervised tradition i.e. regulated channels. Depending on context, these transactions at best may be considered "grey", but more often than not are still not outright illegal in China. As the legal infrastructure in China still somewhat lags behind international standards, these "grey" practices observed in China which may appear to be not outright illegal would be frowned upon by their banking compatriots in other places. For instance, many of the loan institutions in the underground banking industry do not require any form of security or collateral (even if they are trust institutions), and consequently, people without any form of employment are often able to obtain loans easily from these institutions.[35] This would not be possible in most of the developed economies.

Goldman Sachs[36] has categorized the activities of shadow banking in China into five categories: (i) trust loans; (ii) informal loans; (iii) securitized credits; (iv) corporate bonds; and (v) entrust loans. Others have framed the previously mentioned activities differently into the following categories: off-balance sheet lending, often by informal securitization of the loans and banker's acceptance bill; "private loans" between companies and individuals (via third parties, online platforms); trust companies that work with banks by purchasing loans and reselling these loans as "wealth management products"; leasing and loan guarantee companies (which act as guarantor for bank loans in exchange for some payment) and even pawnshops and micro-credit lenders. Deloitte[37] has stipulated the major shadow banking activities as shown in Table 8.1.

*Table 8.1* Major shadow banking activities

| Major forms | Scale (by 2012) |
| --- | --- |
| Bank and trust company cooperation | Sixty-five banks participated in issuing 8,946 financial products from bank and trust company cooperation, with assets of ¥2.54 trillion. |
| Banks acceptance bills | Bank acceptance bills without discount increased by ¥1.03 trillion. |
| Payment by another bank on behalf | The total amount of loans to other banks and financial institutions from 16 listed banks was ¥1.4 trillion, which was an increase of ¥697.50 billion in the first three quarters. Loans to other banks and financial institutions from Industrial Bank experience a new increase of ¥147.10 billion in the first three quarters, showing a sharp increase of 697%. |
| Loan by mandate | Loans by mandate increased by ¥1.3 trillion, which was an additional increase of ¥420.50 million when compared to the same period in the previous year. |
| Financial management products | Commercial issued 14,876 financial products, and the assets of personnel financial management fund products reached ¥13.35 trillion. |

(Source: Deloitte China, 2012)

The Brookings Institution Economics Group[38] has stipulated the activities to involve one of the following instruments:

- Entrusted loans
- Bankers acceptances
- Micro-finance companies
- Financial leasing
- Guarantees
- Pawnshops
- Trust beneficiary rights (TBRs)
- Wealth management products
- Interbank market activities

Amongst all these activities, it is therefore not wrong to say that most institutes and analysts regard the mainstay of the Chinese shadow banking industry has having always been the "loans" sector. The estimates of the "loans" sector of the underground banking also vary hugely across various institutions.[39] It is not hard to understand why many of these underground banks are able to obtain quick and easy money for deposits. With deposits attracting monthly 2% interest, a man who puts in ¥100,000 will obtain one of year income and he did not have to work.[40] For unlicensed moneylenders, essentially "loan sharks" in nature, the returns are even higher.

The sector grew particularly quickly after the 2007–2008 financial crisis, particularly after the government clamped down on availability of easy credit and liberal loan disbursements. While the shadow banking industry is quite common worldwide, the China case is unique in that it has an exceptionally large number of curb-side lenders, about 20–30 online lenders (P2P operators) and private equity financiers, at least 6,000 micro-credit firms and thousands of pawnshops, over 10,000 guarantee companies and numerous trust companies and consumer finance companies.[41] In Zhejiang province, for instance, there are individuals who helm manufacturing companies and are able to obtain loans for their factories at, say, 10% a year. They in turn lend out these loans to real estate companies, for instance, at rates of 2–3% a month.[42] Very often, micro-credit companies make loans to almost anyone with a need to loan money, without the need to fill paperwork, conduct background checks or wait a certain period say, three to four months, before the dispensation for loans – often at rates comparable to bank loans. Consequently, the growth of social capital (or shadow banking loans) in China was and still is multiplying at an alarming rate.

Beyond the category of loans, the other fast-growing sector is the category of financial wealth management products (WMPs). As mentioned previously, they are often structured from high-risk loans to entities/individuals that often do not qualify for formal loans, and are often done off balance sheets and/or are often sold in the legitimate market through its marketing methods. For instance, they are often sold through the branches of state-owned banks to investors. According to ratings agency Fitch, sales of WMPs soared from ¥7 trillion in 2010 by 48% to ¥13 trillion in 2012.[43] These products are immensely attractive, despite government warnings and regulations, because savers are prompted by significantly higher rates of return promised by these products, the bankers by handsome profits and investors by individual returns. These products are precarious, however, because their resilience as investment or wealth generating products are not sustainable in the long run. As they are sold through commercial banks and often draw on pensioners' savings or community funds, they are potential sources of instability. WMPs have grown largely also because investors would have higher returns, prompting consumption and a 'backdoor way to liberalize interest rates'.[44] The Bank of Settlements (BIS) has published a diagram that captures complexity of the Shadow Banking process in the People's Republic of China and this is shown in Figure 8.1.[45]

## Between a rock and a hard place: governmental response to shadow banking

Given the lax regulation, irregular accounting practices and incestuous relationship between banks, companies and corrupt individuals, the Chinese government faces a mounting problem posed by a double whammy of a huge bad debt as well as "wealth management product" time-bombs. As time passes, instances of defaults increased.[46] It is estimated that since 2012, more than 20 trust products totalling US$23.8 billion have ran into difficulties in payment. In October 2013, State-owned bank Hua-Xia Bank's Shanghai branch failed to pay interest of up to 13% to customers who invested ¥140 million after its product reached maturity.[47]

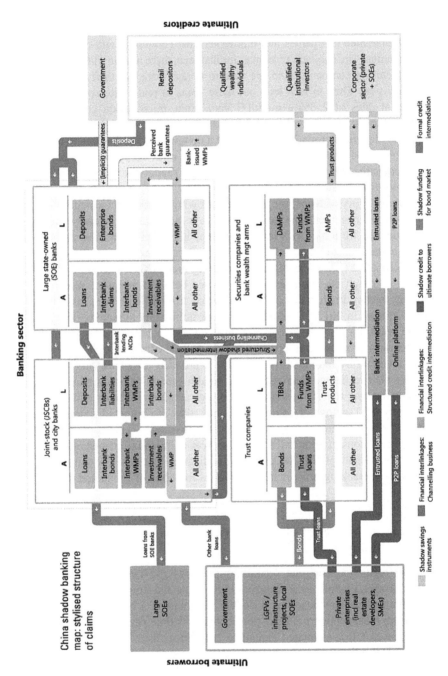

*Figure 8.1* Overview of the shadow banking industry in China

(Source: Ehlers, Kong, and Zhu, 2018)

In the same month, Bank of China Chairman Xiao Gang warned about wealth management products being 'fundamentally a Ponzi scheme'.[48] Beijing University Professor Huang Yiping has suggested that if this is not controlled, it could lead to a Chinese version of the recent subprime crisis in the United States.[49]

The government understands that it cannot be bailing out all of these products, even if they are sold through government-linked intermediaries for many reasons. First, the banking system as a whole will lose legitimacy. Second, a financial crisis stemming out of this will morph into a political one. Third, the shadow banking system does fill a social function that helps cushion the effects of the implementation of banking reforms and more importantly "privatizes" many of the problems facing the government. This highlights the ambivalent role the Chinese government plays. While it wants to portray itself as being "tough" on crime (certainly, sentencing shadow bankers are seen by many as overtly harsh), it still has to take into the account the grievances and resent at the grassroots level.

The government has made it abundantly clear that it will not bail out individuals and institutions engaged in risky forms of shadow banking. This, however, is more rhetoric than reality. The Chinese government is mindful of the political and moral hazard of bailing out various institutions and see their responsibility in preventing unrest and maintaining the integrity of the banking institution through selective "rescue" packages if and when necessary.

In cases wherein the certificates were issued through the state banks, the government actively intervened to prevent a full default of the certificates. In January 2014, more than 700 investors – both wealthy individuals and institutions such as the People's Insurance Company of China (the SOE which is largest life insurer in the PRC) was forced to take a write-down of a ¥3 trillion certificate (Credit Equals Gold No. 1 product) after the mining issuer (Shanxi Zhengfu Energy) ran into difficulties.[50]

The government faces a similar grim situation with regards to the loan sector, as well. With the advent of the global subprime crisis, the Chinese government began a period of financial austerity by tightening regulations to rein in the easy availability of credit. By 2010, many private enterprises were finding it almost impossible to obtain loans from the commercial banks and were turning to shadow bankers to obtain credit. CITIC Securities suggested that only 3% of companies are able to get bank loans in the PRC, with shadow banking funding the rest.[51] The credit crunch against the global recession climate took its toll on the entrepreneurs who had to contend with challenging conditions. By August 2012, more than 80 entrepreneurs had committed suicide or declared bankruptcy in Wenzhou because they weren't able to repay shadow lenders who had resorted to high pressure tactics to recall the loans.[52] Needless to say, this phenomenon attracted the attention of the entire nation, and there was genuine anger at the grassroots level because the big banks had only favoured the lending needs of SOEs, leaving a majority of small businessmen without access to capital. This gave the impression that the government was in cahoots with big banks and enterprises, whilst paying little attention to the small and medium enterprises and the man on the street. There is also the perception that the shadow banking industry filled the gap not provided for by the banks to help these desperate busi-nessmen. It's the opportunity to reap rich profits that drives the industry as much as there is a staggering demand for easy and short-term financing from entre-preneurs, more often than not by desperate ones trying to keep their businesses afloat.[53] For this category of businessmen, high interests mean absolutely nothing in face of impending collapse. Consequently, the state has a hard time suppress-ing these activities from within. The administrative measures implemented did not work because many government departments have a problem abiding by them. Therefore, it is not surprising that there is a growing school of thought that it is the predatory behaviour of China's banks is the primary force behind the thriving underground banks.

The state's power of criminalizing activities might not be a solution for eve-rything. In this instance, curbing the underground industry, banning underground borrowing and shooting underground bankers solves nothing. According to China's National Development and Reform Commission, private entrepreneurs account for 60% of China's total economic activity and provide jobs for 80% of its urban population.[54] The double whammy of economic downturn and curbs (from 2008 onwards) to the private lenders meant that failing businesses and economic slowdown became more important direct consequences of government policy – and the resentment on the ground is deeply felt. Looking for a reconciliatory response, then-Premier Wen Jiabao tapped into popular anger, arguing that banks should not have monopoly over the loan business, as it hands the banks easy access to profits. In other words, state-owned banks should not have as a matter of right access to the best credit customers. Implicit in this is the Chinese govern-ment's reversal of position on "striking hard" at the shadow banking industry. Following this, the Chinese government started a trial run in Wenzhou to legalize the strictly regulated private lending, but it appeared that the pilot scheme failed to bear fruit because the depressed local economy made people in Wenzhou wary of lending money.[55]

To a limited extent, the Chinese government has tried to reform the banking industry, bringing in international practices to the extent possible to increase transparency and accountability where possible; the task has been one fraught with difficulties and challenges.

### *Hot money and capital outflows*

The shadow banking system has challenged the Chinese authorities in different dimensions. Complete financial liberalization is the last thing on the Chinese gov-ernment's mind. As the region and the world weathered crisis after crisis, Beijing is particularly careful to shield China's relatively immature financial sector from speculative attacks. Beijing is also keen to limit capital outflows. Control over the financial sector is an important part of the Chinese government's development strategy to reduce the risks to China's economy and financial markets. Conse-quently, the methods by which shadow bankers and their intermediaries transmit money in and out of China are strictly outlawed. This, however, does not negate the pressing needs of the illicit entrepreneurs and legitimate business people's desire to have free capital mobility across borders.

The methods by which the shadow bankers transmit money are not new, and in fact has been in practice for centuries. The historical basis for the practice of transferring money to and from China is one premised on the principles of convenience and secrecy. In ancient China, rich merchants and corrupt officials would have moved their fortunes and laundered them to prevent investigations and punishment. During the Han dynasty, tomb raiders (a group named *Fan Qiu Jiang Jun*) would hide their criminality from the public and authorities by setting up pawnshops and antique dealership. Pirates would sell their loot in tea-trading areas where merchants from all over the world come to trade rather than cities during the Tang dynasty (618–907 BC).[56] In Republican China, the sons of former President Yuan Shikai were recruited by the Shanghai Underground Triads to assist in laundering the proceeds of crime, and were wholly involved in acquiring the Tong Shang Bank to launder the proceeds.[57] From the mid-19th century onwards, overseas Chinese labourers made use of remittance system or *Fei Chian* (literally "flying money"), utilizing trading system to transmit their hard-earned currency back to China. Very often, this was done without the physical transportation of cash, but rather through a system of "IOU" chits and balanced against export and import trade between two places. The Chinese have traditionally used the system of *Fei Chien*, and in South Asia, the *Hawalla* system, which likewise has been in existent for centuries.[58] The Colombian cartel has a similar system. For example, Colombian drug traffickers sell $3 million of drugs in the United States. Brokers pay the $3 million in pesos to traffickers in Columbia and in turn take orders from businessmen in Colombia in who pay in pesos. The goods are sent (or smuggled) back to Colombia. Neither the traffickers nor $3 million have been physically relocated.[59]

## Transferring money overseas

As the Chinese government intensifies its control over capital, it becomes increasingly difficult and bureaucratic for money to be moved across borders – even when it is legal. Shadow bankers today offer a convenient service in helping people move funds overseas by skirting the constraints put in place by the Chinese government.

For instance, individuals and companies could pay for non-existent services or goods that are invoiced by overseas companies owned by relatives or partners, or perhaps make foreign direct investments (partially real or fake) to overseas holdings or companies. As controls tighten at the time of writing, there have been attempts to transfer money by losing international lawsuits on purpose in order to skirt the law by settling the lawsuit to companies overseas controlled by the Chinese company,[60] or through the purchase of other financial instruments such as insurance which are redeemable overseas.

Today, one of the most serious and prevalent issue is the practice of trade misinvoicing, which is a common practice globally to transfer money to and from a jurisdiction. There are four processes involved: (i) export under-invoicing; (ii) exportover-invoicing;(iii)importover-invoicing;and(iv)importunder-invoicing.[61] For instance, export under-invoicing implies an understatement of a country's reported exports vis-à-vis what partner countries report as having imported from that country. Import over-invoicing indicates an overstatement of imports by a reporting country relative to partner countries' declaration of exports.[62] In the former, firms sell $1 million of goods abroad, and show an invoice for only $500,000 with the other $500,000 staying abroad. In the latter, firms could buy $500,0000 of goods and pay the other the other party for $1 million. This practice is very common in Pearl River Delta cross-border transactions. This phenomenon is not limited to China – mis-invoicing is a major element in the illicit flow of funds worldwide. Figure 8.2 is indicative of the mis-invoicing that occurs within China.[63]

In the Chinese context, these transfers contravene China's capital controls. Such transfers, however, often involve funds that are drawn from evaded tax, criminal proceeds or corruption.[64] Not all funds that flow out with invoicing are from dubious sources. China's large outflows often involved large capital account surpluses, which may often be legitimate funds that are flowing to areas of higher returns; speculative capital that that flows in and out of China in anticipation of Chinese renminbi currency appreciation; high-net-worth individuals who choose to shelter their burgeoning wealth abroad; or simply traders who are experiencing a high turnover of trade volume looking to skip bureaucratic hassles with lagging customs administration.[65] There is, however, no guarantee that sometime somewhere in the mixture of these funds would be a portion of illicit capital outflow. Buehn and Eichler have argued likewise.[66] Their research shows that illegal traders use the illegal black market for Forex to launder money earned from the

*Figure 8.2* China's trade misinvoicing (2000–2011)

(Source: Data drawn from Global Financial Integrity as presented by The Economist Online Edition 27/10/2012)

mis-invoicing of the value of traded goods. Additionally, the evasion of tax on trade (as opposed to income tax) also provides an additional incentive to engage in mis-invoicing. The practice of mis-invoicing as a whole is not just confined to China, but one that have predated the modern banking system and is common to merchants worldwide.

## Micro-perspectives: remittance agents and cross-border financial flow

This section's primary ethnographic data is based on interviews conducted in Shenzhen and Zhuhai. These two cities are important for a few reasons. First, these two cities are Special Economic Zones and have special status that has enabled private entrepreneurial activities to thrive since reforms started in China. These meant that both the licit and illicit sectors are relatively mature compared to those of the inland cities. Second, these two cities have unique geographical localities. Zhuhai borders the Macau Special Administrative Region (SAR), and Shenzhen borders the Hong Kong SAR. They stand at the centre of cross-border traffic of goods, human and capital – both licit and illicit. Hong Kong's special status as the country's eminent financial centre and logistical hub and Macau's reputation as the "entertainment" hub where gaming and vice are legalized give these two cities advantages not available to other Chinese cities. Shenzhen and Zhuhai, therefore, provide a certain allure for any Chinese entrepreneurs hoping to expand their operations beyond China, and certainly the perfect transit point for funds to be transferred out of Hong Kong efficiently. Third, as logistical and financial hubs, Shenzhen and Zhuhai have also been traditional ports of entry for foreign operations wishing to enter the "China" market. Consequently, there is a huge demand on both sides of the border for cross-border financial support and transactions. In particular, "foreign" here also refers to the operations for Taiwanese and overseas Chinese clients based in Southeast Asia. Fourth, because of the unique opportunities accorded by the policy of "One Country, Two Systems" (or three systems, in reality), the differences in legal infrastructure and commercial climate meant that there are plenty of opportunities for Chinese, Hong Kong (HK), Taiwanese, overseas Chinese and foreign business people to do things differently than in other areas of the PRC. Moving funds to these jurisdictions is a major step, as these economies are very much integrated with the global economy. Fifth, the research findings would have important consequences for the way we think about the illicit industries and the implications they have for human security in the region.

Hong Kong and Macau have been significant historical commercial centres with more global connections than many other cities on the mainland – rivalling even Shanghai and Beijing. As global cities go, they are immensely attractive places to live. They have autonomy with regard to their own affairs, with their own currency and laws – something that principal municipal cities like Tianjin, Beijing and Shanghai cannot boast they have. Hong Kong and Macau are cities that many mainlanders want to move to and where many feel safe and shielded from the control of the central government in terms of property rights and individual freedoms. The conventional perspective conjures up an imagery of a "rule-of-law" Hong Kong and a "sinful" Macau versus a "chaotic Guangdong". These imageries are stereotypes and not very useful analytically. Hong Kong and Macau have thrived historically because their unique circumstances maximize the opportunities for entrepreneurs and traders of both the licit and illicit persuasions. In a large part today, even as Hong Kong and Macau maintain a façade of rule of law, they owe their prosperity significantly to the flow of illicit funds and finance. In other words, Hong Kong and Macau are centres of clandestine globalization, and the financial freedom that the SARs enjoy facilitate rather than abate the illicit flow question. Gaining a deeper understanding into these issues would allow us to gain deeper insights into the effectiveness of the public policy and economic measures put in place to curb the flow of "hot money" across the regions. Shenzhen and Zhuhai are therefore important areas of focus as they are effectively the "gateway" for capital flow into Hong Kong, Macau and beyond.

We shall attempt to understand this "underground banking" industry by focusing on studying some of the "frontline" actors involved in the remittance service of this industry. Even though this is a small part of the business compared to the actual "shadow banking" that is being done in relation to loans and other wealth management products, remittances pre-date the current practices of "shadow" banking. Today, on both the Hong Kong/Macau side as well as the Shenzhen/Zhuhai side, we have a network of "grassroots" retailers who engage in money changing and remittance services. While ostensibly they are usually licensed to sell something else, or provide other services, they also offer this service like a full-fledged money changer.

Just like bankers who provide loans, the "grassroots" money changers often provide a service that supplement the shadow banking industry. They will sometimes refer people to a money lending service for a fee, but their real specialty is to assist their clients in sending their money overseas across the border in a no-fuss, safe and secure way. What is most important is that the transactions they make are anonymous. Money changers here simply refer to those individuals, businesses and institutions which engage in the business of transacting different currencies as part of their business, regardless of whether they have a license or not. In fact, this particular scope of this chapter covers those individuals and institutions who *do not* have a license to engage in this trade – for they fall outside the remit of the rules and regulations that govern this trade. It is impossible to estimate how many of these individuals or businesses there are, but it is a safe assumption that most small businesses all seek to engage in this trade, particularly in certain coastal localities in Guangdong province. The fieldwork sites are mainly confined to two urban shopping sites just north of the immigration and customs checkpoint, in and around the Gongbei Underground Mall in Zhuhai and the Lowu Shopping Centre in Shenzhen. These sites are selected because of the tremendous amount of human traffic flow both ways – from residents on the border, cross-border traders, businessmen and traders, and most importantly numerous individuals, shops and businesses which are engaged in the facilitation of money exchange and cross-border monetary transactions.

The main finding here is that that regulations imposed by Chinese authorities do little to curb the flow of illicit capital in and out of China, simply because those who engage in these activities lie beyond the abilities of the authorities to reach them. In fact, the stricter the implementation and enforcement of the anti-money-laundering (AML) framework, the more likely are business entrepreneurs (licit and illicit) to utilize these "services" to remit or receive money. Chinese AML efforts can be divided into three stages. In Phase 1 (1997–2006), the Chinese authorities first formulated AML regulations which remained insufficient. In phase 2, China began to criminalize money laundering on an all-crime basis, and emphasized comprehensive reporting and customer due diligence. In Phase 3, the Chinese pushed for the refinement and internationalization of the AML framework.[67]

Regulation is difficult for a few reasons. First, most of these money changers/remittance agents are "informal", meaning that they do their business openly under the guise of being engaged in another trade. For instance, they operate as general provision shops, selling phone cards, drinks, cigarettes and travel services. These money changers co-exist alongside ones who have met legitimate licensing requirements, and they openly flaunt plying their trade as legitimate money changers and remittance agents. Second, fieldwork results suggest that the licensed money changers are more circumscribed in their solicitation of clients and the range of work they are prepared to do. They do have a "license" to lose. There is, however, no question that the more familiar they are with the clients, they more they are prepared to undertake illicit large-scale transactions for their clients. Third, most of their patrons are regulars who have to change sums of money out of pleasure or work, and even though remittance clients exist, they are usually fewer than the small-transacting clients. Fourth, because of a lack in paperwork, these transactions are hard to prove, much less prosecute. Fifth, the service itself is very much needed, and poses less social harm (from the consumer's point of view) than other illicit industries. Hence, as long as they ply their trade stealthily, ordinary Chinese folks are not bothered by them as the consumption of these services are voluntary and conscious. The remittance service is thus very important, very convenient and very much in demand as a service for the Chinese people, much to the annoyance of Chinese regulatory authorities.

China has in place capital controls to prevent the flow (in or out) of "hot money". All transfers of funds will be subjected to regulations administered by the State Administration of Foreign Exchange.[68] Typically, a wire transfer arranged at a bank will require the remitter to supply very detailed information on the sender and recipient. This means that the remitter would have proof should the government require it that the funds came from legitimate sources and that appropriate taxes (e.g. income or profit taxes) have been paid on for it. Starting in July 2017, Chinese nationals can send up to USD$2,000 per day, with a cap of USD$50,000 a year abroad.[69] For foreigners, there is a limit of USD$500 per day. As at 2017, Chinese nationals would be only allowed to withdraw ¥100,000 using automated teller machines.[70] Banks need to report any overseas transfers by individuals of $10,000 or more.

With regards to the customs regulations at the border checkpoints, there is a physical limit of ¥20,000 that one can import/export into the country. The import (and export, theoretically) of foreign currency is unlimited, but amounts above USD$5,000 must be declared. Consequently, corrupt officials with bribes, embezzlers looking to hide money, criminals and businesses looking to hide and channel profits or even expatriates working in China without proper papers all have reasons not to use the official system for remittances. This is especially true since both the Hong Kong/Macau customs – as well as the Chinese customs – are concerned with people moving large amount of cash across the border. On 15 April 2015, for instance, a Hong Kong woman was arrested at a Shenzhen border checkpoint after mainland customs officers found more than HK$1.9 million in cash.[71] On 8 April 2015, Shenzhen customs arrested seven Hong Kong residents who were carrying a total of US$43,500 and HK$42,000 in cash. On 20 March 2015, a Hong Kong woman was arrested at Shenzhen side of the border with 8 kg of gold, worth HK$2.5 million taped to her body. On 23 October 2014, a Hong Kong man was arrested at the Shenzhen border with US$275,000 into Hong Kong.[72]

It is unclear what organizing principle underpins these money changing syndicates. Initially, the author assumed that it was based on their origins – i.e. the merchants who partake in a particular trade (e.g. counterfeiting of consumer goods, whether on the back-end manufacturing or front-end retail) all came from a particular city in Guangdong or Zhejiang province. This trend might be true in certain localities, but the problem is that these shadow bankers are found in many provinces. Thus, the idea that groups of people from certain area monopolized a certain kind of work is not necessary true in all instances. From personal observations, it would appear that the individuals who partake in the network are usually known to each other, either because of common origins (老家) or based on personal relations (family friend, relatives, etc.). Through mutual introduction, new members are able to join in the network. Consequently, the organizing principle of the network is premised heavily on trust. In each syndicate, there are usually a few operators who are extremely cash rich and well connected, and often they also operate the "wholesale side" of the business (but they also do retail themselves), whilst maintaining a loose network of retailers.

Fieldwork data reveals that one operator might also operate in different localities and across the borders, and/or rely on partner arrangements. A syndicate is quite similar to multi-layered operations – each retail agent is connected to a hub in the network where they can order payments in/out for clients across the border. If the sum is too big or if the "front-end" retailer feels too burdened, they often they will just ask the client to go to see someone in the office of a collaborator with a high trading threshold. Alternatively, some of the wholesale money changing operations run the retail outlet themselves, usually in the form of legitimate/licensed operators at several localities. However, they often supplement and expand their network by incorporating freelance or independent merchants who want to do this on the side.

An informant "L" at Shenzhen side of the border (*lokmachau* crossing) told the author that physical cash seldom changes hands, but there will be frequent attempts to balance the account (算账). For his network, there is usually a delivery service to ensure the outlets have enough capital stock to fund the exchanges. If there is abnormally high demand for certain notes on one side, they would be replenished (e.g. Hong Kong $500 notes on the China side). On the Hong Kong side, there are often specialist couriers who cross the border with certain amounts of cash to queue up at Hong Kong cash machines to deposit cash into accounts through ATM machines.

In terms of the customer base, there is often enough foot traffic each day for him to make a decent living just through normal currency exchanges. For people who utilized his remittance service, many are just business people who would rather use him than the banks or Chinese citizens who do not want to be caught carrying out large amount of cash across the border. There are those who cross from Hong Kong who have come to redeem their cash remittances. "L" is not a licensed money changer. He works out of a general provision shop similar to the one shown in Figure 8.3.

Mr "C" is another money changer who operates a small provision shop right next to a small hotel in Zhuhai. His is a front-end business selling general provisions such as drinks, snacks and cigarettes. Due to his proximity to foot traffic from residents and shoppers, as well as the out-of-towners and tourists from the hotel, he also offers booking services to hotel rooms, transportation, entertainment venues and other services such as provision of tour guides and

*Figure 8.3* An example of a small-scale provision shop which hosts many other commercial activities

(Source: Photograph by author)

even social escorts. However, one of his primary revenue streams comes from money changing activities. Mr "C" relies on three main sources of clients: walk-in clients, usually tourists from East Asia such as Taiwanese and Hong Kongers who are in town for business or pleasure; locals who constantly come to him to change money for use in Macau/Hong Kong, or just to accumulate Hong Kong dollar notes; and businesspeople and traders who request him to swap renminbi for Hong Kong or Macau dollars. Mr "C" has branches in various localities near the Gongbei checkpoint (to Macau). Interestingly, Mr "C" professes that he does not partake in the remittance service. He claims to be a legitimate businessman who does money exchange on the side, although he is happy to help out anyone who wants to send large sums of money to Hong Kong or Macau by referring the person to his "friend" who is located nearby. Mr "C", however, would be able to provide referral services for not only remittance service but also bank loans in his network because he likes to "lend people a hand". During one of the field visits, the author witnessed plastic bags of cash being replenished for his currency exchange by a courier from a different branch.

Another informant, Miss "S", runs a legitimate currency exchange service on the Chinese side of the Hong Kong-Shenzhen border at Lowu. Being a fully licensed changer, Miss "S" has operations in multiple locations in Shenzhen and works with a partner in Hong Kong with branches in Mongkok and Shumshuipo. The trade is brisk, especially on weekends. At first glance, everything appears normal. There are two tellers working out of the windows, where all exchanges are documented (i.e. complete with transaction receipts and the documentation of the identity of the person changing money). Interestingly, two employees, not in uniform, are concurrently engaged with monetary transactions at a side door. For large amount exchanges and also for clients who appear to be "returning" clients, the cashiers at the window direct the clients to the side door and the money is "exchanged" without any records of the transaction or identity of the customer. The dispensation for paperwork is interesting: This is not a case of just remittance, but probably also of tax evasion. The lady who was doing the exchange however was interested in consolidating large notes ($500 or larger denominations of European and U.S. currencies), which she said was needed for ease of payment for large sums of money.

During a fieldwork visit, the author witnessed how the capital stock was refurnished at informant "L"'s general provision store. A delivery entered with a bag and left stacks of notes – approximately ten one-inch stacks of HK$500 notes (assuming a one-inch stack is approximate 232 notes, then this amounts to over HK$116,000 per stack), and more stacks of 500 Macau Pataca (Macau's currency unit) rubber-banded together. This rebalancing of cash is over ¥1 million per transaction – which is staggering to the author, to say the least.

Mr "L" considers these sums "small" compared to places with heavier traffic flows that other operators undertake. Like most of the other merchants, the financial stocks are operating capital, and these merchants would entice customers who are passing by their place of operation to change money. However, there is little incentive for them to outdo each other on the basis of offering a "better" rate to undercut each other, as competitive undercutting would eventually lead the complete erosion of profits. Rather, the strategy undertaken by most of them is to try to gain new customers and retain old ones by offering other services or assistance. In particular, they are extremely accommodating to customers who change huge quantities of money on a regular basis.

Mr "Z" is one of the 30-odd money changers who congregate on the first floor of the Zhuhai underground shopping mall. The stalls typically occupy a space of two to three 1.5-metre glass case cabinets each and the owners pay about ¥40,000 per month for rent. There are another few larger money changing-cum-remittance agents operating in nearby shops. These agents, however, are located in a partitioned room inside these shops (hidden from view); to front the shops, they concurrently sell Chinese medicine, sundry goods or fake consumer electronics or fashion (bags, clothing). Through various conversations, the author learnt that it is not uncommon for them to send up to ¥10–20 million a day across the border into Macau. In Zhuhai alone, the estimates for transactions that occur daily is as high as ¥1 billion per day.[73] In the open area (as seen in Figure 8.4), some 40-odd trading cases have licenses to operate and for years have plied a trade in selling mobile phone subscriber identity module (SIM) cards, top-up vouchers, fake mobile phones, and engaging in side trade of money exchanges. Mr "Z" concedes

*Figure 8.4* The money changers in the Underground Mall Shopping Centre in Gongbei, Zhuhai, China

(Source: Photograph by author)

that since 2010, things have gotten a lot tougher with the authorities cracking down on the fake electronics they were selling. They no longer could display the knock-offs of the iPhones or Nokias prominently on display because of the government inspectors sent to curb pirated/knockoff goods. Now, to a very large extent, almost all the stores rely on making currency exchanges to sustain their business. The overheads are not small, and in order to support the running costs of two or three people working in addition to rental fees, the cost per month could easily come up to ¥50,000–60,000. It would be almost impossible for the stall owners to rely on the sales of telephone SIM cards or phone credit recharge cards to sustain the rent alone. Most of these stalls are most keen to promote money exchanges and remittances as the main business, rather than to sell what they are licensed to trade in.

Theoretically, these money changers make money in at least two ways. The first is derived from the differential in the exchange rates. The second involves the charging of a handling fee/commission or administrative fee – although this is usually not collected by the unlicensed money changer for regular clients changing a small sum of money or if there are many other competitors nearby. There might be instances in the event of "special requirements" of the customer, and under such circumstances a significant portion of the administrative fee might be imposed. Another interlocutor, Mr "X", suggests that many customers do not exchange large amounts of money – usually ¥10,000–30,000. Many of these people are travellers and business people are those who need to make regular transactions in Hong Kong or Macau. These remittance agents often undertake or have connections to other shadow bankers who might be able to undertake money laundering operations for their clients.

There are, of course, regulars who come to make large-scale cash transactions, worth ¥1–2 million per month. The funds cannot be moved physically across the border. The process is as follows: The cash would be paid to the agents on the Chinese side at a designated time and place (usually an apartment or office, or even the stall in the mall). After verification, the agents would then provide the customer a code which then customer brings over to their corresponding agent on the Macau or Hong Kong side (or vice versa). The practice varies, but often a photo or message would be used in place. Usually, the client will agree upon the time for pickup and the partner on the Macau side will be sent a code/message/photo. Whatever this is, the details are kept very private. Many of the money changers interviewed say that they would only dare to carry such transactions if the customers are familiar to them. This method is especially popular because it allows regular customers who want to exchange large sums of money to or from Hong Kong or Macau without having the transactions recorded by the banks or have their identity details recorded to do so.

Mr "X" provides a description of the service on the other end. For those with bags of cash to be dropped at Zhuhai, it is usually because they cannot cross physically with the cash and/or often have a problem with a record of travelling into Macau. This usually means that they are cadres or work in the government, or they have funds which cannot be traced to a legitimate source. For these clients, they can offer to have the money deposited directly into accounts of their choosing in Macau and/or Hong Kong. Alternatively, the clients could collect Hong Kong dollars or Macau Patacas from their partners when in Macau or Hong Kong. Mr "X"'s business also has an "added service" of being able to arrange the payout in the form of chips at the casino's VIP rooms. This allows the chips to be collected as "winnings", and the customer could then legitimately cash the amount in Macau or Hong Kong banks or have it sent back to the PRC. This corresponds to other schemes that operate out of Macau. One common method is to take part in gambling junket. The money is arranged to be paid to an agent on the Chinese side. The person then crosses the border and collects the chips from a junket operator in the casino. This can be cashed as winnings and legitimately redeposited into a mainland account. Dirty money becomes clean as soon as it reaches a Macau casino. Extra commission is usually taken for more complex operations.

There are other methods of aggregating money across the borders. Mainland visitors would be invoiced or charged for services or goods (expensive watches, services or products like paintings, which are not collected) in Macau, and have the cash (minus the commission) returned to the purchaser. In the ground floor of the various casinos, like Venetian and Sands Macau, one can find various elderly ladies walking around in the casinos with a UnionPay machine, charging Chinese gamblers' UnionPay cards and then disimbursing cash immediately (minus their fees) (see Figure 8.5). This provides an avenue to move money to Macau from

*Figure 8.5* Macau Judiciary Police (PJ) officers escort illegal money changers out of the Venetian in Cotai, Macau on 1 February 2018

(Source: Photo reproduced with permission of Macau Post Daily and photographer Long Tat Choi)

the PRC and/or launder money at the same time. Other syndicates often employ groups of people to open bank accounts (described in money laundering narratives as ants), and withdraw cash using these cards in Macau. There are other and more innovative means involving transactions of the UnionPay card (the Chinese equivalent of the Visa card and Mastercard).

The Chinese government has instituted a variety of measures to stem the outflow of cash. First, they have cracked down on Macau casinos by tightening the visa regime, placing limits on the number of civil servants who can visit. They have also tightened regulations involving "junket tours", and have tightened regulations concerning the governance of point of sale machines (used to charged UnionPay cards) and also cracked down on the abuse of bank deposit cards, as well as monitor closely what the remittance agents are doing on the Chinese side of the border. The author learned that the Chinese police have actually mounted sting operations against all these illicit activities at the mall (see Figure 8.6).

When asked if he could reveal what these customers did for a living, Mr "X", the money changer on the Zhuhai side, maintained that most of them had businesses which were significantly profitable and have a high turnover of cash. He stipulated, however, that he "runs" a clean business and has no interest in finding out where his customers' money comes from. It is not certainly not in the interest of his business to pry. What is certain, though, he admits, is that many of his clients are not business people, but probably officials looking to send money overseas without a trace.

What unites them all – the customers and the brokers – is that the transactions are hassle-free, fast and secure (to a certain extent), especially if the customer is dealing with remittance with a physical space where they believe that they can return to. From the conversations with the money changers, it is evident that they do realize that their customer base is varied. In the minds of many of them, changing and transferring money across the border for their customers is not illegal, nor is it illegitimate. To them, these activities are born out of necessity, i.e. them eking out a "living" and providing them a service which might be at best describe as "informal". Mr "X" describes that just like banks, it is very hard for them to tell who has "dirty" or "black" money and who hasn't. Even though their customers might be corrupt officials or hardened criminals, they would not be able to tell. It is, however, "not their business" to care.

What is also true is that for most of the money changers do not see the more "mundane" economic activities as being "criminal", e.g. selling of bootlegged DVDs or fake Prada/Chanel bags, loansharking or proceeds from nightclubs, brothels or gambling dens. The conception of "law" and "illegality" still lags behind the people's desire to make money. It is not important what business one does for a living. As long as the business makes money, then it is one worthy of worship and admiration. Indeed, these unlicensed changers perceive a symbiotic relationship with their customers: They provide a secure, private and convenient service their "high net" worth clients need, almost the equivalent

*Figure 8.6* Chinese police mounting an operation arresting underground bankers on 13 May 2018 on charges of "counterfeit currency usage"

(Source: Internet photo posted on Li Daily)

of a modern investment banker, and see nothing wrong with these cross-border transactions.

## Discussion: micro-macro linkages

The micro-level description of the illicit industry gives us pause for further consideration of the banking industry in China. Studies of this nature, regardless of how "rigorous" they claim to be, all suffer from methodological weakness, usually due to the unreliability and "spotty" nature of the data available. This is true whether it is at the level of analyzing "wealth management products" sold by banks and their intermediaries or the "grassroots" bankers – the loan makers and remittance agents who operate with impunity across the southern and eastern seaboards of the PRC. Consequently, it would be almost impossible to be able to have an accurate estimate of how big this industry is in Guangdong alone, let alone China.

We can however draw a few conclusions. First, the implications of these underground bankers and unlicensed money changers-cum-remittance agents are a lot more significant than ordinarily assumed. Given the amounts they need to sustain their businesses (e.g. rent and other overheads), those businesses that survive are likely to make a healthy turnover from their brisk trade. In the latter category, the numerous establishments that have cropped up all over the city suggest that it is a growing sector. For instance, there are reports of ¥1 billion a day transferred a day across Zhuhai alone. This is likely, but not necessarily authoritative. The fact that the central government has started a major clampdown on these remittance agents in Zhuhai, Shenzhen and other cities (on the China side) and in Hong Kong and Macau of the various channels whereby money could be laundered easily (such as the junkets industry wherein organized groups are brought in to gamble at a casino by operators who in turn offer special privileges, e.g. private rooms with access to gaming chips or those using "UnionPay" where mainland Chinese swipe their credit cards in exchange for cash).

Second, even though the money changers are able to transmit huge sums of money across the border quickly and efficiently, their methods are far from innovative. The methods they have used are "traditional" in the sense that they have been utilized in "informal" banking systems we see in the Indian subcontinent, as well as with overseas Chinese expats in the early 19th century who relied on import/export companies to send their hard-earned money home. Their practices are incredibly simple and at the same time prove to be extremely hard for law enforcement to enforce and prosecute. How does a prosecutor, for example, take a note with a "code" written on it as evidence of a transaction? How can the police deny that the cash of ¥50,000 that a client has just given to a changer is not a "debt" being repaid? The informality of these transactions is what makes the transaction efficient and secure, and also difficult to detect and regulate.

Third, these remittance agents perceive these cross-border flows as a means of livelihood. It would be very difficult to legislate and stem out the "practice", as they do not have licenses to be "suspended" even if the transactions can be proven. These agents perceive themselves to be eking out livelihood and are making a "honest" living by providing this service. When asked if the possibility that they were knowingly participating in money laundering activities – their responses range from the incredulous ('how is it possible? We are just providing a service to travellers and small time businessmen') to denials and outrage ('look at how corrupt our officials are, and what they are doing to "tax" businesses like ours'). The business environment in China has never been one of "regulation"; entrepreneurship amongst these people simply means being able to make money – nothing more, nothing less. Regulations, governance and even the law are at best viewed as annoyances and at worse impediments to be overcome or ignored. But this appears to be the situation is most other cities – that the law is to be overcome. The numerous youth and elderly involved in the industry is staggering. In 2013, a Hong Kong public housing tenant on welfare was convicted of making more than 17,000 bank transfers to launder HK$6.7 million. This 61-year-old Hong Kong lady was reportedly paid only about $4,500 for each month's work. Two months earlier, Luo Juncheng,[74] a 19-year-old delivery man and a school dropout from Guangdong province, was also convicted in Hong Kong court for laundering HK$13 billion in 5,000 deposits and 3,500 withdrawals. He was sentenced to ten years in jail. He was accused of laundering Chinese ¥50 million a day in transactions. Each of these cases had cross-border dimensions and is deeply connected to the shadow banking industry in the PRC.

Fourth, despite the rash of measures implemented to curb money laundering and an attempt to regulate the industry – it does not appear that the industry has taken any sort of a "beating" (see Figure 8.7).[75] In fact, the stricter the "regulation" with the banks, the more it would drive people to send money across the border with these money changers. The higher the number of transactions, the greater the profits and the more people would enter the industry and drive down transaction costs. It would become so commonplace (as it is now) that no one would perceive anything criminal about it.

Fifth, this would have tremendous impact on China's public policy. China's "no capital outflow" rules[76] for foreign enterprises is one of the many reasons why business people, both foreign and Chinese, are trying to move their capital abroad. Of course, there are the usual culprits – corrupt officials, real estate developers and owners of illicit businesses from prostitution dens to fake medicine manufacturers, etc. This channel means that it becomes quite useless to regulate the capital flow business from China itself as Hong Kong and Macau remain the "open" conduit for all these individuals to send and receive funds freely. Even the North Koreans were once in Macau, conducting their businesses and laundering their money – that is, until they angered the Americans and Chinese, who promptly shut them down.[77] The recent US-China trade war has caused many in China to become worried about their Chinese currency holdings and the demand for this illicit service to move money out of China has substantially increased. The availability of these channels during times when there aren't any financial problems already presents a headache for the Chinese authorities who might want to ensure that capital flows are regulated to ensure foreign investments remain in

*Figure 8.7* Customs warning at Hong Kong airport baggage belt. Hong Kong implemented a new law in July 2018 that makes it compulsory for travelers carrying more than HKD$120,000 (USD$15,300) in physical currency or Negotiable Instruments to declare their holdings to customs

country and to prevent volatility from speculative capital outflow. Such underground remittance conduits might undermine this objective if profits from industries (legal or illicit) are leaving the country and other sources are leaving the country via these money changers.[78] One ramification is the possibility of having the renminbi as an international currency. If it is not freely convertible and transferable, why should investors have the confidence to keep the money in China?

Sixth, this would have tremendous implications for human security in the region. Permitting these cross-border transfers allows for profits for many of the illicit industries as well as proceeds of crime across China to be reinvested into legitimate business or reinvested into the illicit industries to further enterprise corruption and illegal activities. The flow of "hot" money into the real estate sector that is driving up property prices, the inability of the central government to rein in inflation, especially in the south, and the "thriving" illicit industries in the Pearl River Delta region is related to this. There is no question that provincial officials will deny this for political reasons, but that does not negate the popularity of shadow bankers and their products. There are important policy consequences – especially for dealing with human security and crime – for us to consider. The biggest worry for local governments is the illicit funds flowing into the legitimate sectors of the economy and having a predatory effect on it.

Last, how would the shadow banking industry and the shadow economy help China in the event of a downturn? One of the most important themes in the scholarly debate is whether China can pull out of its current economic slump. Even though most scholars agree that many of China's economic numbers were "fudged", it is important not to underestimate how much the Chinese government has done to slow down growth. The question for us is the extent that the government's efforts have been useful to curb growth in the underground economy. The official economic forecast made by the Chinese government might not be too high enough to reflect the vibrancy in the underground economy. In fact, the official numbers could be too low. The real reason is that China's underground economy is probably far bigger than the 10–20% of the total economy projected.[79] Therefore, it is vital that the Chinese government is able to rein in shadow banking and money laundering for the sake of getting a grip on the economy.[80]

Given the widespread scale and the high stakes involved for the players, it is unlikely that the Chinese government will be able to curb the shadow banking activities or the outflow of the funds easily. As the adage goes, "capital has no nationality". As much as the Chinese leadership wills it, the flow of capital will continue unabated as long as criminal innovation stays ahead of regulation and governance. In the Chinese case, the stakes are particularly high, and regardless of how hard the Chinese government tries, profit and necessity will ensue that shadow banking remains thriving business in China. Bloomberg reports that Global Financial Integrity, a Washington-based think tank estimates that from 2005 to 2015, the estimated amount is US$1.4 trillion.[81] No one, however, can claim to have an accurate estimate of this.

The key, perhaps, is for the Chinese government to consider legitimizing and legalizing some of the loan and remittance functions played by these shadow bankers. To an extent, this debate is somewhat similar to the debate in the sex industry. Whether or not the government permits this industry, it will continue to thrive as long as there is a demand for it. Legalizing aspects of it will actually provide for more control and revenue, even though the public principle behind attempts to control it (preventing capital outflow) will take a dent. This partial yielding, however, would be an improvement on governance, for it signals the government's willingness to acknowledge that it is keen to increase its accountability instead of pretending that the problem does not exist and sweeping it under the rug. There are other dimensions to this problem. In 2016, police uncovered computers of arrested shadow bankers with up to 10-terabyte hard drives that contained nude photos of young girls who had provided the photos as collateral for loans.[82] This sort of practice no doubt fuel the debate as to whether this industry should be allowed to exist, or legalized. Having said that, it is clear from the number of photos that the demand for loans will continue to exist – but what is shocking is the number of young girls, some working, some still in school, who appeared to be taking these loans. There is therefore an urgent need for the Chinese government to think how to better regulate these shadow bankers. It is not a luxury but a necessity. Given a choice, most of the players in the industry would rather operate under license than illegally, and that in itself would be a big victory for a state that is almost helpless in the current situation, and a big step forward for the enhancement of the financial system in China.

## Notes

1 "No, China will absolutely not collapse", *Forbes*, www.forbes.com/2010/02/03/china-economy-bubble-leadership-citizenship-rein.html
2 D. Kedmey, "How a beige book could shed light on China's shadow economy", *Time*, 5 August 2013, http://world.time.com/2013/08/05/how-a-beige-book-could-shed-light-on-chinas-shadow-economy/
3 "Fifth generation star Li Keqiang discusses domestic challenges, trade relations with Ambassador", 15 March 2007, Wikileaks, https://wikileaks.org/plusd/cables/07BEIJING1760_a.html
4 "China's shadow banking revisited: Size, implications, risks and reforms", *Caijing Magazine* Online, 5 December 2012, http://english.caijing.com.cn/2012-12-05/112336663.html
5 M. Boseler, "Should we be worried about China's $2.2 trillion shadow banking system?", 19 July 2012, http://business.financialpost.com/business-insider/should-we-be-worried-about-chinas-2-2-trillion-shadow-banking-system
6 "Purple palace abandoned shows China shadow-banking risk", *Bloomberg News*, 20 November 2012.
7 E. Cary, "Is shadow banking China's subprime mortgages?", *The Diplomat Blogs*, 21 May 2013, http://thediplomat.com/china-power/is-shadow-banking-chinas-subprime-mortgages/ citing Moody's Report, on *China's Shadow Banking*, available at www.moodys.com/research/Moodys-Chinas-shadow-banking-continues-to-weigh-on-the-banks–PR_273026
8 "China's shadow banking sector tops $5.8 trillion", *Businessweek* 8 May 2013, www.businessweek.com/articles/2013-05-08/chinas-shadow-banking-sector-tops-5-dot-8-trillion-report-says

9  The Four Modernizations were in fact conceived by Zhou Enlai in 1963, and then implemented by Deng Xiaoping in 1978. The Modernizations were to strengthen the fields of agriculture, industry, national defence and science and technology. See B. Naughton, "Deng Xiaoping: The economist", in D. Shambaugh, ed., *Deng Xiaoping: Portrait of a Chinese Statesmen* (Oxford: Oxford University Press, 1995), pp. 36–48.

10  For example, see C. Walter, and F. Howie, *Red Capitalism: The Fragile Financial Foundation of China's Extraordinary Rise* (Singapore: John Wiley and Sons, 2011); for a discussion of bank loans, see J. Chapman, and U. Marshall, *China's Banking System Currency Policy and Economic Conditions* (New York, NY: Nova Science, 2012).

11  K. Okazaki, "Banking system reform in China: The challenges of moving toward a market-oriented economy", *RAND Occasional Papers, 2007*. Santa Monica, 2007, www.rand.org/content/dam/rand/pubs/occasional_papers/2007/RAND_OP194.pdf

12  "World Bank warns China to reform 'distorted' financial system", *Financial Times*, 1 July 2005. The Chinese State controls over 95% of the assets in the Chinese banking system.

13  W. Jiang, "The future of shadow banking in China", *White Paper, Columbia Business School*, 15 September 2015, https://papers.ssrn.com/sol3/papers.cfm?abstract_id=2769603

14  "The flight of the Reminbi, 27th 2012", *The Economist*, Print Edition, www.economist.com.hk/news/china/21565277-economic-repression-home-causing-more-chinese-money-vote-its-feet-flight

15  W.Y. Zhang, "The future of private and state-owned enterprises", in S. Fan, S.M. Ravi Kanbur, S. Wei, and X. Zhang, eds., *The Oxford Companion to the Economics of China*, Oxford: Oxford University Press, 2014 pp. 285–291; also see Gordon Chang, chapter 3 on "Industrial theme parks", pp. 45–70 and Chapter 6, "The banks that sank", pp. 132–144.

16  G. Chang, *The Coming Collapse of China* (New York, NY: Random House, 2001), p. 122.

17  J. Pomfret, and M. Miller, "On China's border, underground banking flourishes", *The New York Times*, 20 May 2013.

18  Ibid.

19  G. Chang, *The Coming Collapse of China*, chapter 6.

20  "Bad debt surfacing with slower Chinese economy: Shang Fulin", *China Times* (Taiwan), 24 April 2013, www.wantchinatimes.com/news-subclass-cnt.aspx?id=20130424000031&cid=1202

21  The author personally knows of a case whereby the local government official in charge of development projects was able to obtain access to cheap loans through connections with the shadow banking industry. The official was able to utilize his connections and bid for a mega project (through proxy) supported by cheap loans from the shadow banking industry. He constructed factories to be sublet out in his development area in Zhejiang. In another case, another local government in Guangdong province who was in charge of inward investments approval was able to obtain capital from shadow bankers to co-invest in investment projects that were made by foreign companies and firms. This was again done via proxy. This pattern of officials exploiting opportunities in their work is not new and seems to be an embedded feature of Chinese capitalism.

22  See A. Sheng, C. Edelmann, C. Sheng, and J. Hu, "Bringing light upon the shadow: A review of the Chinese shadow banking sector", *Fung Global Institute Working paper*, pp. 3–10, cited at www.oliverwyman.com/content/dam/oliver-wyman/global/en/2015/feb/Bringing-Light-Upon-The-Shadow.pdf

23  Ibid, p. 9.

24  C. Koons, "Skepticism on China's nonperforming loans", *The Wall Street Journal*, 3 December 2013.

25  S. Hsu, "China engineers a credit crisis to deleverage shadow banking", *East Asia Forum*, 15 July 2013, www.eastasiaforum.org/2013/07/15/china-engineers-a-credit-crisis-to-deleverage-shadow-banking/

26  Fieldwork interview, 2015,

27  For an economic assessment of shadow banking in the PRC, please see A. Sheng, C. Edelmann, C. Sheng, and J. Hu, "Bringing light upon the shadow", chapter 3 and chapter 4.

28  J. Zhang, *Inside China Shadow Banking: The Next Subprime Crisis?* (Singapore, SGP: Enrich Professional Publishing, 2013), p. VII, ProQuest eLibrary, Web, 8 April 2015.

29  S. Ghosh, I. Gonzalez del Mazo, and I. Otker-Robe, "Chasing the shadows: How significant is shadow banking in emerging markets?", *Economic Premise Paper*, September 2012, No. 88, http://siteresources.worldbank.org/EXTPREMNET/Resources/EP88.pdf

30  Financial Stability Board (FSB), *Global Shadow Banking Monitoring Report 2017*, p. 1, www.fsb.org/2017/05/global-shadow-banking-monitoring-report-2016/

31  IMF Reports, *Global Financial Stability Report, World Economic and Financial Surveys Series*, pp. 65–66.

32  IMF Reports, *Global Financial Stability Report, World Economic and Financial Surveys Series*, p. 66.

33  People's Bank of China, *China: Financial Stability Report 2013* (June 2013).

34  *Caijing Reports*, "China's shadow banking revisited: Size, implications, risks and reforms", 5 December 2012, http://english.caijing.com.cn/2012-12-05/112336663.html

35  Personal Interviews with bankers in Guangzhou, Beijing and Yiwu, Zhejiang China.

36  L. Goldfeld, "Is shadow banking a big risk for China?", *Asian Economic and Financial Market Outlook*, April 2013.

37  D. China, "2012 China banking industry top ten trends and outlook: Enhancing capital management, meeting new challenges", Report posted 28 May 2012, pp. 22–23, www.deloitte.com/assets/Dcom-China/Local%20Assets/Documents/Industries/Finan cial%20services/cn_gfsi_ChinaBankingtop10_280512.pdf

38  D. Elliott, A. Kroeber, and Q. Yu, "Shadow banking in China: A primer", www.brook ings.edu/wp-content/uploads/2016/06/shadow_banking_china_elliott_kroeber_yu.pdf

39  M.C. Chan, http://app1.hkicpa.org.hk/APLUS/2011/12/pdf/36-38-shadow-lending.pdf

40  D. Ren, "Concerns over a collapse in China's underground banking sector resurface", *South China Morning Post*, 9 April 2014.

41  S.J. Chen, "China's economy in banking's shadow", *The Business Times*, 17 August 2013.

42  Ibid.

43  G. Ng, "Shadow banking risks loom in China", *Straits Times*, 4 January 2013.

44  E. Cary, "Is the shadow banking China's subprime mortgages?", *The Diplomat*, 21 May 2013.

45  T. Ehlers, S. Kong, and F. Zhu, "Mapping shadow banking in China: Structure and dynamics", *Bank of International Settlements, Monetary and Economic Department, Working Papers No. 701*, February 2018, www.bis.org/publ/work701.pdf

46  A. Cheng, "China's banking sector poses growing risks to economy", *Institutional Investor*, 7 March 2014, www.institutionalinvestor.com/article/3317208/banking-and-capital-markets-banking/chinas-shadow-banking-sector-poses-growing-risks-to-econ omy.html#.WEHveneZNE4

47  G. Ng, "Shadow banking risks loom in China", *Straits Times*, 4 January 2013.

48  Ibid.

49  Ibid.

50  A. Cheng, "China's banking sector poses growing risks to economy" *Institutional Investor*, 7 March 2014

51 See "China slowdown stymies plan to curb shadow-banking risks", *Bloomberg*, 17 July 2012, www.bloomberg.com/news/2012-07-16/china-slowdown-stymies-plan-to-curb-shadow-banking-risks.html

52 See "China credit squeeze prompts suicides", *Bloomberg*, 6 November 2011, see www.bloomberg.com/news/2011-11-06/china-credit-squeeze-prompting-suicides-along-with-offer-to-sever-a-finger.html; also see "Shadow loans hard to squelch in China City hit by suicide", *Bloomberg*, 27 March 2013, www.bloomberg.com/news/2013-03-26/shadow-loans-hard-to-squelch-in-china-city-hit-by-suicide.html

53 During the trial of Wu Ying (aka "Rich Sister"), the woman sentenced to death for illegally raising funds and engaging in shadow banking in 2009, Wu's lawyer argued that Wu was no different from the estimated 42 million Chinese business owners who rely on the shadow banking system for financing when they cannot get loans from state-owned banks. Wu collected ¥770 million (US$122 million) from private investors between May 2005 and February 2007, according to government prosecutors. She also accumulated more than 100 properties and 40 cars, including a $500,000 Ferrari.

"Shadow banks on trial as China's rich sister faces death", *Bloomberg*, 11 April 2012, www.bloomberg.com/news/articles/2012-04-10/shadow-banks-on-trial-as-china-s-rich-sister-faces-death; in 2013, Lin Haiyin was convicted of illegal fundraising for collecting ¥640 million (US$100 million) from investors. The scheme collapsed in October 2011 and ¥428 million could not be recovered. F. Ji, "China sentences underground bank operator to death", *AP Press*, 20 May 2013.

54 "Shadow banks on trial as China's Rich Sister faces death", *Bloomberg*, 11 April 2012, www.bloomberg.com/news/articles/2012-04-10/shadow-banks-on-trial-as-china-s-rich-sister-faces-death

55 D. Ren, "Concerns over a collapse in China's underground banking sector resurface", *South China Morning Post*, 9 April 2014.

56 X.B. Li, "Money laundering and its regulation in China", Ph.D. Thesis, Cardiff School of Social Sciences, December 2009, UMI Dissertation Publishing, UMI Number U585355 Proquest LLC 2013.

57 Ibid.

58 L.Buencamino, and S. Gorbunov, "Informal money transfer systems: Opportunities and challenges for development finance", *UN Department of Economic and Social Affairs Working Paper No. 26*, November 2002, www.un.org/esa/esa02dp26.pdf

59 R. McCusker, "Underground banking: Legitimate remittance network or money laundering system?", *Trends and Issues in Crime and Criminal Justice, Australian Institute of Criminology Papers*, 300 (July 2005): 3.

60 D. Harris, "Moving money out of China by losing an arbitration", 14 December 2016, www.chinalawblog.com/2016/02/getting-money-out-of-china-by-losing-in-arbitration.html

61 A.Buehn, and S.Eichler, "Trade misinvoicing: The dark side of world trade", *The World Economy*, 34(8) (August 2011): 1263–1287.

62 D.Kar, and S. Fretas, "Illicit financial flows from China and the role of trade misinvoicing", *Global Financial Integrity Paper*, October 2012, p. 3, www.gfintegrity.org/storage/gfip/documents/reports/ChinaOct2012/gfi-china-oct2012-report-web.pdf

63 "Capital outflows: The flight of the Renminbi", *The Economist*, 27 October 2012.

64 D. Kar, and S. Fretas, "Illicit financial flows from China and the role of trade misinvoicing", p. 1.

65 Ibid.

66 A. Buehn, and S. Eichler, Trade Misinvoicing: The Dark Side of World Trade (August 2011), *The World Economy*, Vol. 34, Issue 8, pp. 1263–1287.

67 *Asian Banker Research*, "Identifying anti-money laundering issues in Chinese Banks", p. 5, www.theasianbanker.com/assets/media/dl/whitepaper/Asian%20Banker%20White%20Paper%20-%20China%20Anti-Money%20Laundry%20(English).pdf

174  *Victor Teo*

68  For an overview of the work of the State Administration of Foreign Exchange (SAFE), see www.safe.gov.cn/wps/portal/english
69  As in 2016, it has been reported that the Chinese government is tightening the controls through a variety of enforcement actions and means, and that this is now no longer possible even though this law still exist on paper.
70  "China puts US$15,000 annual personal cap on overseas bank card withdrawals", *South China Morning Post*, 30 December 2017.
71  "Cash smuggler held at Shenzhen-Hong Kong Border with HKD$1.9m in banknotes", *South China Morning Post*, 15 April 2015.
72  Ibid.
73  Reuters reported this after interviewing six retail-level agents at Zhuhai underground mall, site of the paper's fieldwork. The agent is quoted to say that his business has risen by 30% over the period of three years (2010–2013). See J. Pomfret and M. Miller, "On China's border, underground banking flourishes", *The New York Times*, 20 May 2013.
74  "Guangdong man accused of laundering HK$50 million per day for eight months", *South China Morning Post*, 8 April 2013; "Woman banked billions in money laundering case", *South China Morning Post*, 7 March 2013; and "Hong Kong nets only small fry for laundering illegal Chinese money", *South China Morning Post*, 8 April 2013.
75  F. E. R. Abdalla El Sheikh, "The underground banking systems and their impact on control of money laundering: With special reference to Islamic banking", *Journal of Money Laundering Control*, 6(1) (2003): 42–45.
76  For an interesting assessment of China's capital outflow, see F. Xiao, and D. Kimball (2006) "Effectiveness and effects of China's capital controls", conference on WTO, China and the Asian Economies: Economic Integration and Economic Development. http://faculty.washington.edu/karyiu/confer/beijing06/papers/xiao-kimball.pdf
77  Of course, the Americans are perpetually annoyed with the DPRK. They have been lobbying to sanction the bank(s) involved with the alleged money laundering in Macau for years (since maybe 2006), but as of today, the DPRK still appears to be active there. See J. McGlynn, "Banco Delta Asia, North Korea's frozen funds and US undermining of the six party-talks: Obstacles to a solution", *Japan Focus*, 9 June 2007, www.japanfocus.org/-John-McGlynn/2446
78  "The flight of Renminbi", *The Economist*, 27 October 2012, www.economist.com.hk/news/china/21565277-economic-repression-home-causing-more-chinese-money-vote-its-feet-flight
79  S. Rein, "No, China will absolutely not collapse", *Forbes*, 3 February 2010.
80  "Macau Casinos slump on reported China crackdown on money", *Casino Life Magazine*, 17 December 2014.
81  P. Panchhurst, "China's illicit outflows estimated at $1.4 trillion over the past decade", *Bloomberg*, 9 December 2016.
82  L. Hornby, "Chinese borrowers told to post nude photos as collateral", *The Financial Times*, 15 June 2016.

# Index

Note: Page numbers in *italic* indicate a figure and page numbers in **bold** indicate a table on the corresponding page.

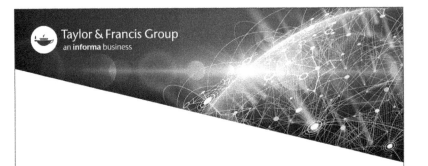

For Product Safety Concerns and Information please contact our EU
representative  GPSR@taylorandfrancis.com
Taylor & Francis Verlag GmbH, Kaufingerstraße 24, 80331 München, Germany

www.ingramcontent.com/pod-product-compliance
Ingram Content Group UK Ltd.
Pitfield, Milton Keynes, MK11 3LW, UK
UKHW021611240425
457818UK00018B/498